Trail Solutions

IMBA's Guide to Building Sweet Singletrack

INTERNATIONAL MOUNTAIN BICYCLING ASSOCIATION

Trail Solutions: IMBA's Guide to Building Sweet Singletrack

©Copyright 2004, International Mountain Bicycling Association. All rights reserved. No part of this work may be reproduced or transmitted in any form or by any means, electronic, photocopy or otherwise, without the prior written permission of IMBA.

Photo copyright IMBA unless otherwise noted.

Project Director/Managing Editor Peter Webber

Writer Vernon Felton

Illustrator Mark Schmidt

Editor Elizabeth Train

Designer Angie Lee, Grindstone Graphics, Inc.

Published and distributed by:
International Mountain Bicycling Association
PO Box 7578
Boulder, CO 80306

Printed in the United States of America.

International Standard Book Number: 0-9755023-0-1

IMBA Disclaimer

Study and utilize the information that is provided in this document but remember: Trailbuilders and landowners are responsible for the safety of their own trails. The design and construction suggestions offered by IMBA in this book do not constitute a standard, specification, or regulation. The publisher, editors, and authors shall not be held responsible for any injuries resulting from the use or misuse of information contained in this book.

FHWA Disclaimer

This book was produced in cooperation with the Recreational Trails Program of the Federal Highway Administration, U.S. Department of Transportation. This document is disseminated under the sponsorship of the U.S. Department of Transportation in the interest of information exchange. The United States Government assumes no liability for its content or use thereof.

The contents of this document reflect the views of the contractor, who is responsible for the accuracy of the data presented herein. The contents do not reflect the official policy of the U.S. Department of Transportation. This document does not constitute a standard, specification, or regulation.

The United States Government does not endorse products or manufacturers. Trade or manufacturers' names appear herein only because they are considered essential to the object of this document.

Cover photo: Flume Trail, Lake Tahoe, Nevada. Photo by Scott Markewitz.

Right: A sustainable trail should be both fun to ride or walk and friendly to the environment. Photo by Lee Cohen.

Table of Contents

Acknowledgments 8

Foreword 9

About IMBA 11

● **Part One: Partnerships** 17

All About Land Managers 18
    Gaining Access 18
    Different Types of Managers 18
    Identifying the Land Manager 21
    Working With Land Managers 22

Creating a Trail Proposal 25
    Ten Critical Elements in Creating a Trail Proposal 25

Coming to an Agreement 28
    Key Elements of an MOU 28

All About Volunteers 31
    Attracting and Keeping Volunteers: Four Steps for Success 31

● **Part Two: Philosophy of Successful Trails** 39

The Core Elements of a Sustainable Trail 40
    Why, Who, and What 40

Why Diverse Trail Systems Work 42

Shared Use or Single Use? 44
    Shared-Use Trails 44
    Single-Use Trails 45
    One-Way Trails 46

The Importance of Singletrack 48
    What Is Singletrack? 49
    Why Is Singletrack Important? 49

The Economic Benefits of Trails 50
    Trails Take Towns from Bust to Boom 51

Bringing Mountain Bikers to Your Area 52
    Fourteen Tips 52

● Part Three: The Principles of Sustainable Trails ... 55

Rolling Contour Trails—Building Great Trails that Last ... 56
    The Problem: Erosion ... 56
    The Solution: Rolling Contour Trails ... 56

Understanding Grade ... 59
    Two Critical Trailbuilding Tips ... 60

The Five Essential Elements of Sustainable Trails ... 63
    1. The Half Rule ... 63
    2. The Ten Percent Average Guideline ... 64
    3. Maximum Sustainable Grade ... 66
    4. Grade Reversals ... 67
    5. Outslope ... 69

Using a Clinometer ... 70
    How to Measure Grade ... 70

Trail Difficulty Rating System ... 72
    Trail Rating Guidelines ... 72
    Criteria to Consider ... 74
    Table: Trail Difficulty Rating System ... 75

Signs ... 76
    Sign Types ... 76
    Sign Materials: Pros and Cons ... 79

Managing Visitors Through Trail Design ... 80
    You Control the Speed ... 80
    Corralling, Chokes, and Turns ... 80
    Spread 'em Out ... 83
    Provide Diverse Experiences ... 83

Understanding Soils ... 84
    Sandy Soil ... 84
    Silty Soil ... 84
    Clay Soil ... 85
    Loamy Soil ... 85

● Part Four: The Trail Design Process ... 87

Eleven Steps to Better Trail Design ... 88
    1. Get Permission and Build a Partnership ... 88
    2. Identify Property Boundaries ... 88
    3. Determine Trail Users ... 88
    4. Identify Control Points ... 94
    5. Configure Loops ... 95
    6. Plan a Contour Route ... 96
    7. Determine Type of Trail Flow ... 97
    8. Walk and Flag the Corridor ... 100
    9. Develop a Construction Plan ... 101
    10. Conduct an Assessment Study ... 101
    11. Flag the Final Alignment and Confirm Permission ... 102

Table of Contents, continued

● Part Five: Tools for Trailwork ... 105

Handling Tools Safely ... 106
    Safety Tips ... 106

The Ten Essential Tools ... 108

Other Useful Hand Tools ... 112

Mechanized Tools ... 121
    The Upside of Mechanized Tools ... 121
    The Downside of Mechanized Tools ... 122
    A Short Guide to Mechanized Tools ... 124
    Choosing the Right Machine ... 127
    Tips for Using Mechanized Tools ... 129
    Other Useful Mechanized Tools ... 132

● Part Six: Trail Construction ... 135

Clearing the Trail Corridor ... 137
    How Wide? How High? ... 137

Bench Cut Trails ... 140
    Building a Full Bench Trail with Hand Tools ... 142

Building Climbing Turns, Switchbacks and Insloped Turns ... 149
    Climbing Turns ... 149
    Switchbacks ... 151
    Four Steps for Building a Switchback ... 153
    Insloped Turns ... 154
    Four Steps for Building an Insloped Turn ... 157

Retaining Walls ... 159
    Key Steps to Building Retaining Walls ... 159

Armoring—Using Rock to Harden Trails ... 162
    Five Ways to Armor with Rock ... 163
    Ten Tips for Rock Armoring ... 166
    When Armoring, Always. ... 170
    Man-Made Soil Hardeners ... 174

Wetlands and Water Crossings ... 176
    Stream Corridor Function and Dynamics ... 176
    Five General Guidelines for Water Crossings ... 177
    Armored Crossings ... 179
    Culverts ... 180
    Bridges ... 183
    Wetlands ... 185

How Long Will It Take? How Much Will It Cost? ... 187

Part Seven: Trail Maintenance ... 191

Assessing the Condition of The Trail ... 192

Maintaining the Trail Corridor ... 195

Identifying Trail Problems ... 197
- User-Caused Erosion Problems and How to Solve Them ... 197
- Water-Caused Erosion Problems and How to Solve Them ... 200

Drainage Solutions ... 201
- Deberming and Maintaining the Outslope ... 201
- Knicks ... 203
- Rolling Grade Dips ... 204
- Waterbars: Good Intentions, Bad Results ... 206
- Armoring ... 207

Special Conditions: Wet, Flat, and Sandy ... 208
- Wet Areas ... 209
- Flat Areas ... 209
- Sandy Areas ... 210

Rerouting and Reclaiming Damaged Trails ... 211
- Time to Reroute? ... 211
- Ten Tips for Rerouting and Reclaiming a Trail ... 211

Part Eight: Building Challenging Trails ... 217

Freeriding ... 218
- The Ups and Downs of Freeriding ... 218
- Freeriding: Hype or Reality ... 219
- IMBA Freeriding Position ... 221

Freeriding and Risk Management: Fifteen Steps to Success ... 222

Building Technical Trail Features ... 231
- Three Ways to Create a Challenging Trail ... 231
- Using Existing Natural Trail Features ... 233
- How to Design a Drop-Off ... 234
- Construction Guidelines for Wooden Technical Features ... 235
- Ten Tips for Building a Ladder Bridge ... 239

Downhill Trails ... 242
- Fifteen Tips for Building Excellent Downhill Trails ... 242

Afterword ... 248

Appendix A: Natural Resource Impacts of Mountain Biking ... 249

Appendix B: Sources for Tools, Bridge Supplies, and Signs ... 255

Appendix C: IMBA-Affiliated Professional Trailbuilders ... 257

Appendix D: Recommended Reading ... 258

Glossary ... 259

Index ... 270

Acknowledgments

Project Director/Managing Editor Peter Webber

Writer Vernon Felton

Illustrator Mark Schmidt

Editor Elizabeth Train

Designer Angie Lee, Grindstone Graphics, Inc.

Contributors

Attila Bality	Vernon Felton	Mark Liebig	Gary Sprung
Tim Blumenthal	Jim Hasenauer	Scott Linnenburger	Elizabeth Train
Tony Boone	Aaryn Kay	Mike Riter	Dan Vardamis
Judd De Vall	Woody Keen	Jim Schmid	Peter Webber
Rich Edwards	Joey Klein	Mark Schmidt	Lora Woolner

Photographers

Bob Allen	John Gibson	Joe Lindsey	Bryan Moody
Kevin Bauman	Chuck Haney	Sterling Lorence	Seb Rogers
Lee Cohen	Dean Howard	Scott Markewitz	John Shafer
Rich Etchberger			Stephen Wilde

Special Thanks

A number of people and organizations made the publication of this book possible. We'd like to thank Christopher Douwes of the U.S Department of Transportation's Federal Highway Administration, Subaru of America, and our many other corporate sponsors whose financial support enables us to spread the good word.

Professional trailbuilders Kurt Loheit and Tony Boone started to create innovative trail solutions with mountain bikers in mind even before IMBA was born. They have inspired us and supported trailbuilders around the globe for nearly 20 years. Mike and Jan Riter refined and spread these techniques as the first Subaru/IMBA Trail Care Crew. Since then, a half dozen other IMBA teams have followed their lead. Much of the information in this book is the direct result of their hard work and commitment.

In addition to the contributors listed above, credit is due to Ric and Holly Balfour, Mauro Bertolotto, Dafydd Davis, Jen Edwards, Kim Frederick, Scott Frey, Jim and Cathy Haagen-Smit, Glen Jacobs, Jim Jacobsen, Philip Keyes, Bob Moore, Ken Neave, Rita Nygren, Jan Riter, Harvey Schneider, Kathy Summers, and Bill Victor. Sandy Husmann provided the tool illustrations. Special thanks go out to IMBA's staff, regional representatives, board members, and founders, who provided invaluable input and support along the way.

Many of the concepts presented in this book are built on a foundation of knowledge and experience developed by the U.S. Forest Service, Bureau of Land Management, National Park Service, Appalachian Mountain Club, Appalachian Trail Conference, and Student Conservation Association. We pledge to keep working with these and other partners in the trails community.

Finally, we want to express our gratitude to all of IMBA's members and affiliated clubs. Without your support and volunteer commitment, mountain biking wouldn't be half the sport it is today...or will be tomorrow. Thank you.

Foreword

If you've visited Italy or studied Julius Caesar in high school, you probably know that the civil engineers of the Roman Empire were pretty talented. Their aqueducts, bridges, and roads were amazing feats of construction, and they created design techniques that guide the way we build roads and trails today.

But lots has changed in the last 1,500 years. More than six billion people now inhabit the planet, straining the delicate balance between man and nature. Today, millions of people use trails not only for transportation but also for recreation.

A recent development is the growth of mountain biking—now one of the most popular types of use on trail systems around the world. The boom of off-road cycling has sparked a new generation of trail volunteers and many innovative techniques for the construction and management of trails. The primary goal of this book is to catalog and share these techniques in order to help land managers and volunteer groups develop and support better trail experiences.

While the unique angle of this text is its emphasis on mountain biking, the trailbuilding concepts and management strategies presented here are intended to benefit all trail users. Building and managing trails is an art and a science. This book is a compilation of proven methods and current trends aimed at providing solutions to common problems. Alaska, Italy, California, Iowa, Wales—IMBA's staff travels the world teaching trailbuilding techniques to trail users and land managers alike. In the course of our journeys, we've seen what works and what doesn't work when it comes to building and maintaining trails. We've also paid special attention to designing trails that provide the types of experiences visitors want.

There will always be several solutions for each problem you encounter when building a trail. One approach may have been developed on the Mediterranean a millennium ago, while another may have been devised by an IMBA expert in 2003. The solution you choose will depend on several factors including your location, annual rainfall, soil type, available resources, and the type and number of trail users the trail will serve. It's up to you—the trailbuilders, land managers, and volunteers—to choose the most appropriate methods and techniques for your particular situation. The information in this book can help you make the right decision.

About the Federal Highway Administration's Recreational Trails Program

The Federal Highway Administration's Recreational Trails Program provided the funding for this book. Since 1993, the Recreational Trails Program (or RTP) has utilized federal fuel taxes to help communities develop and maintain thousands of miles of trails in all 50 states. RTP funding benefits all trail users. Hikers, bikers, trail runners, equestrians, cross-country skiers, snowmobilers, and OHV enthusiasts all profit from the program. In fact, it's fair to say that society as a whole benefits from the RTP.

Convenient trail access combats obesity by encouraging Americans to go outside and be active. Most of us are aware that obesity poses a serious risk to the health of this country. Few realize, however, that health conditions related to inactivity (heart disease, diabetes, and high blood pressure, for instance) cause an estimated $180 billion in additional medical costs and 300,000 premature deaths each year. An investment in America's trail network is a cost-effective and appropriate response to this public health crisis.

IMBA would like to thank the Federal Highway Administration for its foresight and dedication to improving our country's trails.

Photo by Sterling Lorence.

About IMBA

IMBA was founded in 1988 by a group of California mountain bike clubs concerned about the closure of trails to cyclists. These pioneering clubs believed that mountain biker–education programs and innovative trail management solutions should be developed and promoted. While this first wave of threatened trail access was concentrated in California, IMBA's pioneers saw that crowded trails and trail-user conflict were fast becoming worldwide recreation issues. This is why they chose "International Mountain Bicycling Association" as the organization's name.

IMBA's mission has always been to create, enhance, and preserve trail opportunities for mountain bikers worldwide. In addition, we actively promote responsible mountain biking, support volunteer trailwork, assist land managers with trail management issues, and improve relations among trail user groups.

IMBA has members in all 50 United States and 30 other countries. This group includes 32,000 individuals, 500 bicycle clubs, 300 bicycle retailers, and 130 corporate supporters. IMBA's Rules of the Trail promote responsible recreation and are recognized worldwide as the standard code of conduct for mountain bikers. IMBA members annually contribute more than one million hours to trailwork projects on public land. To date, these volunteers have created more than 5,000 miles of new trails worldwide.

IMBA continues to bring out the best in mountain biking through education, trail construction, volunteer support, management advice, cash and grants for trail improvement, and worldwide leadership. IMBA gives mountain bikers a national and international voice that is heard and respected by federal land managers,

IMBA's board of directors, staff, and regional reps. Location: Moab, Utah. 2002. Photo by Bob Allen.

The Subaru/IMBA Trail Care Crews have led more than 1,000 trail improvement projects since 1997.

environmental groups, the mainstream media, and other trail users. IMBA works closely with the U.S. Forest Service, Army Corps of Engineers, Bureau of Land Management, and many National Park Service units. We also partner with a variety of state, local, and international agencies.

IMBA's key projects and endeavors include the Subaru/IMBA Trail Care Crew, the National Mountain Bike Patrol, IMBA Trailbuilding Schools, IMBA Epic Rides, IMBA Urban Hot Spots, IMBA Trail Solutions, and a wide range of educational efforts. IMBA works to keep trails open and in good condition for everyone.

For more information, visit imba.com or call or write our headquarters: IMBA, P.O. Box 7578, Boulder, CO 80306 USA; 303-545-9011.

About the Subaru/IMBA Trail Care Crew

Since 1997, Subaru of America and IMBA have sponsored an effort to help local groups assess and improve trail conditions in their communities. Two fulltime, professional teams of trail experts travel year-round throughout North America and beyond, leading trailwork sessions, meeting with government officials and land managers, and working with IMBA-affiliated clubs and associations to improve mountain biking opportunities. To date, the Trail Care Crews have worked on more than 1,000 trail projects and trained more than 100,000 people. The Crews also lead more than 60 IMBA Trailbuilding Schools each year. Trailbuilding Schools are generally hosted by IMBA-affiliated clubs and blend interactive learning, hands-on trailwork, and top-notch instruction to develop skilled trailworkers and environmental stewards.

IMBA's Trailbuilding Philosophy

Building a constituency for outdoor recreation is vital to ensuring the future of open space. If people visit and enjoy the outdoors, they'll support preservation of natural and undeveloped land. The challenge is to encourage more Americans to explore the outdoors without trampling it underfoot (so to speak) and spoiling its natural beauty.

IMBA supports the development of trails that encourage the public to get out and enjoy natural settings without harming ecosystems. IMBA promotes sustainable trailbuilding techniques that produce paths that withstand erosion, provide designated users with their desired experiences, and minimize user conflict.

Almost all of these techniques are borrowed from great trailbuilders in history: the Civilian Conservation Corps of the 1930s, the U.S. Forest Service, and even the road builders of ancient Rome. Some of the techniques presented in this book are new to the world of trailbuilding and are tailored specifically to the needs of mountain bikers. Much of IMBA's trailbuilding philosophy, however, is based on long-standing lessons learned from successful shared-use trails.

What is a sustainable trail?

Throughout this book you'll hear us repeatedly mention the term "sustainability." No, we don't get a kick out of being redundant or boring our readers, we just can't overemphasize the importance of this concept.

The National Park Service's definition states it well.

A Sustainable Trail:
- Supports current and future use with minimal impact to the area's natural systems.
- Produces negligible soil loss or movement while allowing vegetation to inhabit the area.
- Recognizes that pruning or removal of certain plants may be necessary for proper maintenance.
- Does not adversely affect the area's animal life.
- Accommodates existing use while allowing only appropriate future use.
- Requires little rerouting and minimal long-term maintenance.

—From the National Park Service, Rocky Mountain Region, January 1991

Why are these elements so important?

When you design a trail correctly and build it to withstand erosion, you create a trail that's enjoyable to ride. What's more, you create a trail that doesn't require constant maintenance. Minimizing the need for maintenance is critical. Land managers don't have the time, money, or manpower to constantly rebuild each trail under their jurisdiction. Likewise, anyone who has led a crew of trailworkers knows that there is always a shortage of volunteers. The less time, labor, and money needed for trail maintenance, the more likely trails will remain open for mountain biking and other public use. Achieving that perfect balance between resource protection and recreation is what good trail design and construction are all about.

Here's another way of looking at it: good trails are both sustainable and fun. Poorly designed trails can be no fun to ride or walk and are a steady drain on professional and volunteer resources.

IMBA Rules of the Trail

The way we ride today shapes mountain bike trail access tomorrow. Do your part to preserve and enhance our sport's access and image by observing the following rules of the trail. These rules are recognized around the world as the standard code of conduct for mountain bikers.

Ride On Open Trails Only.

Respect trail and road closures (ask if uncertain); avoid trespassing on private land; obtain permits or other authorization as may be required. Federal Wilderness areas are closed to cycling. The way you ride will influence trail management decisions and policies.

Leave No Trace.

Be sensitive to the dirt beneath you. Practice low-impact cycling. Recognize different types of soils and trail construction. Wet and muddy trails are more vulnerable to damage. When the trailbed is soft, consider other riding options. This also means staying on existing trails and not creating new ones. Don't cut switchbacks. Be sure to pack out at least as much as you pack in.

Control Your Bicycle!

It's fine to get in the zone, but zoning out can cause problems. Obey all bicycle speed regulations and recommendations.

Always Yield Trail.

Let your fellow trail users know you're coming. A friendly greeting or bell is considerate and works well. Anticipate other trail users around corners or in blind spots. Show your respect when passing others on the trail by slowing to a walking pace or even stopping. Yielding means slowing down, establishing communication, and being prepared to stop if necessary in order to pass safely.

Never Scare Animals.

All animals are startled by an unannounced approach, a sudden movement, or a loud noise. This can be dangerous for you, others, and the animals. Give animals extra room and time to adjust to your presence. When encountering horses always be prepared to dismount, yield the trail and allow the horse and rider to pass. If the horse seems frightened, dismount, remain downslope of the animal, and keep yourself between the horse and the bike so the horse focuses on you. Speak to horses in soothing tones, and encourage equestrians to stay on the trail. Finally, running cattle and disturbing wildlife is a serious offense. Leave gates as you found them, or as marked.

Plan Ahead.

Know your equipment, your ability, and the area in which you are riding, and prepare for your trail experience accordingly. Be self-sufficient at all times, keep your equipment in good repair, and carry necessary supplies for changes in weather or other conditions. Always wear a helmet and appropriate safety gear.

Photo by Chuck Haney.

Photo by Seb Rogers.

Part One: Partnerships

You've probably heard the saying, "It takes a village to raise a child." Well, without getting too touchy-feely, we're going to suggest that the same thing is true of building and maintaining trails. Your trail project won't succeed unless you have support and approval from land managers, volunteers, other users, and your community.

Building just one mile of trail might require, for example, that a local mountain bike club work with a federal agency, the city council, a private landowner, and several local hiking and equestrian clubs. Before you move a speck of dirt, you must gain legal access to the land through which your proposed trail will pass, create a detailed trail proposal, and ensure that all of your partners in this project are on the same page.

Volunteers can be helpful in every stage of the trailbuilding process—from planning the trail's route to building and maintaining its tread. It's important to involve volunteers in the early stages of the trail project and to cultivate this important partnership by showing your appreciation for their efforts.

In This Part ...

- **All About Land Managers** 18
  - Gaining Access 18
  - Different Types of Managers 18
  - Identifying the Land Manager 21
  - Working With Land Managers 22
- **Creating a Trail Proposal** 25
  - Ten Critical Elements in Creating a Trail Proposal 25
- **Coming to an Agreement** 28
  - Key Elements of an MOU 28
- **All About Volunteers** 31
  - Attracting and Keeping Volunteers: Four Steps for Success 31

All About Land Managers

Gaining Access

Before you can consider designing, building, or maintaining a trail, you need to gain legal access to the property through which the trail passes. This means getting permission from the person who owns or manages the land. Receiving permission is the first, and perhaps most important, step in the process.

Be warned—obtaining permission takes time and effort. You need to determine who owns or manages the land, you need to anticipate that person or public agency's concerns; and you need to create a cooperative relationship with the land manager and the local community based in mutual trust and respect.

Different Types of Land Managers

Where you live has a lot to do with whether your proposed trail runs through private or public lands. Much of the open space in the eastern United States is privately owned. The reverse is true in the West. More than 90 percent of the forestlands in Maine, for instance, are privately owned, whereas 83 percent of the land in Arizona is in the public domain. The important thing to know is this: *Different types of landowners will have different types of concerns about trails on their property.* Here's a breakdown on the various kinds of property owners you may encounter.

Private Landowners

There are essentially two types of private landowners: corporate owners and residential owners.

Corporate landowners include paper companies, timber harvesting firms, and real estate developers. While some corporate landowners embrace the idea of allowing trail users on their land (it can boost their public image or serve to strengthen permit applications for future developments), most will be concerned that a proposed trail will adversely affect the value of their holdings and increase their liability. After all, they possess the land with the intention of making a profit from it. As trailbuilders, you should be concerned with the property's future, too. There's not much point in dedicating 500 hours of trailwork to a piece of property if the landowner plans on covering the trail with condos within two years.

Residential landowners may live on or near the property in question and are frequently concerned with issues of parking, littering, noise, and lawsuits should visitors injure themselves on their property. Anticipate these questions and formulate accurate and convincing answers prior to contacting the landowner. We'll cover common landowner questions and appropriate responses later in the sections ahead.

Public Land Managers

Public lands account for roughly 600 million acres—or approximately one third of the United States. A variety of different government agencies manage these lands. If we were to make one generalization regarding public land managers, it would be that they tend to be most receptive to trail proposals that will accommodate a wide variety of trail users. After all, as public employees, part of their job is to provide recreational opportunities for the general public. Pitching a mountain biking or hiking-only trail system to a public land manager, for example, may not fly, as it would exclude other users.

Trail Solutions

Trails on public lands are treasured community resources. Their success and longevity depends on strong partnerships between land managers and volunteer trail stewards.

Here's a quick rundown on key federal, state, and other land agencies.

U.S. Bureau of Land Management

The Bureau of Land Management (BLM) manages 264 million acres of public land in 12 western states. The BLM, which is part of the Department of Interior, has a long record of support for mountain biking and IMBA's work.

U.S. Forest Service

The Forest Service, part of the Department of Agriculture, manages 192 million acres of forests and grasslands in 42 states and Puerto Rico. This land includes more than 100,000 miles of trails. The Forest Service has historically been supportive of mountain biking, and a first MOU, or Memorandum of Understanding, between IMBA and the Forest Service was signed in 1994.

Part One: Partnerships

U.S. National Park Service

The National Park Service manages 384 parks, monuments, battlefields, buildings, and recreation areas, and more than 80 million acres of U.S. public land. It is the flagship branch of the Department of Interior.

Bicycling—on pavement or off road—hasn't been a priority for Park Service management, and cycling is severely limited in many parks. Recently, the Park Service's perspective on bicycling has begun to change, and opportunities to ride in parks are slowly emerging. In 2002, IMBA and the Park Service's Rivers, Trails, and Conservation Assistance (RTCA) program signed a Memorandum of Understanding—in effect, a five-year agreement to:

- Develop four to six trail projects annually.
- Encourage the design of trail systems with broad appeal.
- Develop and promote mountain biking success stories.
- Develop a model "Urban Trails Park" concept.

U.S. Army Corps of Engineers

The Army Corps of Engineers is part of the U.S. Department of Defense and is responsible for building and operating water resources and other civil works projects and managing the construction of military and governmental facilities. The Corps hosts nearly 400 million recreation visits per year—more than any other land management agency—and is the steward of 12 million acres of land and water resources, including 5,000 miles of trails. In 2002, IMBA and the Corps signed an agreement to partner on trail projects across the country.

U.S. Bureau of Reclamation

The Bureau of Reclamation, another arm of the Department of Interior, is best known for the dams, power plants, and canals it has constructed in the 17 western states. It is the largest wholesaler of water in the country, administering 348 reservoirs. Reclamation helps manage 308 recreation sites visited by 90 million people each year.

State Forests

More than 11 million acres of U.S. wild lands are managed by state forestry departments. Mountain biking access in state forests varies from state to state.

State Parks

State parks provide most of the opportunities for mountain biking in the East and Midwest. Even in California and Colorado—both states with huge amounts of federal public land—state parks are vital sources of recreational trails.

City/County Parks

Estimating the amount of land managed by city and county land agencies is difficult. Nevertheless, it's fair to say that city and county parks are an important resource for urban mountain bikers. As with state parks, mountain biking access varies from park to park in cities and counties.

Identifying the Land Manager

The first thing you need to do is determine who owns the private property or manages the public land that your proposed trail will cross. Occasionally, the answer will be immediately apparent—the land may be posted with signs—but sometimes you'll need to do some sleuthing. Here are several places to turn for all the dirt on who owns the dirt.

Research Town Tax Maps

Your City or County Assessor's Office will typically keep tax maps indicating acreage and boundary lines along with each property owner's name and contact information. These maps are considered public information and are definitely worth reviewing.

Examine Deeds

Deeds are another useful source of information. Your county recorder's office is the place to go. The recorder's office is typically responsible for maintaining legal documents that determine property ownership.

Query Elected Officials

There are a number of elected officials whose staff may be of service. Your county board of supervisors or city council/town selectmen's office can point you in the right direction if your search isn't yielding results. Always be polite when making inquiries. Elected officials are typically overworked and underappreciated. Besides, these people may prove to be vital supporters of your trail in the future.

Question Surveyors

Surveyors often work a specific territory for years and may therefore be familiar with property ownership and specifics about the lay of the land. They are particularly good sources of information regarding public lands. Check with your county surveyor's office.

Check with Conservation Officers

County forestry departments, soil and water conservation districts, open space or greenway departments, and agents from state fish and game departments may manage the land or be familiar with the landowners in their regions. If you've struck out with everyone else, give them a call.

> **Bright Idea**
>
> **Talk to the Locals.** The local populace can be a vital source of information. Neighbors are often familiar with the owners of property adjacent to their own. They may also know the land's history and the owner's conservation ethics. Be prudent, however, when probing locals for information. Some residents may harbor fears that new trails will bring noise, litter, and mayhem to their stretch of paradise. Be prepared to allay such concerns—you don't want to seed opposition to your trail before you've even begun.

Working with Land Managers

Land managers have to juggle internal politics with external pressures and have a limited capacity to respond to clubs and individual volunteers. Likewise, private landowners may be wary of the "extreme" mountain bike image and of costly lawsuits. The following steps will help you effectively communicate the need for a new trail, or the rationale for saving an existing one from closure.

Focus and Fact-Finding

Decide what you want and what you don't want.

Make a list of your trail proposal's goals. Break them down into objectives and actions. Don't forget to list things you don't want as well. Why? Because time (yours) is precious and every thing you do must directly help the cause.

Do your homework.

Learn as much as you can about the park or private property. Likewise, identify other potential trail users, stakeholders, and your likely opponents. What arguments might be made for and against your proposal? Estimate the cost and time involved in the project, including the value of volunteer hours you have already put into other trails. Research your state's recreational liability laws. Almost every land manager you work with will have questions concerning liability. Be prepared. See page 222 for more information on liability.

Successful trails benefit from close working relationships among user groups, land managers, and community leaders.

Trail Solutions

Be strategic.

Break your proposal into bite-size chunks and phases. The last thing you want to do is over-commit yourself so you are unable to follow through on your end of the deal. You may have to compromise, so decide what you are prepared to negotiate for and what you are willing to do without.

Develop a list of supporters and identify potential detractors.

If dealing with public land, learn who on the park's staff is the best person to contact for a meeting. There is usually someone designated to work with trail users, but it never hurts to send a copy of your letter to the local supervisor as a matter of protocol. It is also helpful to make a list of people you can rely on for assistance as well as people who may oppose the project.

Bright Idea

There's Strength in Numbers. Delegate! You are going to need help. The last thing you want to do is burn out half way through the process. Having more partners will help spread the workload and add credibility to your cause. Look beyond your group for partners. The most attractive proposals have multiple proponents, shared commitments, and broad community support.

Play the Game Fairly

Be professional.

The success of your interactions with land managers has a lot to do with the degree of professionalism you show. Keep your conversations, letters, and e-mails clear and concise, and be vigilant about checking for typos in written material. Above all, don't be confrontational.

Find common ground.

Look for an issue you can both agree on and work from there. Typical community concerns include trash dumping, park budget cuts, or the threat of development on adjacent land. Ask how you and your group can help solve these problems.

Be honest, be fair, and be prepared to "agree to disagree."

Nothing garners respect more quickly than up-front honesty and the ability to move past disagreements. Don't get stuck on obstacles. Make a note and come back to the issue later if you think it is worth your time and integral to the project.

Understand before you seek to be understood.

This proverb is essential to a successful partnership. Educate yourself about the priorities and constraints facing land managers and property owners. Investigate the budget cycle, availability of support staff, and the other priorities a land manager must handle. The politics, traditions, and trends associated with the park may also shape a land manager's decisions, so it is important that you are aware of these factors.

A well-designed trail balances environmental stewardship with the needs of trail users. Location: Yukon Territory, Canada. Photo by John Gibson.

Follow-Up is Critical

Be persistent.

End each conversation with a summary of your agreement, what each of you will do with the information, and a date for your next meeting. Remember, persistent and annoying are entirely different qualities. Follow through on your efforts, but avoid irritating the people whose help and support you seek.

Cultivate other sources of support.

There are many people and organizations whose mission is to assist people like you. Your IMBA state or regional representative is one such person. Local politicians may also be of service in charting the political waters. Sometimes local academic institutions have information that can help you understand the bigger picture, with studies on recreation trends, economic impacts, and demographics. Chambers of commerce, bureaus of tourism, and bike shops can also be sources of support.

Keep it clear by keeping good notes.

You will be more effective, learn more, and leave a better legacy of your efforts if you take good notes. Keep everything associated with the proposal—such as a calendar, a notebook, and a project binder—in one place for quick and easy reference. Maintain accurate records so additional participants can get up to speed rapidly and to ensure that new people aren't reinventing the wheel if you must leave the project or the park staff changes.

Creating a Trail Proposal

People will take you and your proposed trail more seriously when you present your ideas in a thorough, well-presented document. An effective trail proposal clearly outlines your goals and the benefits the trail project will bring to the community. Successful trail proposals also anticipate and answer questions that the community may have regarding your project. The exact format is up to you. Just make sure the proposal appears professional and is easy to read.

10 Critical Elements in Creating a Trail Proposal

Your proposal should answer the following critical questions:

1. Who are you?
2. Who will benefit from this trail?
3. Who will build the trail?
4. Who will manage the trail once it's built?
5. How long will it take to complete this project?
6. How much will it cost to build the trail and who will pay for it?
7. Where (on a map) will the trail be located?
8. What steps will be taken to ensure that trail users won't stray from the trail and wander onto neighboring property?
9. How do you plan to deal with parking and litter?
10. Will the public be able to participate in the planning of the trail?

1 Who are you?

Naturally, you are familiar with your own qualifications, but odds are good that your name or the name of your club alone will only illicit blank stares from most land managers or property owners. So who are you? What are your qualifications? Have you or other members of your group received trails training? Have you already built successful trails in the area? More important, who else will be working on this trail? One-person projects don't stand much of a chance of being approved or of being completed, so name some other people who will be supporting your endeavor. If you belong to an official mountain bike club that will assist the project, include the club's name. Will other trail-user organizations (hiking or equestrian clubs, for example) help too? Trail proposals face better odds when supported by a diverse group.

2 Who will benefit from this trail?

This is a particularly crucial question on public lands where land managers are usually directed to deliver the greatest benefit to the greatest number of people possible while also protecting the resource. Identify other trail users who will reap the rewards of this trail project, but don't stop there. Will a trail or trail system bring needed tourism dollars to the area? Will it improve the community's health by giving more people access to trails near their homes? Think big.

3 Who will build the trail?

Big ideas are great, but at some point this trail just needs to be built. Who will do the work? Will you solicit volunteers from your mountain bike club or another trail-user organization? Will you hire professional trail-builders? Will IMBA provide training or assistance through the Subaru/IMBA Trail Care Crew or IMBA Trail Solutions (IMBA's professional trailbuilding program)? Be specific.

4 Who will manage the trail once it's built?

Are you creating this trail only to dump the long-term maintenance responsibilities onto an already over-worked land manager? That approach probably isn't going to sit well with the authorities. Be clear about whether or not your club will perform routine volunteer maintenance on the trail and whether the club is willing to staff a mountain bike patrol to help instill a responsible riding ethic. (Check imba.com for more information on our National Mountain Bike Patrol program.) Be realistic—don't make promises you can't keep.

5 How long will it take to complete this project?

Will this project take a month, six months, or a year to complete? When during the year will it be built? Building trail—the right way—takes quite a bit of time, particularly if it is done by hand. Refer to page 187 for project time estimates.

Trail proposals should include a clear map that shows exactly where the new route(s) will be located.

6. How much will it cost to build the trail and who will pay for it?

The coffers of most parks departments are not exactly overflowing. So who will pay for the construction and maintenance on the trail? Will the club volunteer its time and manpower to build the trail and maintain it over the years? See page 187 for tips on how to estimate (and cover!) costs associated with trailbuilding.

7. Where (on a map) will the trail be located?

You need to be crystal clear about where the trail will run and how long it will be. Plot your route on a topographic map. This isn't a one-day project; it takes time and you may need permission to scout the terrain in advance.

8. What steps will be taken to ensure that trail users won't stray from the trail and wander onto neighboring property?

Your greatest source of opposition often comes from people whose properties border the trail. Such individuals may understandably be concerned that trail users will wander onto their land. Be sure that you've anticipated this situation and devised ways to resolve it. Maintaining a buffer zone between the proposed trail and the property's boundary lines, for instance, will help keep visitors off of private property.

9. How do you plan to deal with parking and litter?

Poorly managed trailheads can quickly become magnets for late-night parties, loud music, and litter. How will you address these common problems? Make sure you've spoken to local law authorities or park staff about ways to tackle such issues prior to submitting your proposal. Can the current trailhead facilities accommodate the increased traffic that a new trail might attract? If not, your proposal should include plans to expand the trailhead facilities.

10. Will the public be able to participate in the planning of the trail?

People want to be involved in their communities. At the very least, they want to know that they can chip in their two cents. Make sure you've determined a way for the community to get involved in the planning of the project. You can participate in public information meetings on the trail system or encourage the formation of a citizen's advisory committee. Your trail proposal should outline some strategy for involving the community—we'll leave the exact tactics to you. Just remember that ignoring the local community poses great risk to your proposed trail.

Don't Forget...

Ask Questions. If considering a trail on private property, you need to know whether the owner plans on selling or developing it in the near future. If the property is public, you need to know if there are any protected species or archeological sites on the property that may restrict trail development. Different land management agencies employ different protocols for reviewing and approving proposals. Knowing the administrative processes of the land manager in question will save you time.

Coming to an Agreement

Collaboration is a key aspect of trailbuilding. If everyone puts insight, muscle and goodwill into a project, the end result can be a trail that meets a broad spectrum of needs. Successful collaborations, however, require that everyone be on the same page—all stakeholders must have clear agendas, responsibilities, and roles. That's where an MOU comes into play.

MOU stands for **Memorandum of Understanding.** An MOU is a document that clearly spells out a project's goals and each stakeholder's role in getting that project completed. In short, MOUs ensure that everyone involved is "on the same page."

An MOU is not, however, a legally binding document. Instead, it's more of a public statement of your goals and duties. Think of it as a means of reducing potential misunderstanding and conflict between you and your trailbuilding partners.

Key Elements of an MOU

The content of an MOU will vary depending on the organizations involved and the collective goals you hope to achieve. The important thing to remember is that an MOU should clearly answer the following questions:

- **Which organizations will be involved in this project?**

- **What is the goal of the partnership?**

- **Who (by name) will represent the interests of each organization?**

- **What trail or specific section of land will be included?**

- **What, specifically, will be done in the name of trailwork?**
  Will new trails be built? Will corridors be trimmed? Will bridges be installed?

- **What design philosophies will be employed?**
  Will you be building grade dips or rerouting certain sections of trail?
  Carefully describe the specific design strategies you will utilize to achieve your goals.

- **Who will be responsible for what?**
  Representatives from each organization should be responsible for specific actions. Delegation increases accountability and efficiency.

- **What's the timeline?**
  The MOU should specify completion dates for various stages of the project as well as the entire trail.

Working with Other Trail User Groups—Hoof and Tire Unite in Michigan

Mountain bikers and equestrians are sometimes at odds when it comes to trail access. Lack of communication between the two groups escalates tensions. One such conflict came to a head in Michigan in the late 1990s at Pontiac Lake Recreation Area, a popular destination for mountain biking and horseback riding about an hour from metro Detroit.

"It was an ugly, ugly situation," said Michigan Mountain Bike Association executive director Todd Scott. "More than 600 folks attended a meeting to discuss the problem, and things were hostile. Equestrians argued that they were losing trails they had ridden for decades. Mountain bikers were worried that they would simply have no place to ride if Pontiac Lake was deemed off-limits."

The land management agency of the park, Michigan's Department of Natural Resources, wasn't sure what to do with the two battling groups. They didn't want to close trails, but they also needed local mountain bikers and equestrians to come to a truce. The DNR presented a challenge to both groups: Get along or lose trails.

As a result, leaders from the IMBA-affiliated Michigan Mountain Bike Association and the Michigan Horse Council sat down to discuss solutions. It was a landmark moment. The two groups had agreed to disagree for as long as anyone could remember, yet by actually talking face to face they were able to create some remarkable strategies.

First, the two groups agreed that the volume of traffic on the Pontiac Lake trails made a shared-use system challenging. They concluded that the ideal situation would be separate loops for mountain bikers and equestrians. In order to retain a stacked loop system for bikes and to eliminate problem intersections, miles of new trail would need to be constructed in the coming years.

With help from the Subaru/IMBA Trail Care Crew, Michigan Mountain Bike Association, and the Michigan Horse Council, volunteers worked together to build new trails that added to the existing network.

Cynics might say that the two groups never really got along until they agreed to use different trails. Todd Scott disagrees, saying, "Given the high volume of users on these trails, we decided that separate use was the best solution. But the real key was just opening the lines of communication. They understand what we want now, and we're more educated to their needs."

Location: Chile Photo by John Gibson.

Want an Example?

You'll find several examples of successful MOUs at **imba.com**.
We particularly recommend that you review the following:

MOU between North Tennessee Mountain Bike Association and Cherokee National Forest
This MOU sets forth guidelines that govern how the two organizations go about dealing with one another on a daily basis. While no specific trailwork is discussed, the MOU lays the groundwork for a successful relationship between a club and a land manager. Every club should consider creating one of these.

Sample MOU Between Biking Club and Land Management Agency
This MOU deals with a specific trailwork project between a hypothetical bike club and the land manager. After reading this MOU, you have a perfectly clear idea of who will be doing what and how the club plans on achieving its goals.

All About Volunteers

Building and maintaining trails takes time and effort. Who's going to do the work? Land management agencies are generally underfunded, understaffed, and overworked. They barely have time to manage existing trails, much less to build new ones. As a result, quite a bit of today's trailwork is done by volunteers.

There's a definite benefit to having volunteers build trails. *Trailworkers are better trail users.* After all, once you've invested 10 hours of sweat into rebuilding a switchback, you'll never skid through that corner again. But attracting volunteers and convincing them to come back next Saturday is the hard work. The information in this section will help both land managers and trail advocates recruit and maintain a core group of volunteer trailworkers.

Attracting and Keeping Volunteers: Four Steps for Success

Step 1: Get the Word Out.

You need help. You know this, but your potential volunteers don't. Your first challenge is to reach out to your prospective work crew.

Use the Media.

Invite local reporters to a planning meeting or a trail maintenance day. Local newspapers, television, and radio stations are all interested in stories about people pulling together to improve their communities. Here's your chance to build support for your project and solicit help from area volunteers. Send a press release to all three types of media. Press releases should explain why you're building a trail, where it will be, how it will benefit the community, and how people can get involved. Include contact information and a calendar of work days.

Contact Local Cycling Clubs.

Ask the leader of your local club to explain your cause to members at the next meeting. Also try to disseminate your message through the club's email system, website, or printed newsletter.

Start a Website.

The Internet is a great place to reach volunteers, present the project, and show the progress you're making. Dedicate a website to the project and link it to your local cycling club's site.

Find Trail Users Where They Congregate.

Create a flyer soliciting volunteers and post it at places where outdoorsy types gather. Bike shops, coffee shops, outdoor-recreation shops, stables, trailhead signboards, and races are all excellent starting points. Be sure to include contact information and a calendar of upcoming work days.

Every weekend, thousands of dedicated volunteers help build and maintain trails in their communities. How do you persuade these people to spend their precious weekends bent over a shovel? Read the next few pages for the answer.

Find Creative Sources of Volunteers.

Don't restrict your efforts to cyclists. Be inclusive. There are plenty of people looking to help their communities. Here are some potential sources:

- **College Students:** Many fraternities and sororities have community service days—get on their list.
- **High School Students:** Some high schools have mandatory community service. Another great resource? The horde of kids trying to pad their resumes to get into college.
- **Girl and Boy Scouts:** Think Eagle Scout project.
- **National Service Organizations:** Americorps and the Student Conservation Association are great examples.
- **People in Orange Jumpsuits:** Many city, county, and state corrections departments provide well-organized, hard-working, and enthusiastic work crews. Great trails have been built by these groups.

Trail Solutions

Step 2: Be Prepared.

If you're not well organized, you won't get much done on your first workday. Worse yet, you'll run the risk of losing volunteers. People will only volunteer their time if they feel their effort is making an impact. If you're running a ramshackle show, word will spread, and you'll attract fewer volunteers. Check these items off your list before your first trail day.

Develop Goals and Strategies.

Make a list of your project goals and break them into objectives and tasks. List all the actions needed, including meeting with the land manager, organizing tools, and finding local business support (local businesses can help by donating schwag or food). Estimate how much time it will take and how many volunteers you need to complete each task. (See page 187 for estimates on trail costs and volunteer hours.)

Get Help.

Delegate. You can't do it all yourself effectively and you risk burnout if you try. Develop a good back-up plan and a group of crew leaders who could take over if necessary. You'll also find that some people will jump at the chance to provide leadership, and they will play a more active role in the project if they are given a bit of authority.

Be Prepared for Any Kind of Turnout.

A crowd of volunteers may show up. Then again, you may only get enough do-gooders to pack a phone booth. Be prepared with several different work plans so that your workday is productive either way.

Train Crew Leaders in Advance.

The last thing you want is 40 workers, side-by-side, swinging sharp, heavy tools within inches of each others' heads. You want to build trail—not the patient list at your local hospital. Thus, your work day will be much safer and more effective if you split the volunteers into small groups. Each group should be led by a trained crew leader. If you don't have any experienced crew leaders, ask the land agency, if applicable, to train a few of your club members, or contact IMBA for info on crew-leader training.

Begin every volunteer trailwork day with a quick meeting to run through introductions, offer a safety briefing, and explain the day's project.

Part One: Partnerships

Step 3: Manage Your Volunteers.

Brief Your Crew.

Begin by introducing any park staff present, the crew leaders, and the individuals (name tags are helpful). Remind people to sign up, complete waiver forms (if required), and then run through a safety briefing and the day's format. Count heads and assign crew leaders, leaving one person to greet the late arrivals.

Promote Safe and Proper Tool Use.

When you brief your crew, take a few minutes to also explain the proper way to handle tools (see Part 5) and the basics behind a few critical construction techniques.

Bright Idea

Reach Out to Other Trail Users. Venture outside your circle and seek volunteers from organizations that represent other trail user groups who'll benefit from the trail. Local equestrian, hiking, and trail-running groups all hold potential. Your trail will also benefit greatly from the design input of other users.

Don't forget to invite the kids! They love getting dirty and will learn how to care for trails and the land. Just be safe, particularly when using trail tools.

Volunteers gain an appreciation for the hard work it takes to build trails and will try hard to minimize their impact when they return as visitors.

Provide Leadership.

Your trailbuilding crew needs inspiration, encouragement, and direction in order to complete the project efficiently. As their leader, you must to ensure that your volunteers are excited about the work, aware of their progress, and focused on the task at hand. They will look to you for guidance, so you should be prepared to provide it!

Care for Your Crew.

Your volunteers are sacrificing their weekend to help build this trail. Do you have water, snacks, and lunch for everyone? Remember, this is a volunteer trailbuilding day, not an episode of *Survivor*. If possible, avoid scheduling work days during the hottest months. Don't work your volunteers for more than five or six hours at a time and be sure to take breaks. You want to be sure you'll see these folks again. . .in volunteer mode!

Keep Track of What's Going On.

Working alongside volunteers is important, but keeping the work flowing safely, providing encouragement, and monitoring progress is essential. Give clear instructions and explain your goals so that volunteers and crew leaders are all on the same page.

Keep Records.

Record the time you put into the project preparation, the number of volunteers you've used, and the total number of hours the project takes to complete. This information will help in planning future events and shows commitment—a requirement for some grant applications. Use a camera to record "before and after" shots of the work.

Be Considerate of Other Trail Users.

Place notices or signs at the trailhead or work site to promote safety and to encourage others to join or attend the next work party. Don't let your volunteers harass or "guilt trip" other trail users into helping as they pass the worksite, however. Be positive and encourage visitors to help next time.

Avoid Leaving a Job Half-Finished.

If you and your workers are unable to finish a section of trail, be sure to leave it in a condition that won't pose a risk to trail users. Consider closing the trail, posting clear signs around areas of danger, or rerouting users on a detour around the construction site until you and your volunteers can come back and complete the job.

Step 4: Keep 'em Coming Back!

Provide a Sense of Accomplishment.

Volunteers will return if they feel they accomplished something. To ensure this happens, match crews to tasks that are within their capacity. Every once in a while, step back and encourage your volunteers take a look at what they've achieved.

Make It Enjoyable.

Trailwork is tough, but it should also be fun. Don't take it too seriously, use a little humor, and include a fun element afterward such as a BBQ, a group ride, or a get-together at the local pub or cafe.

Stay in Touch.

Have volunteers register. Get their names, addresses, phone numbers, and email addresses, so you can keep them involved. This is particularly important with first-timers. New volunteers are likely to return if they leave feeling welcomed and appreciated. Never shame people into coming back.

Show Your Appreciation.

Volunteers need to know their hard work is valued. List volunteers in newsletters or put photos of workers on your group's website. Many trail groups have rewards programs with schwag as an incentive for volunteering a certain number of hours. Consider holding a party at the end of the season to recognize volunteers.

Be Consistent/Repeat Step One.

Most trailbuilding efforts take time—think months, instead of days. Develop a regular schedule and publicize it. Work days can be held once a week, once a month, or once a year. Predictability is what will keep people coming back. Reaching out to past and potential volunteers is an ongoing task. Consider delegating this responsibility to a reliable volunteer who is a savvy communicator.

Don't Make the Mistake of. . .

Setting Unreasonable Goals. Trailworkers should not be expected to work miracles. Giving them an unreachable goal is a primary cause of volunteer burnout. Consider all the factors, from the job you hope to accomplish to the tools available and the physical condition of your volunteers, and set your sights on a goal that will be attainable. Remember to give trailworkers support and encouragement along the way and to recognize their efforts. The satisfaction of a job well done will bring them back for the next project.

Creating and Sustaining a Successful Club—Going Out on a Limb in Montana

Low Impact Mountain Bikers (LIMB), of Missoula, Montana, is a perfect reflection of its larger community—not too big, low-key, and fun-loving. The group is also working hard to preserve the region's abundant open space, and particularly its trails. Every year since 1990, LIMB has been bringing groups of 10 to 30 volunteers on work projects to improve Missoula's paths. In the last few years, they've become the major force in the local trails community.

LIMB was formed in response to growing conflicts between bikers and equestrians, and members began by attending a Backcountry Horsemen event to familiarize horses with bikes. Relations quickly improved.

According to Bill Jacko, a founding member, LIMB's early goal was simply "to try to dispel the notion of the mountain biker as some idiot in the backcountry tearing things up."

To that end they made presentations to local school children and worked to build relationships with city agencies. The local Forest Service was involved from the beginning—one Forest Service employee was even on the first LIMB Board of Directors—supplying tools and directing LIMB trailwork efforts.

This growing partnership with the Forest Service was aided by four visits from Subaru/IMBA Trail Care Crews. By 2001, thanks largely to IMBA Trailbuilding Schools and trailwork led by the Trail Care Crew, the Forest Service had authorized LIMB to cut new trail on the mountains overlooking town. Since then, the Bureau of Land Management has sought the club's expertise to design and build an entirely new, mountain bike–focused trail network near Missoula.

While trailbuilding success has built LIMB's profile, the club keeps its 100 or so members happy with social events like its weekly, Thursday-night rides and LIMB "pint nights" at local breweries. LIMB has also been the lead organizer of New Belgium Brewing's annual Tour de Fat bike festival in Missoula, which raises money for future trailwork.

Photo by Rich Etchberger.

Part Two: Philosophy of Successful Trails

Now that you've read about gaining access and proposing your trail project, you're probably eager to dig in and learn some construction techniques. Perhaps you saw the title of this section and groaned aloud, fearing that we'd fill the next few pages with theoretical, pie-in-the-sky mumbo jumbo. Maybe, you're even tempted to skip the discussion on philosophy in search of something more tangible to sink your teeth in. . . . Well, don't.

This Part will be useful to seasoned land managers as well as first-time trailworkers. It includes both the very basics and cutting-edge theories for designing sustainable singletrack trails that will provide delightful experiences for diverse user groups and enrich your community.

In This Part ...

- **The Core Elements of a Sustainable Trail** 40
  Why, Who, and What 40
- **Why Diverse Trail Systems Work** 42
- **Shared Use or Single Use?** 44
  Shared-Use Trails 44
  Single-Use Trails 45
  One-Way Trails 46
- **The Importance of Singletrack** 48
  What Is Singletrack? 49
  Why Is Singletrack Important? 49
- **The Economic Benefits of Trails** 50
  Trails Take Towns from Bust to Boom 51
- **Bringing Mountain Bikers to Your Area** 52
  Fourteen Tips 52

The Core Elements of a Sustainable Trail

A sustainable trail. . .
- Protects the environment.
- Meets the needs of its users.
- Requires little maintenance.
- Minimizes conflict between different user groups.

If any one of these four values is overemphasized at the expense of another, the trail could cause irreparable damage to the environment, provide an unsafe or negative experience for visitors, or deplete your maintenance budget. If, in planning your trail, you find that you can't balance these components, you should strongly consider whether it is wise to build the trail at all. There's no point in creating a trail that's destructive, unsatisfying, or expensive to maintain.

Why, Who, and What?

Before you begin designing a trail, you must ask yourself three questions.

1. Why do we need a new trail?
2. Who will use the trail?
3. What kind of experience are we trying to create?

If you don't have sound answers to these questions, you're in trouble. Read on. . .

Why Do We Need This Trail?

Before you invest precious time and money into building a new trail, you need to make sure that the existing trail system is working to its full potential.

Do you have carte blanche to build a new trail system? Okay, design away. In truth, however, this is rarely the case. People often build a new trail because the old one isn't holding up or satisfying users. In this case, you need to determine why the existing trail isn't working before you create a new one. Often, some maintenance and slight rerouting of an existing trail may be all that's needed to remedy the situation.

Who Will Use the Trail?

If you build a shared-use trail that only meets the needs of one user group, the trail is doomed from the start. As a designer, you must know the types of visitors your trail will attract and support. The vast majority of trails are shared-use. Thus, you should consider what makes a quality trail from a number of different user-group perspectives. Hikers, mountain bikers, horseback riders, runners, and birdwatchers (to name just a few) all have specific expectations for their trail experience. Your job as a designer is to anticipate and account for those expectations. Which leads us to the next question…

What Kinds of Experiences Are We Trying to Create?

Once you know who will be using the trail, you must determine what they want to experience on the trail. Do they seek solitude, exercise, an adrenaline rush, or all three? Designing the trail becomes much easier when you know who its users will be and you've determined what they want to get out of their time on the trail.

Here's an example:

Imagine you've teamed with a land manager and conducted a survey of people entering the park where you'll be building trail. Surveys show that hikers, mountain bikers, equestrians, and anglers would like a connecting route between two existing trails. This would increase the variety of available loops. For anglers, it would also allow easier access to a popular fishing hole. By reviewing maps, you have discovered that the most convenient point at which you can tie these two trails together is about 3 miles from either existing trailhead. The new connecting trail will be about 1.5 miles long.

Using this information, you can infer that there will be lots of user interaction on the new trail, in part because it will make the established trail system more appealing and therefore busier. One group—the anglers—will consistently use the trail to access a favorite spot.

The length of any trail determines its users. By adding the connector, the new one-way overall distance of the trail will be 7.5 miles. A trail this long will appeal to hardy hikers and anglers. Most cyclists and equestrians will find the new loop just enough of a challenge.

Armed with this information, you can anticipate that the trail will attract the following groups:
- Beginner and intermediate cyclists
- Beginner to advanced equestrians
- Anglers
- Experienced hikers

Now, should the new section be rugged and full of twists and turns? Probably not. A wide variety of visitors will be using this trail, so it needs to incorporate good sightlines and a fair amount of passing room. An open and flowing trail is in order. Such a trail will appeal to all the different groups, enable communication between them, and mitigate conflict.

Why Diverse Trail Systems Work

By now, you may realize how difficult it is to create a single trail that meets everyone's needs. How can you balance a freeride mountain biker's desire for technical challenge, a birdwatcher's need for serenity, and a trail runner's quest for a fast workout—all on a single path? In many cases, *you can't*.

Don't get us wrong; you can build a shared-use trail that meets the needs of several types of trail users. You can even build different trail experiences into a single trail corridor—say, a technical boulder-ride alongside an easy section of trail—but there are times when some user's needs are simply incompatible with others. That's okay. Diverse trail systems help resolve these kinds of problems.

A system of intersecting trail loops enables you to design a network of trails that will meet everyone's needs. The beauty of the arrangement is this: If you build a system of trails—with wide-open easy trails near the trailhead(s) and rugged, difficult trails farther away—you can open the network to all users, and they'll gravitate to the trails that appeal to them. By creating a system that features trails of varying difficulty, you provide something for everyone.

Advanced mountain bikers usually crave long, technically challenging rides; they'll quickly pass by

A diverse trail network with a variety of trail styles ensures happy visitors.
Location: St. George, Utah. Photo by Bob Allen.

Trail Solutions

Preserving the Environment—Blending Access Work and Conservation in New England

The New England Mountain Bike Association's (NEMBA) commitment to conservation has garnered respect and political clout in environmentally minded New England.

NEMBA's solid conservation work earned special recognition when the New England office of the U.S. Environmental Protection Agency presented NEMBA with their 2003 Environmental Merit Award, recognizing the group's "commitment, teamwork, and perseverance. . .to bring about meaningful and lasting environmental protection and improvements."

NEMBA also raised more than $200,000—mostly from individual mountain bikers—to purchase a hilly, wooded, 47-acre land parcel near the headwaters of the Charles River in Milford, Massachusetts. NEMBA plans to place a conservation restriction on the land to protect it from development, and they will implement a trail management plan to allow all non-motorized users free access to this popular area. NEMBA hopes that the site will become a model for an environmentally sound trail system and a laboratory for trailbuilding techniques. They also hope to inspire other nonprofit groups to preserve open space for conservation and recreation and to build their own trail systems.

The New England Mountain Bike Association is the largest regional, nonprofit, cycling advocacy organization in the United States, with more than 4,300 members and 17 chapters.

---

the wide, smooth trails just a short jaunt from the parking lot. As a result, they generally leave those trails to slower, novice riders, as well as hikers and equestrians.

Likewise, the mom and dad who are taking their young children on a Sunday stroll won't hike 5 miles to the start of the advanced trail that suits avid mountain bikers, backpackers, and runners. Their kids would tire and begin yammering long before they reached their destination.

Diverse trail systems work. They reduce congestion and trail wear by distributing visitors throughout the park instead of concentrating them on one or two trails.

The Bigger Picture

You may have read all this thinking, "Yeah, well I've only got two trails in my park." The good news is if your current trails are working well, you can often use them as the basis for a wider system of trails.

A trail system can also consist of trails within a specific region (as opposed to a single park). A high-use park close to town, for instance, might contain wide, smooth trails that can be enjoyed by the masses, while a park 10 minutes farther down the road contains a mix of trails, and the park 20 minutes away contains more technical and challenging trails. Though the playing field is larger, the result is the same.

Shared Use or Single Use?

Shared-Use Trails

Some land managers believe separate trails will eliminate user conflict, with one trail for mountain bikers, one trail for hikers, and so on. Separating trail users is a commonplace strategy in recreational land management. The problem with this policy, however, is that responsible bike use is, in fact, compatible with most other types of trail use. When all visitors observe basic trail etiquette, their encounters with other users will be harmonious, and most people will have a satisfying experience on the trail.

From day one, IMBA has advocated shared-use trails. This position is based on the following seven beliefs:

1. **Shared-use trails best accommodate the needs of the most users.** Open trails disperse users across an entire trail system, while single-use or restricted-use trails tend to concentrate users, increasing negative social impacts through crowding.
2. **Sharing trails helps build a trail community.** Visitors are encouraged to cooperate in order to preserve and protect a common resource. Encountering other types of users on a trail offers the opportunity to meet and talk, which helps to establish mutual respect and courtesy. Separate trails, on the other hand, can sometimes breed ill will, territoriality, and rivalries.
3. **Shared trails are most cost effective for land managers.** They require fewer signs and less staff, which simplifies monitoring and enforcement.
4. **Shared trails empower responsible, experienced users.** Novices and "outlaws" are exposed to conscientious, courteous users, and the opportunity for peer regulation is enhanced.
5. **Shared-use trails take better advantage of the available space.** Quite simply, they provide more trail for everyone to enjoy.
6. **Shared trails require less trail miles and therefore have less impact.** Building additional trails for individual user groups increases the ecosystem impacts including potential habitat fragmentation and water sedimentation.
7. **Shared-use trails manage the most visitors.** Trails that lead to major destinations, such as waterfalls and scenic vistas, should be shared-use, since all visitors will want to see a point of interest. For the same reason, trails that serve as major travel corridors are more efficient when shared.

Shared-use trails help build a trail community to support a common resource.

Single-Use Trails

Separate, single-use trails disturb more land and can breed resentment. Mountain bikers, in particular, feel frustration when they ride up to a beautiful, twisty singletrack only to discover that it is posted with a NO BIKES sign.

That said, IMBA recognizes that local conditions vary and that there are cases where single-use trails do make sense. Here is a list of situations where separating visitors may be the best option.

Crowded Trails: Popular trail systems with very crowded trails can have a blend of shared and single-use routes. Visitors won't enjoy a traffic jam when they are seeking relaxation and a connection with nature. Different routes for hikers and bicyclists can help provide a desirable experience.

Crowded Trailheads: Trail systems can have separate access points that cater to specific users. One entrance can be designated for equestrians and include horse-trailer parking. Another parking area can be designated for hikers and bikers. The trail network can blend shared and single use.

High-Speed Trails: A designated trail can allow advanced runners and riders to race-train at higher speeds without bothering other visitors. Phoenix, Arizona, has an outstanding network of trails ringing the city, highlighted by a few trails called "competitive tracks" designed for high-speed use.

Challenge Parks: A mountain bike playground can be set-aside for riders to hone their skills in isolation. A practice area with a wide variety of challenging obstacles, from easy to difficult, will allow for skills progression. A challenge park is a perfect place to offer skills clinics.

Nature Trails: A single-use trail can be created to provide hikers or birdwatchers with the seclusion they desire. Likewise, trails for disabled visitors may benefit from restricted use.

Extraordinary Mountain Biking Trails: The experience of riding a narrow, roller-coaster trail where twists and turns unfold under your wheels in a rocking rhythm is highly valued by mountain biking diehards. These types of trails envelope riders in a zone of exhilaration and are most successful when they are specifically designated for mountain bikers.

Part Two: Philosophy of Successful Trails

Bells Ring in Santa Barbara

Bike bells have successfully minimized trail-user conflict in many popular riding areas. In Santa Barbara, California's Los Padres National Forest, Santa Barbara Mountain Bike Trail Volunteers (an IMBA affiliate) and Kona Bicycles have taken the concept to the next level, providing free bells to cyclists who are heading downhill on particularly popular trails. Bell boxes, stocked with loaner mini-cowbells that attach to a mountain bike's handlebar, have been built at busy trailheads. Riders can grab bells at the upper trailhead, use them on their way down, then deposit them at the bottom. The bells are receiving widespread praise from other trail users, including equestrians who say the familiar cowbell sound is less likely to spook horses than traditional bike bells.

One-Way Trails

Sometimes shared-use trails can be designated as one-way routes, so that users must travel them in only one direction. There are both benefits and disadvantages to one-way trails.

Pros:
A one-way trail can. . .
- Alleviate congestion on a crowded trail.
- Provide a more predictable experience (no on-coming trail users).
- Reduce the number of passes between users.

Cons:
A one-way trail can. . .
- Lead to uneven wear on the trail tread.
- Limit the experience, as visitors often like to travel in both directions.
- Be difficult to monitor/enforce.
- Create animosity among users.
- Require consistent signage so first-time visitors know what to do and don't invoke the wrath of other users.

Trail Solutions

Here are three examples of one-way trails:

1. A one-way, mountain bike–only trail. If the park in question is primarily visited by mountain bikers, you might designate one trail as a one-way, mountain bike–only trail. The one-way trail allows for tight single-track with short sightlines and blind corners, without the risk of collisions.

2. A shared-use trail where mountain bikes travel in one direction and all other users travel in the opposite direction. This scenario requires clear sightlines in order to be effective, but it allows you to channel slower visitors in one direction and faster users in the other to help reduce conflict. You don't want mountain bikers riding at warp speed, but you *do* want visitors to see and safely anticipate encounters with one another.

3. A shared-use trail on which the direction of travel and/or access restrictions change on alternating days.
This approach seems to work well in high-volume areas with short sightlines and on trails where speed is a problem and design changes can't be made. However, it definitely adds a management wrinkle. It can be difficult to get pedestrians to buy into the idea that they can only use a specific trail on Mondays, Wednesdays, Fridays, and Sundays, while convincing mountain bikers that they can only ride the trail on Tuesdays, Thursdays, and Saturdays. If you can get your community to support this idea, and you do an excellent job of posting signs that clearly spell out the policy, this might be a good solution for you.

Reducing Trail-User Conflict: Fast Tracks in Phoenix

Phoenix, Arizona, boasts some of the best trails of any urban area in the world. The warm, dry climate and hilly topography lend themselves perfectly to outdoor recreation. The region has an outstanding network of trails ringing the city, highlighted by something called "competitive tracks." Competitive tracks are single-direction trails designed for high-speed, nonmotorized use. The first competitive track was opened in 1998, thanks to sponsorship from Specialized Bicycles and volunteer trailbuilding help from the Mountain Bike Association of Arizona and IMBA. Since then, Maricopa County has expanded the network of competitive tracks to three separate parks and approximately 35 miles of trail. The tracks operate on a fee basis. Revenues are used to enhance and maintain the competitive track system. "It's been a huge success," said Rand Hubbell, marketing coordinator for Maricopa Parks and Recreation. "The parks get a ton of use from local residents. Competitive tracks have also been used by the 24 Hours of Adrenaline, the local state championship series, and manufacturers testing new gear in the spring." Since the competitive tracks were built, reports of user conflict on other trails in Maricopa County have drastically decreased. Most important, recreational mountain bike access to shared-use trails has continued.

The Importance of Singletrack

Some officials and citizens object to singletrack bicycling. Seeing narrow trails as inherently dangerous, they advocate that bicyclists should be restricted to riding on roads or very wide trails. This perspective doesn't recognize the nature of mountain biking.

Cycling on narrow, natural-surface trails is as old as the bicycle. In its beginning, *all* bicycling was essentially mountain biking, because bicycles predate paved roads. In many historic photographs from the late 19th century, people are shown riding bicycles on dirt paths.

"Mountain biking on singletrack is like skiing in fresh powder, or matching the hatch while fly fishing, or playing golf at Pebble Beach." —Bill Harris, Trail Advocate

During World War II the Swiss Army outfitted companies of soldiers with bicycles to more quickly travel on narrow trails through mountainous terrain. In the 1970s, when the first mountain bikes were fashioned from existing "clunkers," riders often took their bikes on natural-surface routes. When the mass production of mountain bikes started in the early 1980s, more and more bicyclists found their way into the backcountry, and the geometry of mountain bikes was changed to improve handling on narrow trails. At first cyclists used existing hiking, motorcycle, game, and livestock trails. In recent years many new trails have been designed with mountain bike use in mind.

What is Singletrack?

A singletrack trail is one where users must generally travel in single file. The term "hiking trail" is an improper synonym for singletrack, because it defines a type of user, not the physical structure of the trail.

The tread of a singletrack trail is typically 18- to 24-inches wide, though it can be as narrow as 6 or as wide as 36 inches. Singletrack trails tend to wind around obstacles such as trees, large rocks, and bushes. As compared to roads, singletrack trails blend into the surrounding environment, disturb much less ground, and are easier to maintain. The tread of singletrack is almost always natural surface, in contrast to the gravel or pavement of roads.

Why is Singletrack So Important?

Most trail enthusiasts prefer narrower trails. Whether they are riding a mountain bike, running or hiking the trail, or exploring on horseback, these users want to experience a close connection to nature. Singletrack provides this better than roads and separates recreationists from the world of the automobile. Trees and shrubs may create a tunnel of green, tall flowers may reach eye level, wildlife may cross the path, immersing visitors in the natural world. The experience just isn't the same on an open, wide road.

Many singletrack enthusiasts also seek a higher degree of challenge than can be found on most jeep trails or forest roads. The narrow nature of singletrack makes these trails exciting for a variety of users and provides an invigorating backcountry experience.

Singletrack Fosters Slow Speeds

Those who object to mountain biking on singletrack envision riders bombing along a 12-inch-wide trail at supersonic speeds. They imagine bicyclists launching headlong into startled hikers and equestrians who have no place to escape on the narrow trail. This scenario, while alarming, is generally unfounded.

Singletrack trails tend to slow mountain bikers—particularly on shared-use trails where they anticipate encountering other visitors. The narrow and frequently rough nature of singletrack demands constant focus and a slow to moderate speed, and its tight and twisty nature is exhilarating on its own. While there are always a few renegades who push the limits, most mountain bikers are responsible, conscientious trail users who seek an enjoyable experience, not excessive speed.

It's almost counter-intuitive, but speed and danger tend to increase when mountain bikers are confined to wide roads. Bored and unchallenged, bicyclists quickly attain speeds that can bring them into direct conflict with other visitors.

The Economic Benefits of Trails

When you meet with land managers and community leaders, you may encounter a common question: *How will new trails benefit our community?* It is a perfectly reasonable query, given that the community will (in one form or another) invest resources into developing these trails. Your answer should be: *In a variety of ways and quite a lot.* A well-designed trail system can bring an influx of valuable tourism dollars to your area and increase property values—all while enhancing the quality of life for residents.

The Outdoor Industry Association conducted a study in 2002, which revealed that bicycling on narrow singletrack trails is one of the most popular outdoor activities in the United States. The study showed that 43.1 million Americans rode their mountain bikes off road that year, and 7 million of those were considered enthusiasts.

Fruita, Colorado, has become a worldwide mountain biking mecca thanks to the combined efforts of local mountain bikers and the BLM. Photo by Rich Etchberger.

Trail Solutions

The region around Medora, North Dakota, has emerged as a popular mountain biking destination.
Photo by Chuck Haney.

Consider the following success stories…

Trails Take Towns from Bust to Boom

Fruita, Colorado

In the early 1990s Fruita was a dusty, western Colorado desert town with little tourism. The local oil refinery closed in the late 1980s, and many farms were subdivided into housing developments.

Today Fruita is known worldwide as a mountain biking mecca. Fruita's leaders teamed with the local mountain bike community and the Bureau of Land Management to develop two outstanding trail networks: the Kokopelli and the Book Cliffs Trail Systems. In less than five years, Fruita went from being one of Colorado's most economically depressed towns to being one of its more prosperous. Fruita's revival is commonly attributed to the development of these trails.

Maah Daah Hey Raises Medora to Mecca

A few years ago the state of North Dakota sat alongside Papua New Guinea and the Sahara on the average mountain biker's radar. Fortunately for the village of Medora, that has changed. Now cyclists are a regular sight in this tiny, remote tourist town of 100 near the border of North Dakota and Montana. According to Loren Morlock, co-owner of Medora's only bike shop, Dakota Cyclery, "You go [to Medora] now and it's car after car after car with bikes on top."

It's only taken one trail to transform Medora into this veritable velo-hotbed—one 100-mile-long singletrack named the Maah Daah Hey. Officials from the surrounding Little Missouri National Grassland conceived the Maah Daah Hey for equestrians, but input from Morlock and his wife Jennifer, along with IMBA, convinced them to make it a shared-use trail. In 1999, Subaru/IMBA Trail Care Crew leaders Mike and Jan Riter participated in the trail's opening ceremonies, and they returned in 2000 to lead an IMBA Trailbuilding School. A year later, the Maah Daah Hey was designated an IMBA Epic. The number of mountain bikers visiting Medora has been increasing ever since.

Bringing Mountain Bikers to Your Area

Whether you're a trailbuilder, a government official, a bike-shop owner, or an enthusiastic member of a mountain bike club, there are several things you can do to make your community more appealing to mountain bikers. The following tips include something for everyone.

14 Tips for Bringing Mountain Bikers to Your Area

1 Provide and promote trails for all abilities.

Beginners enjoy lightly traveled paved roads, dirt roads, and wide dirt paths. Intermediate and advanced riders seek twisting, forest trails, challenging singletrack, and downhill routes. Providing all of these experiences in abundance, and promoting trails through websites, tourism brochures, and mountain bike clubs, will help establish your area as a first-rate mountain biking destination. Be sure to advertise a whole system of trails instead of just one in order to avoid over-use.

2 Develop sustainable singletrack trails.

IMBA provides advice on designing and building trails that require minimal maintenance. Mountain bikers crave singletrack, and designing interconnecting singletrack trails will bring them in droves.

3 Showcase the land's natural beauty.

Design and recommend rides that visit sites with historical interest and beautiful views.

4 Sign your trails well.

Riders who get lost may have a bad experience. Design, produce, and post accurate trail signs to supplement the signs and markers that may already be in place. No one likes too many signs, but simple, attractive markers that direct mountain bikers will be well received. Make sure to coordinate this effort with other trail groups.

5 Great maps make it easy for visitors.

Create excellent maps that clearly show the best trails for mountain biking. Elevation profiles and concise ride descriptions are helpful, as are estimates of ride difficulty, descriptions of ride features, and weather and safety considerations. Maps should include parking and facility information. Use map revenues to improve trails and mitigate tourism impacts.

6 Help your community understand mountain biking.

Some people don't know the difference between mountain bicycling and motorcycling. Help residents understand that mountain biking is a low-impact, quiet, muscle-powered, off-pavement sport. Reference one of the studies in Appendix A that shows the similarities between and biking and hiking in terms of their effects on trails and wildlife. Show that with proper trail management and design, all trail-user groups can recreate in harmony. Take town leaders on a ride.

7. Get your community involved.

Build community support for bicycle tourism by emphasizing the economic benefits. Cyclists spend money on gas, food, lodging, and souvenirs, and businesses that are friendly to riders will reap the rewards.

8. Seek support from local bike shops.

Tourists don't want to work to find out where to ride, lodge, eat, and shop. . .they usually just ask at the local bike shop. Shops can train their staff to be area ambassadors, which makes for happy bikers and satisfied customers. Giving mountain bikers the lay of the land, telling them where to park, and posting pictures of the area trailheads in the shop reduces travel hassle and anxiety for first-time visitors. Staff can also mention helpful tips for responsible riding and trail use.

9. Provide lodging with cyclists in mind.

Cyclists look for convenient places to stay that complement their lifestyle. Campgrounds near trailheads, bed and breakfasts, and hotels that provide secure bike storage are all appealing. Hut-to-hut (or inn-to-inn) rides have become popular in Colorado and Utah because they allow cyclists to ride light and free. Italy Bike Hotels, a group of more than 50 cooperating businesses, offer discounts to IMBA members, as well as guided tour packages, a place to store your bike, and pre- and post-ride snacks, and they'll even wash your bike and cycling clothes daily!

10. Photograph your trails professionally.

A picture really is worth a thousand words. Commission a photographer to capture your trails on film, and send slides or digital files to magazines, newspapers, and tourism bureaus. Moab, Utah; Fruita, Colorado; Medora, North Dakota; and Slatyfork, West Virginia have built stellar reputations as mountain bike destinations through photographs of happy riders on beautiful trails. IMBA has a database of professional photographers for your reference.

11. Advertise other amenities in the area.

Mountain bikers are active, adventurous people, and hiking, climbing, surfing, and other activities might appeal to them. Cyclists also love to eat (especially following a long day in the saddle), so a list of easy restaurant options is also appreciated. If you are advertising in a mountain bike–specific publication, or on your bike club's website, be sure to highlight other activities that might be of interest to cyclists.

12. Create package deals.

Develop package offers that appeal to mountain bikers by combining lodging, meals, and bicycle-shop support.

13. Woo the media.

Offer all-expense-paid mountain bike trips for the media—not only to editors at cycling magazines but also to editors at general magazines and journalists at daily newspapers.

14. Quantify your success.

To help ensure continued community buy-in and investment in infrastructure improvements, it is essential to quantify your success. It will take several years of promoting and tracking to get an accurate reading on the positive impact of bike tourism on your community, but this information is essential in order to garner and maintain local support. Start by examining sales tax, lodging, and traffic counts.

Location: Imperial Gulch, Idaho. Photo by Sterling Lorence.

Trail Solutions

Part Three: Principles of Sustainable Trails

What makes a trail sustainable? A sustainable trail balances many elements. It has very little impact on the environment, resists erosion through proper design, construction, and maintenance, and blends with the surrounding area. A sustainable trail also appeals to and serves a variety of users, adding an important element of recreation to the community. It is designed to provide enjoyable and challenging experiences for visitors by managing their expectations and their use effectively. The following sections will help you to understand and implement the core principles of sustainable trails.

In This Part ...

- **Rolling Contour Trails—**
  - Building Great Trails that Last 56
    - The Problem: Erosion 56
    - The Solution: Rolling Contour Trails 56
- **Understanding Grade** 59
    - Two Critical Trailbuilding Tips 60
- **The Five Essential Elements of Sustainable Trails** ... 63
    - 1. The Half Rule 63
    - 2. The Ten Percent Average Guideline 64
    - 3. Maximum Sustainable Grade 66
    - 4. Grade Reversals 67
    - 5. Outslope 69
- **Using a Clinometer** 70
    - How to Measure Grade 70
- **Trail Difficulty Rating System** 72
    - Trail Rating Guidelines 72
    - Criteria to Consider 74
    - Table: Trail Difficulty Rating System 75
- **Signs** 76
    - Sign Types 76
    - Sign Materials: Pros and Cons 79
- **Managing Visitors Through Trail Design** 80
    - You Control the Speed 80
    - Corralling, Chokes, and Turns 82
    - Spread 'em Out 83
    - Provide Diverse Experiences 83
- **Understanding Soils** 84
    - Sandy Soil 84
    - Silty Soil 84
    - Clay Soil 85
    - Loamy Soil 85

Rolling Contour Trails— Building Great Trails that Last

The Problem: Erosion

Erosion is the natural process through which rock and soil are worn away by wind and water. It's also a trail's worst enemy. Left unchecked, erosion can destroy trails and damage the environment. Trail erosion is accelerated by a combination of trail users, gravity, and water. *All* trail users loosen soil, especially on steeper grades where they resist the force of gravity.

Water compounds the problem if it's allowed to channel or "focus" down the trail. Focused water can do more damage to a trail than any user. It gains velocity and energy, washing away precious soil and cutting deeper into the tread each time it flows.

The Solution: Rolling Contour Trails

Fortunately, you can build trails that will resist erosion—**rolling contour trails**. A contour trail is a path that gently traverses a hill or sideslope. It's characterized by a gentle grade, undulations called **grade reversals**, and a **tread** that usually tilts or **outslopes** slightly toward the downhill edge. These features minimize tread erosion by allowing water to drain in a gentle, non-erosive manner called **sheet flow**. When water drains in thin, dispersed sheets, dirt stays where it belongs—on the trail.

Rolling Contour Trail

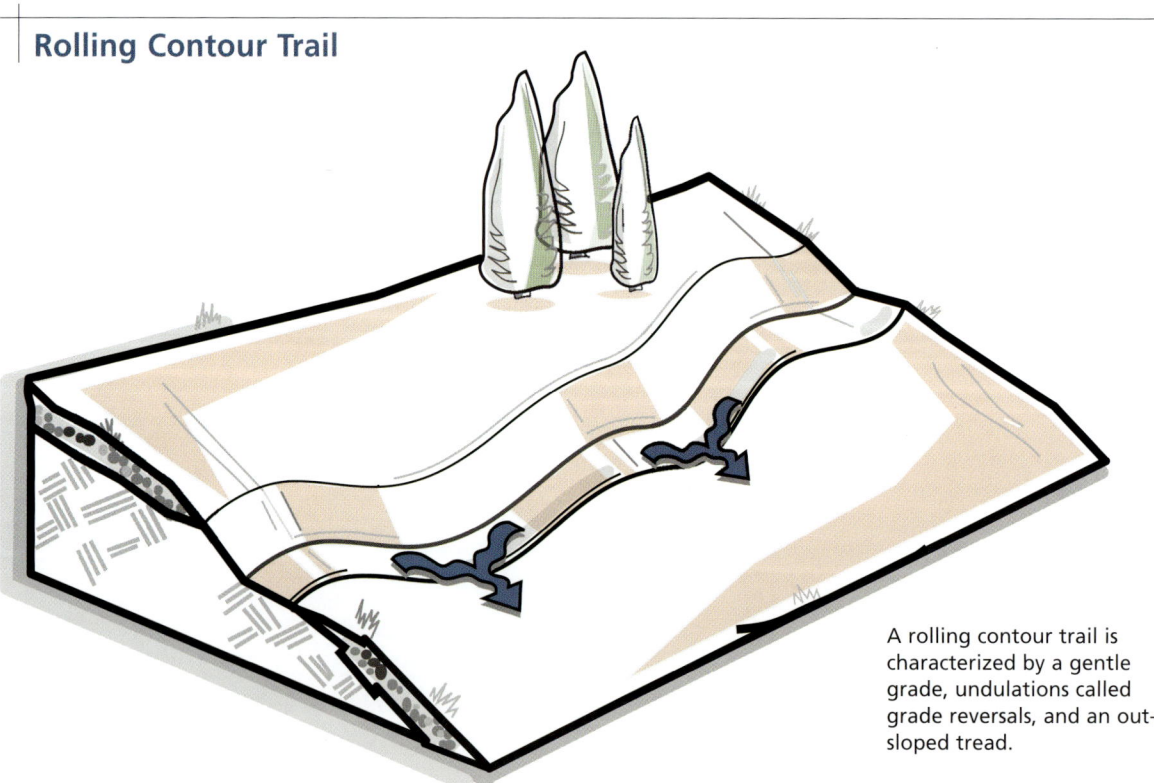

A rolling contour trail is characterized by a gentle grade, undulations called grade reversals, and an outsloped tread.

Trail Solutions

Erosion can destroy trails and damage the environment.

Part Three: Principals of Sustainable Trails

This hillside displays contour lines normally only visible on a topographic map.

Don't Make The Mistake Of...
Falling for the Fall Line. Fall-line trails are erosion nightmares. They turbo-charge natural and user-created erosion, expose rocks and roots, and quickly become a scar on the landscape. To build trails that last, pay careful attention to grade.

Understanding Trail Grade

One of the biggest trailbuilding mistakes is creating trails that are too steep. As we noted earlier, these trails funnel water and quickly erode. To avoid this mistake, you first have to understand the concept of trail **grade**—essentially an objective measure of steepness. Grade is expressed as a percentage and should not be confused with angle, which is expressed in degrees. Percent grade is used to measure the slope for roads, landscaping, and trails because it's easier to calculate than degrees.

If calculating grades sounds confusing, you can rest easy knowing there are ways to measure trail grade that don't involve calculators, slide rules, or NASA supercomputers. We'll cover these methods of determining trail grade in a minute.

What is Grade?

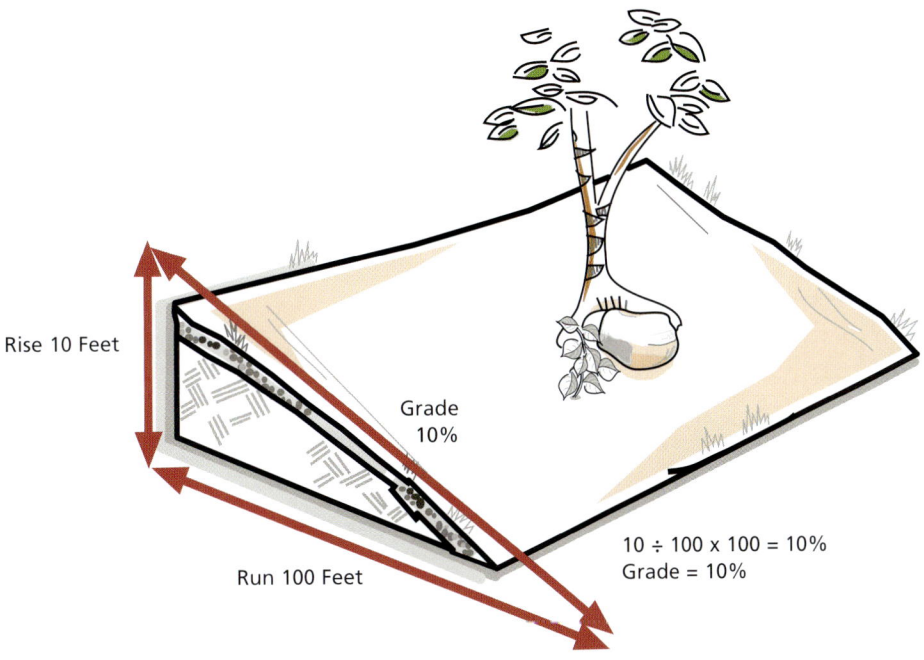

Grade is determined by dividing the elevation gain between two points by the linear distance between them. Percent grade equals rise over run multiplied by 100.

Two Critical Trailbuilding Tips

1. Avoid the Fall Line.

Fall-line trails usually follow the shortest route down a hill—the same path that water flows. The problem with fall-line trails is that they focus water down their length. The speeding water strips the trail of soil, exposing roots, creating gullies, and scarring the environment.

2. Avoid Flat Areas.

Flat terrain lures many trailbuilders with the initial ease of trail construction. However, if a trail is not located on a slope, there is the potential for the trail to become a collection basin for water. The trail tread must always be slightly higher than the ground on at least one side of it so that water can drain properly.

Fall-Line Trail

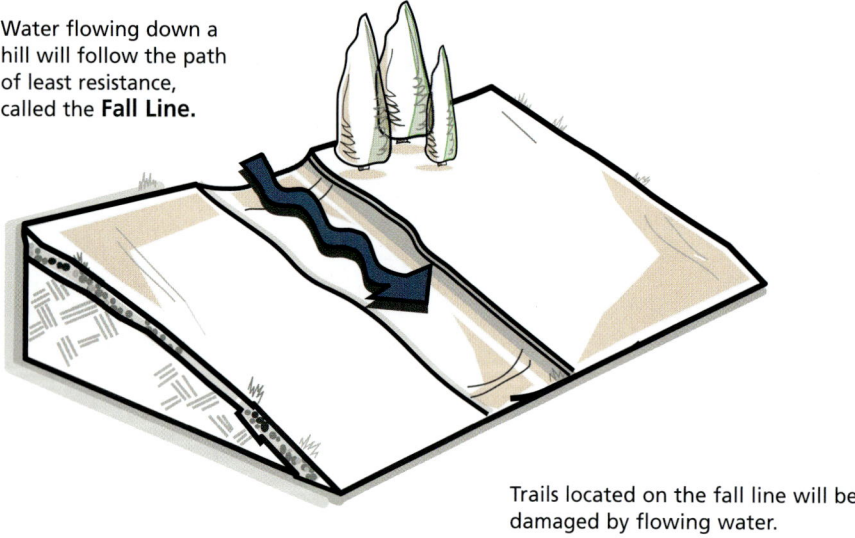

Water flowing down a hill will follow the path of least resistance, called the **Fall Line.**

Trails located on the fall line will be damaged by flowing water.

Here are some key terms to help you understand grade:

Tread: The actual surface of the trail upon which users travel.

Grade: Slope expressed as a percentage.

Fall Line: The prevailing slope and the direction water will naturally flow.

Sideslope: The natural slope of a hillside measured on the fall line.

Average Trail Grade: The average slope of the trail from one end to the other. Also called *overall trail grade*.

Average Trail Segment Grade: The average slope of a certain trail segment.

Maximum Trail Grade: The steepest trail slope that is longer than approximately 10 feet.

Half Rule: A trail's grade shouldn't exceed half the grade of the sideslope. If the trail grade is steeper than half the grade of the sideslope, it is considered a fall-line trail.

The 10 Percent Average Guideline: Generally, an *average* trail grade of 10 percent or less is the most sustainable.

Outslope: A method of tread construction that leaves the outside edge of a hillside trail lower than the inside, in order to shed water.

Grade Reversal: A reverse in the trail grade—usually a short dip followed by a rise—that forces water off the trail.

Fall-line trails funnel water and quickly erode—even if they are surfaced with gravel.

Part Three: Principals of Sustainable Trails

Trails that follow natural contours (like the side of this hill) are much more sustainable than trails that go straight up and down the slope. Location: Giants Causeway Headlands, Northern Ireland.

The Five Essential Elements of Sustainable Trails

1 The Half Rule

2 The Ten Percent Average Guideline

3 Maximum Sustainable Grade

4 Grade Reversals

5 Outslope

❶ The Half Rule

A trail's grade shouldn't exceed half the grade of the hillside or sideslope that the trail traverses. If the grade *does* exceed half the sideslope, it's considered a fall-line trail. Water will flow down a fall-line trail rather than run across it.

Measure the sideslope with a clinometer (we'll discuss how to do this shortly), then be sure to keep the tread grade below half of that figure in order to ensure good drainage. For example, if you're building across a hillside with a sideslope of 20 percent, the trail-tread grade should not exceed 10 percent.

The half rule is especially important in gently sloping areas. A common mistake occurs when trails are routed down gradual slopes, based on the assumption that erosion won't be a concern in nearly flat areas. Yet, water will funnel down trails and ruin them even on gentle slopes. A trail passing through an area with a mere 6 percent sideslope must have a trail tread grade less than half of that figure—only 3 percent—in order to escape the fall line.

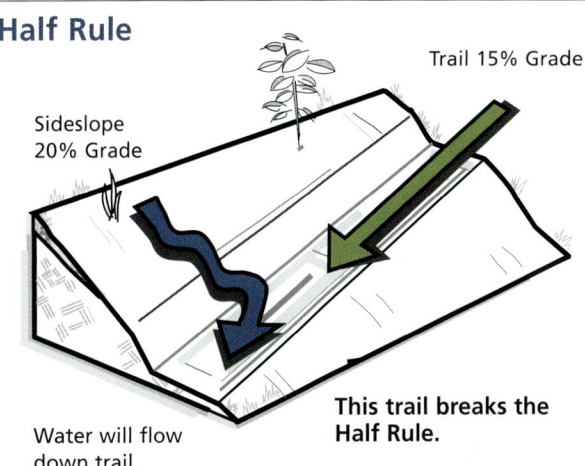

Half Rule

Sideslope 20% Grade
Trail 15% Grade
Water will flow down trail.
This trail breaks the Half Rule.

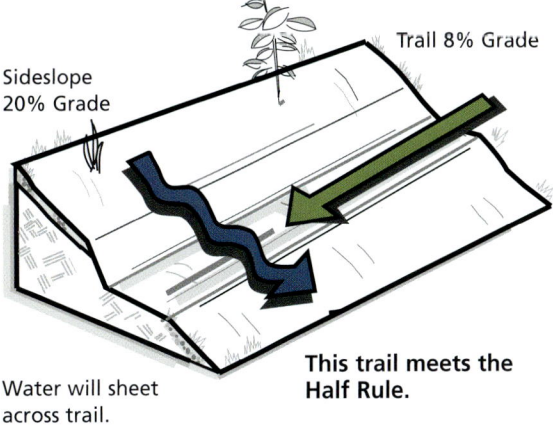

Sideslope 20% Grade
Trail 8% Grade
Water will sheet across trail.
This trail meets the Half Rule.

Part Three: Principals of Sustainable Trails

There is an upper limit to this half rule: You must also apply knowledge about maximum sustainable grades. Very steep trails will erode even if their grade meets the half rule. For example, a trail with a grade of 24 percent that traverses a steep, 50-percent sideslope may be unsustainable even though it complies with the half rule.

② The Ten Percent Average Guideline

Generally, an *average* trail grade of 10 percent or less is most sustainable. Also called *overall trail grade*, average trail grade is the slope of the trail from one end to the other.

This does not mean that *all* trail grades must be kept under 10 percent. Many trails will have short sections steeper than 10 percent, and some unique situations will allow average trail grades of more than 10 percent.

A trail's average grade is calculated by dividing total elevation gain by total length, multiplied by 100 to convert to percent. For example, a trail that gains 1,000 feet of elevation and is 2 miles long would have an average grade of 9.4 percent. (1,000 ft. /10,560 ft. x 100 = 9.4%)

For trails that undulate rather than climb or descend consistently, **average trail-segment grade** can be calculated for certain sections. For example, a trail that is relatively flat with only one small climb may have an average trail grade of only 2 or 3 percent. In this case, it would be more helpful to evaluate the average trail-segment grade in a critical climbing section only.

Average Trail Segment Grade

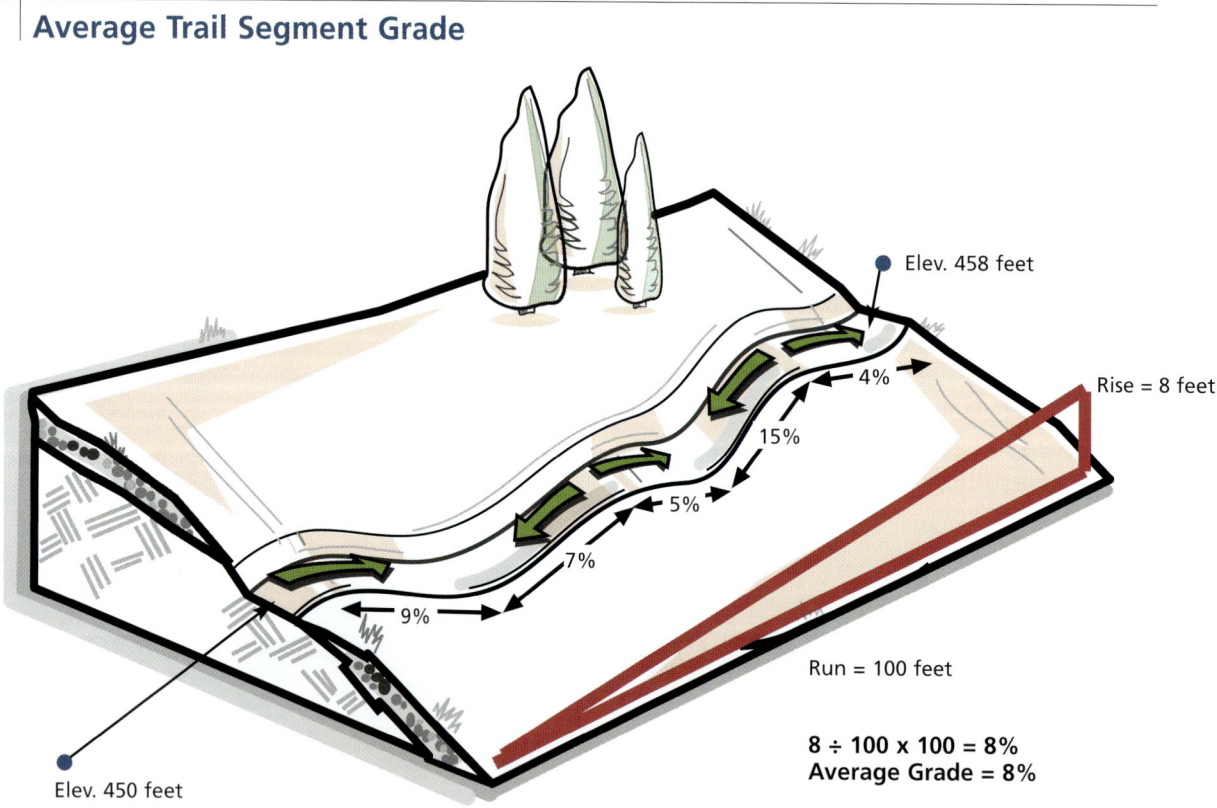

Elev. 458 feet
Rise = 8 feet
Run = 100 feet
8 ÷ 100 x 100 = 8%
Average Grade = 8%
Elev. 450 feet

Trail Solutions

Why 10 Percent?

Aids Planning

The 10 percent average figure provides a framework for sustainable design and can be very helpful when conceptualizing a trail. You'll be able to calculate the approximate length of trail needed to reach the top of a given hill at a sustainable grade, and you'll be able to plot possible trail corridors with sustainable grades on a topo map.

Applies to Most Soil Types

There are many types of soil and each has different qualities of cohesion and drainage. Some soils support steeper trail grades than others. By employing a 10-percent average, you won't need to rely on your soil-identification skills. A 10-percent average grade is a trustworthy guideline for sustainable trails in all but the most unique soil conditions. (See page 84 for a more thorough discussion on soil.)

Minimizes User-Caused Erosion

Average grades of 10 percent or less help minimize erosion caused by users. Sustained grades of more than 10 percent can increase the amount of soil loosened by visitors who must work harder to travel up or down the slope. This loosened material is more easily carried off by water and gravity, resulting in a damaged trail.

Allows Design Flexibility

A trail that climbs at conservative grades allows flexibility in case there is an obstacle in the path. By staying at or below a 10 percent average, you can adjust the route without necessarily starting at the beginning or routing the trail too steeply to reach your targeted destination.

Helps Future Reroutes

Future reroutes are much easier if the average grade is roughly 10 percent. For example, if a trail with an average grade of 20 percent develops an erosion problem, a reroute around the problem area may require very steep grades or a switchback to reach the destination. When average grades are closer to 10 percent, there is greater flexibility for the trail's future.

Accommodates Undulations

Average grades of 10 percent allow the trail to rise and fall without resulting in overly steep sections. Visualize a trail climbing to a targeted destination at an average grade of 20 percent. The trail dips slightly to cross a drainage and then resumes climbing. Following the dip, the trail must now climb at 25 percent—an unsustainable grade—in order to reach the destination. A better design would have the trail climb at an average of 8 to 10 percent, with short sections of 15 percent when needed (as long as the sideslope grade is greater than 30 percent, to ensure the trail meets the half rule).

Bright Idea

Begin flagging the trail with conservative grades below 8 or 10 percent. This allows flexibility in case you run into something like a water seep or major tree and need to route the trail around the object. By using shallow grades as you move along, you can steepen the route periodically without necessarily reconfiguring the whole trail.

3. Maximum Sustainable Trail Grades

The 10 Percent Average Guideline advises that, generally, an *average* trail grade of 10 percent or less is most sustainable. But what about *maximum grade?*

Maximum grade is the steepest section of trail that is more than about 10 feet in length. When designing a trail, it is essential to determine early in the process the precise maximum trail grades the trail will be able to sustain in your local conditions. This target figure will help guide your layout and ensure sustainability. Although maximum sustainable trail grade is typically about 15 to 20 percent, it is site-specific and fluctuates based on several factors. The variables to be considered when setting your target maximum trail grade include:

- **Half Rule** A trail's grade shouldn't exceed half the grade of the sideslope. If the trail grade is steeper than half the grade of the sideslope, it is considered a fall-line trail.

  Note: the maximum sustainable grade on a gentle hillside will be half the grade of the sideslope.

- **Soil Type** There are many types of soil and each has different qualities of cohesion and drainage. Some soils will support steeper trail grades than others. See page 84 for a more thorough discussion of soil types.

- **Rock** Trail grades can be steeper on solid rock. However, steep earthen sections between rocks may need to be fortified or armored to prevent soil loosening and erosion.

- **Annual Rainfall Amount** Trails in regions with either very high or very low annual rainfall may need to be designed with gentler trail grades. Lots of rain can lead to water-caused erosion. Low rain levels can lead to very dry and loose tread surfaces.

- **Grade Reversals** A grade reversal is a short dip followed by a rise, forcing water to drain off the trail. It is an essential technique for preventing water from channeling down the trail. Frequent grade reversals will allow for slightly steeper trail grades. We'll describe grade reversals more thoroughly in a moment.

- **Type of Users** Trails restricted to relatively low-impact visitors such as hikers and mountain bikers can sustain maximum grades as high as 15 to 25 percent for short distances depending on soil and rainfall. Trails open to visitors with higher impact, such as horses or motorized users, should have more gentle maximum grades.

- **Number of Users** Trails with high anticipated use may need shallower maximum trail grades.

- **Difficulty Level** Trails with a higher level of technical challenge may incorporate steeper grades, but construction techniques such as frequent grade reversals and armoring may be necessary to ensure sustainability.

Calculating the maximum sustainable trail grade is a complicated process that requires a high level of trail-building knowledge and experience. When in doubt, design trails with conservative grades until you have had the opportunity to observe the effect of a variety of trail grades in your local conditions.

4 Grade Reversals

A **grade reversal** is just what it sounds like—a spot at which a climbing trail levels out and then changes direction, dropping subtly for 10 to 50 linear feet before rising again. This change in grade forces water to exit the trail at the low point of the grade reversal, before it can gain more volume, momentum, and erosive power. Grade reversals are known by several different terms, including grade dip, grade brake, drainage dip, and rolling dip.

Frequent grade reversals are a critical—and often overlooked—element of sustainable trail design. Most trails will benefit from grade reversals every 20 to 50 feet, depending on soil type and rainfall. Bear this in mind: *It's much easier to build a trail with grade reversals in it than to come back a year later and try to retrofit them into a poorly designed trail. For best results, incorporate them in your design from the start!*

Grade reversals can help trails endure, even with minimal maintenance. Older trails often have a deeply compacted, concave trail tread that collects water. With regular grade reversals, this water will only be trapped on the trail for a short distance before it can drain. Grade reversals effectively divide the trail into short, individual watersheds, so the drainage characteristics of one section of trail won't affect any other section.

Grade reversals also make a trail more enjoyable. For mountain bikers, long runs of constant grade encourage excessive speed on a downhill and they're boring on an uphill. Short climbing interludes on a downhill provide variety, challenge, and let cyclists get off their brakes for a bit. Brief descents mixed into long climbs help all users regain their momentum and catch their breath.

Grade Reversal

Water may become trapped on trail and flow long distances if there are no grade reversals.

A grade reversal forces water to drain off the trail.

The trail on the top has no grade reversals and could trap or channel water, while the trail on the bottom rolls gently up and down, and will drain water efficiently.

An ideal trail will *simultaneously* incorporate all five sustainable trail principles:

The Half Rule

The 10 Percent Average Guideline

Maximum Sustainable Grade

Grade Reversals

Outslope

Trail Solutions

5. Outslope

As the trail contours across a hillside, the downhill or outer edge of the tread should tilt slightly down and away from the high side. This tilt is called **outslope**, and it encourages water to sheet across and off the trail instead of funneling down its center. Outslope is one reason why contour trails last for years and years. IMBA recommends that all trail treads be built with a 5-percent outslope.

Outslope can be difficult to maintain in loose soils. Tires, feet, and hooves constantly compact the center of the trail and push loose soil to the sides, creating a concave tread. Frequent grade reversals are essential in order for water to drain in this situation.

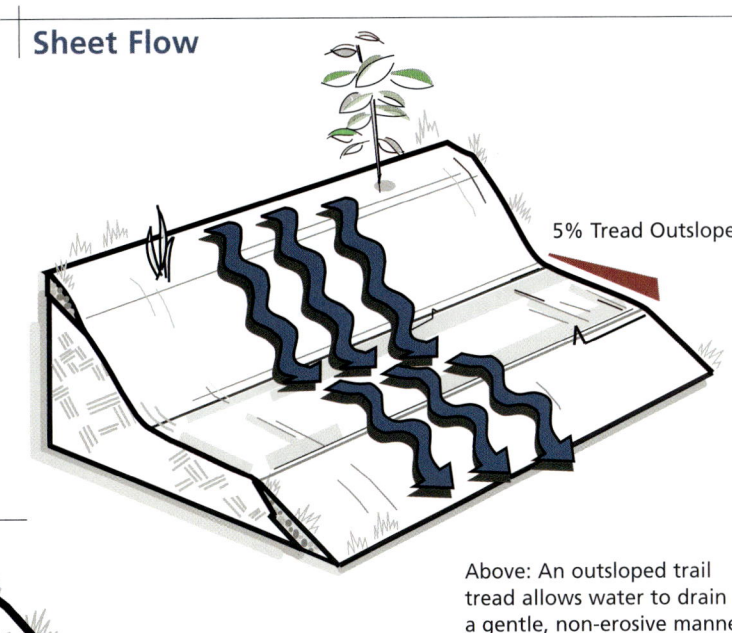

Above: An outsloped trail tread allows water to drain in a gentle, non-erosive manner called "sheet flow."

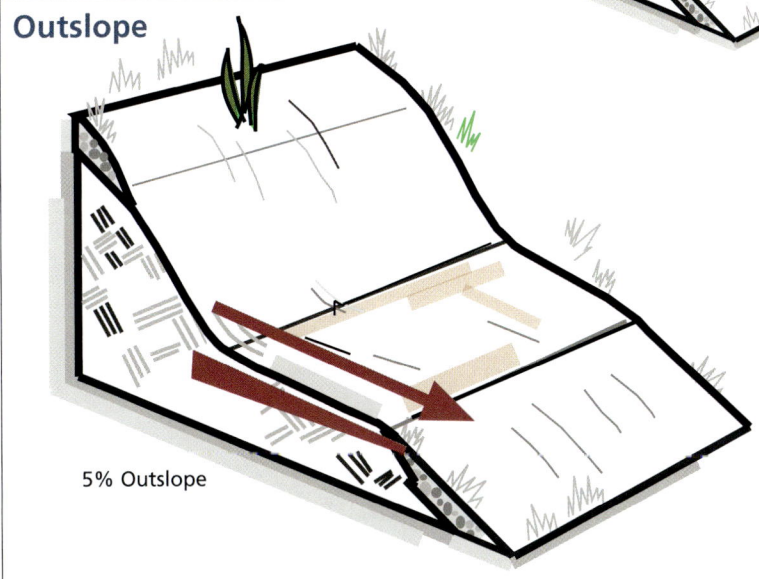

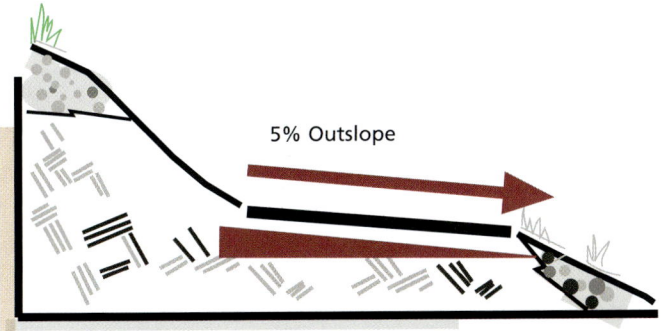

Part Three: Principals of Sustainable Trails

Using a Clinometer

A variety of tools ranging in sophistication can be used to measure grade. The tool of choice by IMBA is the clinometer because it is accurate, user friendly, relatively inexpensive, and fits in your pocket.

A **clinometer** measures a grade in degrees or percent. For highways, roads, and trails, percent is used.

How to Measure Grade

To determine grades you need to establish a visual target—another trailbuilder will serve this function perfectly. Follow the next three steps with your partner and you'll soon be able to read grades with this tool.

Step 1: Get Familiar with Your Clino.

Hold the clinometer to your dominant eye. (To determine your dominant eye, see the tip below.) With your dominant eye open and your other eye closed, look into the clinometer's viewfinder. The first thing you will notice is a rotating scale. There are numbers printed on both sides of the scale; one side is in degrees and the other side is in percent. By rotating the clinometer all the way toward the sky, you will see labels identifying the degree and percent scales. Ignore the degree side (unless you want to visit the sines and cosines of high-school trigonometry).

Bright Idea

Which eye is dominant? Try using the thumb test. Stick your thumb up at arm's length in front of you. With both eyes open, line up your thumb with any target in the background, such as a tree, a door knob, etc. Close one eye, then open it and close the other eye. Your thumb will appear to move. Determine which eye doesn't "move" your thumb, and that is your dominant eye.

Trail Solutions

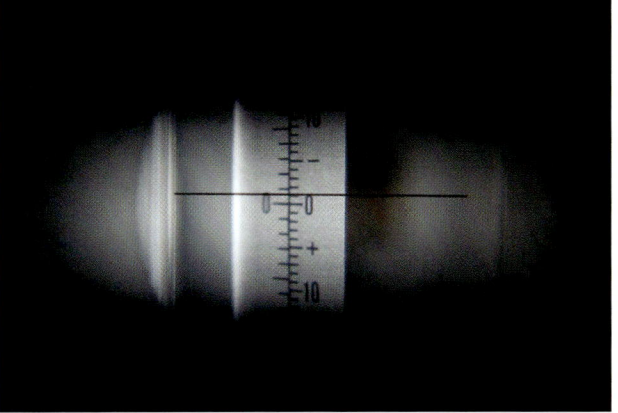

Take a minute to get familiar with the clinometer. Notice the horizontal line in the center of the viewfinder. This is the line you will use to measure grade. As you move the clino up and down, the scale will move while the horizontal line stays put.

Step 2: Locate the "Zero Point."

Once you are familiar with the tool, it's time to "zero out." Find a partner, preferably someone similar in height. Stand 10 to 15 feet apart on exactly level ground. The floor of a building is ideal since most will be perfectly level. Face your partner and hold the clino to your dominant eye with your opposite eye closed. Find the 0s, line them up to the horizontal line, and open your other eye. Binocular vision will superimpose the line across your partner's face. The point where the horizontal line intersects your partner's face is your target or "zero point." This is the spot you will be focusing on to determine grades.

If you are the same height as your partner, the zero point will fall across your partner's eyes. If you are taller, the line will be above your partner's eyes. Don't forget where the zero point is, and remember to always stand tall when reading grades. If you start to slouch throughout the day, the grades that you read will be inaccurate.

Don't Make the Mistake of...
Guessing the Grade. Some people believe they can judge the grade of a section of trail just by eyeballing it. They can't. Always use a clinometer or Abney Level to confirm grades.

Step 3: Practice.

Ask your partner to stand on a chair, a step, or a slope, and then stand about 10 to 15 feet away, facing your partner. Hold the clino up to your eye, and with both eyes open, put the horizontal line on your partner's zero point. Now read the percent number on the scale. You have just measured the grade of the slope you have created between you and your partner. If you move closer to your partner, the grade will be greater, and if you move farther away, the grade will be less. This is because you are keeping the rise constant, but changing the run in the equation (remember that grade = rise/run).

Part Three: Principals of Sustainable Trails

Trail Difficulty Rating System

The IMBA Trail Difficulty Rating System is a basic method used to categorize the relative technical difficulty of recreation trails.

The IMBA Trail Difficulty Rating System can:
- Help trail users make informed decisions
- Encourage visitors to use trails that match their skill level
- Manage risk and minimize injuries
- Improve the outdoor experience for a wide variety of visitors
- Aid in the planning of trails and trail systems

This system was adapted from the International Trail Marking System used at ski areas throughout the world. Many trail networks use this type of system, most notably resort-based mountain biking trail networks. The system applies to mountain bikers best, but also is applicable to other visitors such as hikers and equestrians. These criteria should be combined with personal judgment and trail-user input to reach the final rating.

Trail Rating Guidelines

 Rate Technical Challenge Only.

The system focuses on rating the technical challenge of trails, not the physical exertion. It is not practical to rate both types of difficulty with one system. Consider, for example, a smooth, wide trail that is 20 miles long. The technical challenge of this trail is easy, yet the distance would make the physical exertion difficult. The solution is to independently rate technical challenge, and indicate physical exertion by posting trail length, and possibly even elevation change.

 Collect Trail Measurements.

Use the accompanying table and collect trail measurements for each criteria. There is no prescribed method for tallying a "score" for each trail. Evaluate the trail against the table and combine with judgment to reach the final rating. It is unlikely that any particular trail will measure at the same difficulty level for every criteria. For example, a certain trail may rate as a green circle in three criteria, but a blue square in two different criteria.

The IMBA system includes five levels of difficulty.

○	Easiest
●	Easy
■	More Difficult
◆	Very Difficult
◆◆	Extremely Difficult

Four objective, measurable criteria are used to determine these ratings:

- Tread width
- Tread surface
- Trail grade (maximum & average)
- Natural obstacles and technical trail features

72

Trail Solutions

3. Include Difficulty and Trail Length on Signs and Maps.

Trail length is not a criterion of the system. Instead, trail length should be posted on signs in addition to the difficulty symbol. A sign displaying both length and difficulty provides lots of information, yet it is simple to create and easy to understand.

Likewise, elevation change is not a criterion. The amount of climbing on a trail is more an indicator of physical exertion than technical difficulty. Mountainous regions may consider including the amount of climbing on trail signs.

4. Evaluate Difficulty Relative to Local Trails.

Trails should be rated *relative* to other trails in the region. Don't evaluate each trail in isolation. Consider all the trails in a region and how they compare to one another. This will help you rank the relative difficulty of each trail and will help trail users select an appropriate route. Trails will rate differently from region to region. A black diamond trail in one region may rate as a blue square in another region, but the ratings should be consistent locally.

5. Use Good Judgment.

Rating a trail is not 100 percent objective. Its best to combine tangible data with subjective judgment to reach the final rating. For example, a trail may have a wide range of tread surfaces—most of the trail is easy, but some sections are more difficult. How would you rate it? Use your personal experience to consider all elements and select a rating that best matches the style of trail.

6. Consider Other Trail Qualities.

Don't forget to consider trail qualities beyond the objective criteria. A wide variety of features could contribute to a trail's difficulty. For example, **exposure**—the feeling of empty space next to and below the trail tread—provides an added psychological challenge beyond the steepness or roughness of the trail. A 3-inch rock seems like a boulder when a 50-foot drop looms on your side! Other qualities to think about are **corridor clearance** and **turn radius**.

7. Use Common Sense and Seek Input.

No rating system can be totally objective or valid for every situation. This system is a tool to be combined with common sense. Look at trails with a discerning eye, and seek input from trail users before selecting the rating.

Remember, a diverse trail network with a variety of trail styles is a great way to ensure happy visitors. Provide both easy and difficult trails to spread visitors and meet a range of needs. By indicating the length and difficulty of trails with a clear signage system, visitors will be able to locate their preferred type of trail easily.

Criteria to Consider

Tread Width
The average width of the active tread or beaten path of the trail.

Tread Surface
The material and stability of the tread surface is a determining factor in the difficulty of travel on the trail. Some descriptive terms include: hardened (paved or surfaced), firm, stable, variable, widely variable, loose, and unpredictable.

Trail Grade (maximum and average)
Maximum grade is defined as the steepest section of trail that is more than approximately 10 feet in length and is measured in percent with a clinometer. Average grade is the steepness of the trail over its entire length. Average grade can be calculated by taking the total elevation gain of the trail, divided by the total distance, multiplied by 100 to equal a percent grade.

Natural Obstacles and Technical Trail Features
Objects that add challenge by impeding travel. Examples include: rocks, roots, logs, holes, ledges, drop-offs, etc. The height of each obstacle is measured from the tread surface to the top of the obstacle. If the obstacle is uneven in height, measure to the point over which it is most easily ridden.

   Technical Trail Features are objects that have been introduced to the trail to add technical challenge. Examples include: rocks, logs, elevated bridges, teeter-totters, jumps, drop-offs, etc. Both the height and the width of the technical trail feature are measured.

Photo by Bob Allen.

Trail Solutions

Trail Difficulty Rating System

	Easiest White Circle ⚪	Easy Green Circle 🟢	More Difficult Blue Square 🟦	Very Difficult Black Diamond ◆	Extremely Difficult Dbl. Black Diamond ◆◆
Trail Width	72" or more	36" or more	24" or more	12" or more	6" or more
Tread Surface	Hardened or surfaced	Firm and stable	Mostly stable with some variability	Widely variable	Widely variable and unpredictable
Average Trail Grade	Less than 5%	5% or less	10% or less	15% or less	20% or more
Maximum Trail Grade	Max 10%	Max 15%	Max 15% or greater	Max 15% or greater	Max 15% or greater
Natural Obstacles and Technical Trail Features (TTF)	None	Unavoidable obstacles 2" tall or less Avoidable obstacles may be present Unavoidable bridges 36" or wider	Unavoidable obstacles 8" tall or less Avoidable obstacles may be present Unavoidable bridges 24" or wider TTF's 2' high or less, width of deck is greater than 1/2 the height	Unavoidable obstacles 15" tall or less Avoidable obstacles may be present May include loose rocks Unavoidable bridges 24" or wider TTF's 4' high or less, width of deck is less than 1/2 the height Short sections may exceed criteria	Unavoidable obstacles 15" tall or greater Avoidable obstacles may be present May include loose rocks Unavoidable bridges 24" or narrower TTF's 4' high or greater, width of deck is unpredictable Many sections may exceed criteria

Signs

It is important to develop a comprehensive signage system for your trail network. Signs should be placed at the main trailhead, at trail intersections, and at other key locations. When planning signs, consider the location. Trails with high use should be well signed. Conversely, trails deep in the backcountry should have far fewer signs. Signs can intrude on a visitor's outdoor experience, so use them with care.

Sign Types

Trailhead Kiosks

Trailhead kiosks are larger signs positioned at the beginning of the trail or trail system. Well-designed kiosks include a complete map and description of all the nearby trails. The main trailhead kiosk is the ideal place to describe trail length and relative difficulty. Visitors armed with this information can make smart decisions about which trails to travel. Trailheads are also excellent places to promote trail etiquette, explain local rules, list emergency contact information, and recruit volunteers for future trailbuilding efforts.

Directional Signs

Directional signs provide navigational information—everything from a simple blaze or trail name to the length of a route—and should be repeatedly posted along the trail. These signs can be small, so long as they are obvious and clearly mark the way. Be careful not to overuse them, especially if the route is easy to follow. More frequent placement may be needed for trails that are hard to follow, such as on slickrock or paths that are frequently snow-covered.

Warning Signs

Warning signs are used to caution trail users of upcoming hazards and should be placed close to the trail so they're easy to see. Be sure to position them well in advance of the hazard so that visitors have enough time to read the sign and react. It is particularly important to sign before very challenging technical trail features, like big drop-offs, narrow bridges, or other elements of increased risk.

Difficulty-Level Signs

These should be posted at the main trailhead and at every access point. Signs should be large enough to clearly display the trail's difficulty level as well as its length. Signage should be particularly clear at the intersections of trails with differing difficulty levels.

Regulatory Signs

Regulatory signs delineate rules, such as the direction of travel, or designate user groups. When creating regulatory signs, keep the tone constructive and upbeat. Visitors are more apt to obey rules that are presented in a positive way.

Rustler's Loop Teaches While You Ride

Rustler's Loop, near Fruita, Colorado, is an educational trail with about 25 interpretive signs that teach visitors mountain biking skills and responsible riding techniques.

Rustler's Loop, near Fruita, Colorado, is a great example of a trail with outstanding interpretative signs. Local mountain bikers partnered with the Bureau of Land Management to provide a beginner singletrack experience for visitors. Together they constructed 5 miles of scenic, smooth singletrack in 2001. Rustler's Loop is part of the famous Kokopelli Trail system, which provides a myriad of options for visitors of all abilities.

Rustler's Loop winds through desert red rocks on a natural bench above the Colorado River. Approximately 25 interpretative signs teach visitors about the natural environment, responsible trail use, and mountain biking skills. The signs are small and placed low to the ground to complement the scenery.

Educational Signs

Educational signs interpret natural or cultural points of interest along the trail and should be placed farther from the trail tread—roughly 4 feet away. Trail users will stop to read these signs, and you don't want them to block the trail for extended periods. Post the signs in clear areas that are easily accessed (you don't want vegetation to be trampled while people read the sign). Educational signs are most useful when they are near the elements they describe.

Part Three: Principals of Sustainable Trails

Way-Marked Routes

In a way-marked route system, certain trails are identified by unique blazes that enable users to follow a designated route on interconnecting trails. Marking routes in this manner is a convenient and effective way of giving visitors a self-guided experience without the need for frequent map checks. Way-marked routes usually link trails of similar difficulty.

In a way-marked route system, certain trails are identified by unique blazes that enable users to follow a designated route on interconnecting trails. Location: Seven Stanes Project, Scotland.

Don't Forget...

Proper Size, Placement, and Tone are Critical. If your signs are too small or are improperly placed along the trail, most trail users will simply ignore them. Keep the tone positive, inspiring trail users to obey the rules.

Trail Solutions

Sign Materials: Pros and Cons

Signs can be crafted from a wide range of materials—everything from flexible plastic strips to immovable stone cairns. Here are the pros and cons of each.

Plastics are widely available and come in a range of colors. Durability varies, so do your research. Plastics tend to expand and contract with temperature changes—something to consider if you live in an area marked by extreme temperature swings. Vandals are more likely to break a plastic sign than a stout steel sign, so keep that factor in mind if the trail is in a high-use urban setting.

Wood is an aesthetically pleasing material and can be fairly affordable, but it is easily damaged by vandals. Be sure to use rot-resistant wood.

Aluminum is lightweight and doesn't corrode. However, aluminum is expensive and doesn't blend with nature as well as wood or stone.

Steel is affordable and durable, but it is prone to rusting and must be galvanized to resist corrosion. For some reason, there is a special breed of vandal who takes pleasure in shooting steel signs. One company actually produces signs that appear to have already been shot by a shotgun, as vandals are less likely to shoot a sign that's already been hit. It's a "beat 'em to the punch" approach that, while not terribly attractive, might keep your sign from being shredded by a shotgun blast.

Stone is durable, but it limits the amount of information that can be posted on the sign, as carving stone is tedious and therefore expensive. Stone is best used in rock cairns that simply inform trail users that they are, in fact, still on the trail. Stone cairns can be made more permanent by corralling the stone in a wire framework.

Note: Appendix B provides information on obtaining signs.

Managing Visitors Through Trail Design

You Control the Speed

Some trails attract inexperienced mountain bikers who are still learning how to manage their speed. Sometimes they'll ride too fast and make other visitors uncomfortable, other times they'll brake too suddenly when approaching a turn or obstacle and damage the trail. For these reasons, speed is best controlled by the designer, not the rider. There are numerous ways to keep bicyclists from traveling too fast.

Corralling, Chokes, and Turns

Corral the Trail

Include objects to define the sides of the trail and emphasize turns. Also called **trail anchors,** these can be large rocks, logs, trees, or other obstacles staggered on either side of the trail that serve as physical and visual barriers to keep visitors on the trail and slow riders.

Install Chokes

Create a slight narrowing of the trail with rocks or plants to control speeds. Also called **gateways**, these should be installed just prior to spots in the trail where users will need to slow down, such as sharp turns and trail intersections. Chokes encourage riders to gradually apply their brakes well in advance of sensitive areas. *(Hmmm…it looks like the trail gets more technical up ahead. I better slow down before I get there.)* Make sure the narrowing flows naturally with the trail. Otherwise people may find it annoying and may create a new route around it.

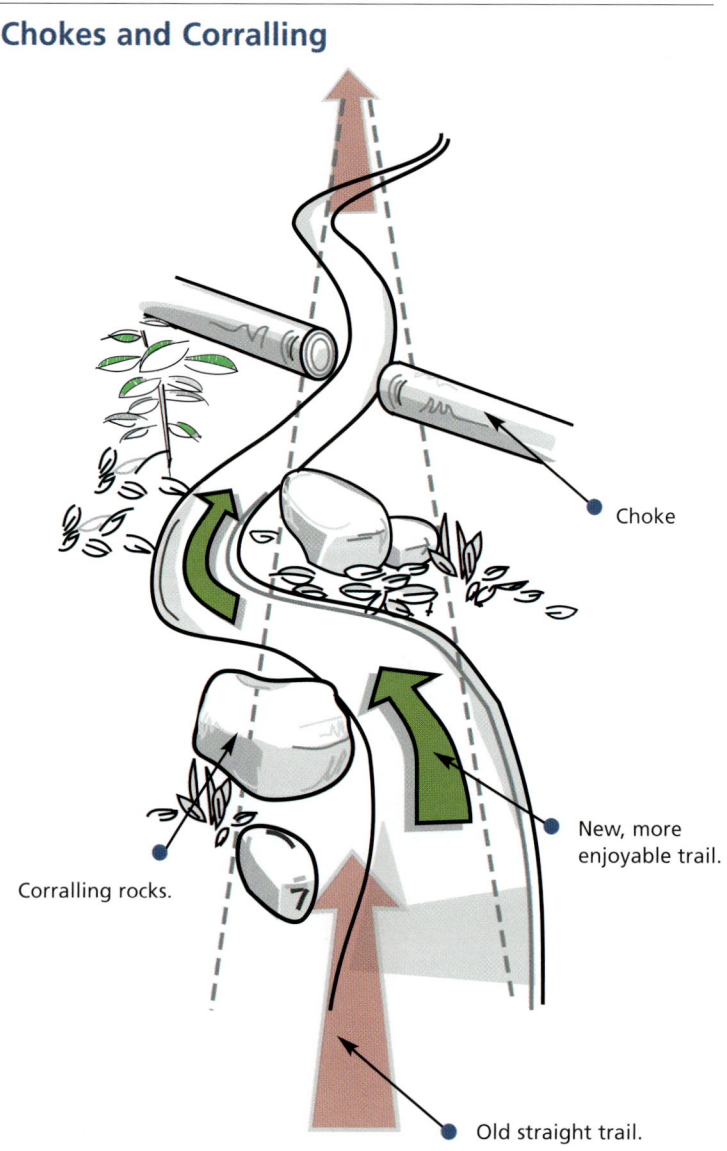

Chokes and Corralling

Choke

New, more enjoyable trail.

Corralling rocks.

Old straight trail.

Trail Solutions

Use Turns

You can also build a tight and twisty trail, with constant ups, downs, lefts, and rights. Since trail users must stay focused on an always-changing trail, they feel like they are traveling faster than they actually are. Tight and twisty singletrack gives the illusion of speed without allowing trail users to actually go very fast. Gradual transitions are essential between changes in trail flow.

Corral the trail with rocks to emphasize turns and anchor the trail to the landscape.

Utilize chokes to create a slight narrowing of the trail to control speeds. Location: Wales.

Part Three: Principals of Sustainable Trails

Tight and twisty singletrack is fun to ride and keeps the speed of mountain bikers in check. Location: Fruita, Colorado

Spread 'em Out

The key to managing a high-volume trail system is to evenly spread visitors over the trail network. Locate easier, shorter trails close to the trailhead so that casual visitors can conveniently access them. Entice more skilled pedestrians and bicyclists to travel on other trails by locating the longer, more technical sections farther away from the trailhead. Be sure to post signs that clearly indicate the difficulty level of trails and enable visitors to select the routes that best meet their needs.

Provide Diverse Trail Experiences

Most popular trail systems have to accommodate weekend crowds and a wide variety of users. A diverse network of trails is the best solution. See Part Four for more advice. But when many different trails aren't available, consider creating a variety of trail experiences within a single trail corridor. Technical trail features can be added to the side of the main trail as an optional path for riders who are seeking a more challenging line. For more information about adding technical features to your trails, see Part Eight.

Trails in Urban Settings

Urban parks pose a challenge for trailbuilders. Because of their proximity to population centers, urban parks receive a large volume of visitors searching for a wide range of experiences. Parents with strollers, joggers, kids on BMX bikes, bird watchers, and just about every other user group must vie for space on trails that are frequently old and poorly designed. Many of the trail-design suggestions presented in this book can solve these urban challenges, so read carefully and don't be afraid to manage visitors through trail design.

Photo by Bob Allen.

Understanding Soils

Soil types vary widely all over the world. In fact, you may find several distinct soil varieties on a single trail. Soil type is largely characterized by texture. Texture, in turn, is determined by the size of the soil particles.

There are three basic types of particles: *sand, silt,* and *clay*. Each differ in size and shape, and therefore affect different physical properties of the soil, such as its ability to drain. The ability to categorize soil is important to successful trailbuilding.

Sandy Soil

Sand is the largest of the three kinds of soil particles. Sand doesn't hold many nutrients, and because the voids (or pores) between sand particles tend to be large, water drains through it quickly. While quickly draining trails seem preferable, there is a downside to sand. Individual particles are noncohesive, meaning they don't hold together well. Sand doesn't compact well, and trail users often try to avoid loose sections of sand by going around it, thereby widening the trail.

You know you have a sandy trail when. . .

Dry: It's loose and feels rough. You can see individual grains of sand.

Moist: Squeeze a handful of it. Sand will form into a ball that crumbles apart easily and does not stain your fingers.

Silty Soil

Silt particles fall somewhere between sand and clay in size. Silt is essentially very small sand, although it doesn't feel gritty and the particles can't be seen by the naked eye. Pores between silt particles are much smaller (and far more numerous) than those in sand, meaning silty soils retain more water and don't drain as well as sand. When wet, silt particles don't exhibit much cohesion, causing them to be washed away easily by flowing water.

The science of dirt: Understanding different types of soil is important to successful trailbuilding. Photo by Joe Lindsey.

You know you have a silty trail when. . .

Dry: It feels smooth and powdery—like flour.

Moist: It feels smooth, but not sticky, and crumbles apart.

Clay Soil

Clay is the smallest of the three soil particles. Though there are many different types of clay, they all tend to be shaped like tiny flakes or flat platelets, which gives clay particles very large surface areas relative to their size. This surface area and the prevalence of very small pores, gives clay a tremendous capacity to hold water. Hence, clay soils don't drain well. However, clay particles tend to stick together when the soil is dry, making it very hard and durable.

You know you have a clay-dominant trail when. . .

Dry: Clods are almost impossible to break with your fingers.

Moist: It is sticky, easily forms into a ball, and leaves stains on your fingers.

Loamy Soil

Loam is a mix of different types of soil particles, in which neither sand, clay, nor silt predominates. Loam is the ideal soil for trailbuilding purposes as it drains well, holds together well, and is easy to work with.

You know you have a loamy trail when. . .

Dry: Clods are moderately difficult to break and somewhat gritty to the touch.

Wet: It is neither very gritty nor sticky; it forms a firm ball when squeezed.

Soil Properties and Behavior Relevant to Trailbuilding

Property	Sand	Silt	Clay
Water-holding capacity	Low	Medium to High	High
Drainage rate	High	Slow to Medium	Very Slow
Compactability	Low	Medium	High
Susceptibility to water erosion	Low	High	Low (if aggregated) High (if not)

Exceptions occur based on soil structure and clay mineralogy. Table adapted from *The Nature and Properties of Soils*. N.C. Brady and R.R. Weil. 12th Ed. p. 125. Prentice-Hall, Inc. Upper Saddle River, NJ. 1999.

Soil Information

Anticipating what soil types you'll encounter during trailbuilding can help in developing a sustainable trail. Unfortunately, there is little region-specific information on the use of soils for trailbuilding. To compensate for this, soil surveys can provide basic background information on the soils you'll be working with. In addition to maps delineating different soil types within an area, soils surveys contain detailed descriptions of properties (such as texture) that can help you better understand what soil-related challenges you may face during trail construction. Your local library, Natural Resource Conservation Service (NRCS), or county agricultural extension offices are good sources for locating a soil survey for your region. (Soil surveys are published for each county within the United States.)

Marquette, Michigan. Photo by Kevin Bauman.

Building Better Trails

Part Four: The Trail Design Process

As we've discussed in previous sections, the fundamentals of good trailbuilding include more than just construction, and many key steps must be implemented well before the first shovel-full of dirt is lifted from the ground. Forming partnerships with land managers and volunteers, determining the users and their expectations, examining topography, and assessing the environment with particular attention to fragile ecosystems and possible control points are all important aspects of trailbuilding. The following sections will help you build the foundation of a sustainable trail.

In This Part ...

- **Eleven Steps to Better Trail Design** 88
    1. Get Permission and Build a Partnership ... 88
    2. Identify Property Boundaries 88
    3. Determine Trail Users 88
    4. Identify Control Points 94
    5. Configure Loops 95
    6. Plan a Contour Route 96
    7. Determine Type of Trail Flow 97
    8. Walk and Flag the Corridor 100
    9. Develop a Construction Plan 101
    10. Conduct an Assessment Study 101
    11. Flag the Final Alignment and Confirm Permission 102

Eleven Steps For Designing Great Trails

Most trail management problems, from erosion to user conflict, stem from poor design. A poorly designed trail—no matter how well you build it—will almost always fall apart and be the source of strife for managers and visitors. The advice in this section will help you avoid the most common trailbuilding pitfalls.

Step 1: Get Permission and Build a Partnership

We covered this pretty thoroughly in Part One, but it bears repeating: It is never better to ask for forgiveness than for permission. *Always* get permission before you begin building a trail. Forming a strong partnership with the landowner or land manager from the start will accomplish more and create a situation in which everyone wins. Let land managers know you're part of an organized group. Present a written proposal describing how and where you want to implement or improve a trail system. Remember that clear and frequent communication is the backbone of all good relationships.

It is also important to seek input from various users when beginning a trail project. Involving different user groups gives everyone a sense of ownership and ensures the trail's future. Great trails often result from a blend of ideas.

Breaking ground on Federal land may require a National Environmental Protection Act (NEPA) study. Some trail projects fall under a Categorical Exclusion that can save land managers time and money. It may take a while to secure approval, but it must be done. Protection of the land always comes first. Be patient and willing to compromise.

Step 2: Identify Property Boundaries

Locate and mark the property boundaries on a topographic map. Naturally, you can't build your trail on land that's off limits, but have you considered whether your trail's proximity to private property might tempt users to wander into restricted areas? In some cases, trails should direct people away from boundaries. There may also be off-limits areas *within* the property boundaries (a sensitive archeological site, for instance) that need to be protected.

Step 3: Determine Trail Users

Think about the people who will use your trail. Does the trail system accommodate their needs and desires?

- What experiences do they want?
- What trail length will appeal to them?
- What level of fitness and ability do they have?
- How often will they use your trail?

Consider the future as well. What elements can you include to serve a growing population and an evolving mix of users?

A trail's design shapes the experiences of those who use it. The best trail systems offer something for everyone by recognizing that each trail user is unique. It would be wrong to assume that all mountain bikers want challenging terrain or that all hikers want solitude. Nevertheless, it's possible to make a few generalizations about the following kinds of trail users.

Where can (and can't) the trail go? Never forget to roll out the maps to determine property boundaries before designing a trail.

Pedestrians

Walkers are usually interested in getting a little exercise. For the most part, they prefer short trails that provide a direct path from one natural feature to another.

Hikers tend to be familiar with the outdoors and enjoy a more strenuous and adventurous experience than walkers. They can handle difficult terrain and steep grades. They will generally stay on trails that are direct yet interesting.

Backpackers yearn for a backcountry experience and will travel many miles to reach it. Even though they have an intended destination, they are less apt to shortcut because they carry heavy loads that hinder maneuverability. Gentle trail grades linking natural features help keep long-distance foot travel interesting. Water sources should be regularly spaced and near suitable camping sites.

Part Four: The Trail Design Process

Trail Runners enjoy connecting trail loops to add variety in their workouts. Most runners want several miles of rolling trail with occasional challenging sections.

Rock Climbers use trails to reach climbing areas. Contour trails may be too indirect for them. They prefer short, direct access to the rocks.

Endurance Athletes, including trail runners, mountain bikers, and equestrians, like to push their limits. These people seek trail networks that are as much as a hundred miles long. A large network is more appealing to these users than multiple laps of a short loop.

Disabled Trail Users

The Americans with Disabilities Act is a 1990 federal law that helps disabled people gain equal access to public facilities. Due to improved skill, endurance, and equipment such as off-road wheelchairs, more trail opportunities are being sought by disabled athletes. Suitable trails have a wide, smooth tread with a gentle grade (an average of 5 percent) and no staircases. Some small obstacles may be allowed as long as this is indicated by appropriate signage at the trail entrance.

Equestrians

Equestrians are the heaviest, widest, and tallest nonmotorized users. Their trails require a wider corridor and a higher ceiling than those designed for pedestrians and bikers. Contour trails with a durable tread and frequent grade reversals are the most suitable. Some equestrians seek technical trails in order to push themselves and their horses, while others prefer gentle grades and wider tread.

Trail runners and mountain bikers often seek similar trails because their travel speeds are nearly the same.

Equestrians are the heaviest, widest, and tallest nonmotorized users. Their trails require a durable tread and frequent grade reversals to shed water.

Building Better Trails

Motorized Users

ATVs (all-terrain vehicles) require a 4- to 5-foot-wide tread that's open and flowing. Their horsepower and wide tires allow travel on sandy or rocky trails. Since the year 2000, this has been the fastest growing group of trail users. Fitted with racks, ATVs are popular with hunters, anglers, and others who take loads into and out of the backcountry. Land managers and trail crews find ATVs useful in many work situations.

Off-Road Motorcycles require more operator skill than ATVs and can be used on narrower trails. Riders prefer trails that are open and flowing, and they can cover more than a hundred miles a day.

Don't Forget...
Design Your Trail with Its Users in Mind.
While all trail users want to be outside in a natural setting, each type of trail user has different needs. The best trail systems offer variety, challenge, and sustainability. They keep visitors on trail by providing the experiences they want.

Mountain Bikers

As is the case with trail runners and endurance athletes, trails are not only a source of recreation for mountain bikers but also a source of exercise. Typical mountain bikers will not simply ride a trail once every Saturday, they may ride the trail three or four times a week in order to stay fit. Keep this in mind when deciding how much trail to build.

Beginner Cross-Country Riders tend to like gentle, relatively short trails. As they become more skilled, they often seek longer, more difficult routes. Rough, arduous, or twisty sections satisfy the need for technical challenge and help control speed. Trails that are fun discourage mountain bikers from riding off trail to find more exciting routes.

Avid Cross-Country Riders are comfortable in the backcountry. These experienced cyclists are typically self-sufficient and carry tools, water, food, clothing, and sometimes a first-aid kit. Avid riders seek trails that let them cover from 10 to 100 miles in search of solitude, nature, and challenge. Desirable trails feature several miles of connecting loops with natural obstacles.

Beginner mountain bikers prefer gentle, relatively short trails and dirt roads.

Part Four: The Trail Design Process

Freeriders like challenges such as drop-offs, elevated bridges, and dirt jumps. Freeriding has its roots in the North Shore region of British Columbia, but has since become popular worldwide. Photo by John Gibson.

Avid cross-country riders are comfortable in the backcountry and look for trails with natural obstacles that feature several miles of connecting loops.
Photo by Seb Rogers.

Downhillers are usually advanced riders who use sophisticated equipment specifically designed for descending steep and technical trails. The most sustainable trails for downhillers are rocky contours with many grade reversals. Since downhill bikes are heavy, it's helpful to have access to a road for a vehicle shuttle to the top. Ski areas that provide summer lift service are popular with downhillers.

Freeriders like challenges such as drop-offs, ledges, logs, elevated bridges, dirt jumps, and teeter-totters. Some freeriders want these technical features within cross-country rides, while others prefer them as stand-alone experiences. One solution is special-use areas (similar to snowboard parks at ski resorts) called **challenge parks**, also referred to as terrain parks or skills areas. On backcountry trails, technical features should blend with nature and be built well. Freeriding has its roots in the North Shore region of British Columbia, but has since become popular in all parts of the world.

Part Four: The Trail Design Process

Step 4: Identify Control Points

Hit the Maps First…

Save time in the field by studying maps, aerial photographs, master plans, and so on. In some areas, a Geographic Information System (GIS) study may have already been done. A detailed GIS map might display many layers of information, including ownership boundaries, topography, hydrography, soils, vegetation, wildlife management, and slope grades. Use these resources to become familiar with the area and begin establishing control points.

Then Head Into the Field.

Time spent in the field is the best way to get a sense of the terrain. Once you've finished studying maps, head out with your compass, map, and altimeter. A global positioning system (GPS) is also a valuable tool. It can help you pinpoint boundaries, control points, and trail lengths. In forested areas, the ideal time to survey is during autumn or winter, when visibility is at its best. It is also important to return in wet season (if there is one) to check water levels at their highest.

Identify Control Points.

The most important goal of your field trip is to identify significant control points. **Control points** are places that influence where a trail goes. The beginning and end of your trail are basic control points. Other control points include parking areas, trailheads, structures, slopes for turns or switchbacks, road or water crossings, and other trails.

Positive control points are places you want trail users to visit. These include scenic overlooks, waterfalls, rock outcroppings, lakes, rivers, and other natural features or points of interest. Consider the mix of users and the control points or terrain that will appeal to them. Design the trail to connect these places, keeping the route interesting along the way.

If you fail to design positive control points into your trail, people will quickly trample their own, unsustainable **social trails** to the waterfall or scenic overlook you should have included on your route.

Negative control points are places you want users to avoid. Examples are low-lying wet areas, flat ground that may hold water or sand, extremely

Potentially Positive Control Points

- ✔ Water
- ✔ Scenic vistas
- ✔ Old-growth forest
- ✔ Large trees or unique vegetation
- ✔ Historic, cultural, and archeological sites
- ✔ Certain slope aspects
- ✔ Rock outcroppings
- ✔ Interesting boulders or ledges
- ✔ Appealing sounds and scents
- ✔ Gentle sideslopes
- ✔ Sustainable turning platforms (where climbing turns and switchbacks can be built)
- ✔ Sustainable drainage crossings
- ✔ Existing rail, road, or water crossings

Potentially Negative Control Points

- ✘ Water
- ✘ Historic, cultural, and archeological sites
- ✘ Private property
- ✘ Unpleasant views
- ✘ Wetlands, riparian zones
- ✘ Sensitive wildlife habitat
- ✘ Sensitive plant communities
- ✘ Property boundaries
- ✘ Flat areas

Building Better Trails

Positive control points, like this scenic overlook, are places you want trail users to visit.

Negative control points, like this wet area, are places you want visitors to avoid.

steep sideslopes, fall lines, environmentally sensitive wildlife habitat or plant communities, certain water crossings, riparian areas, sensitive archeological sites, safety hazards, and private property. If there's a negative control point, keep trail users well away from it—otherwise more social trails may appear.

Water crossings present special challenges as control points. Can a stream be forded or should a bridge be built? Geography and regulations usually provide the answer. Consult land managers and check other trails in the area to see what's customary. In general, design trails to avoid frequent water crossings. (See page 176 for more details on water crossings.)

As freeriding and technical trails become more popular, boulders and rock outcroppings are important positive control points to seek for their usefulness in creating highly challenging yet sustainable trails.

Step 5: Configure Loops.

Trail systems with loops are appealing because they offer variety. People love the adventure of starting down one path and returning to the same point by way of a different trail. Loops let visitors enjoy trails of varying distances, difficulty, or ecosystems in the same outing.

Several different types of loops can work for a trail system, depending on its geography. A park that parallels a river may use linked loop trails that follow the water; each loop is like a link in a chain. Visitors can choose a small loop, a combination of loops, or the large, outer loop. In mountainous terrain, a trail may climb one drainage to a summit and then descend another drainage. Stacked-loop trail systems make optimal use of available land.

Stacked Loop Trail System

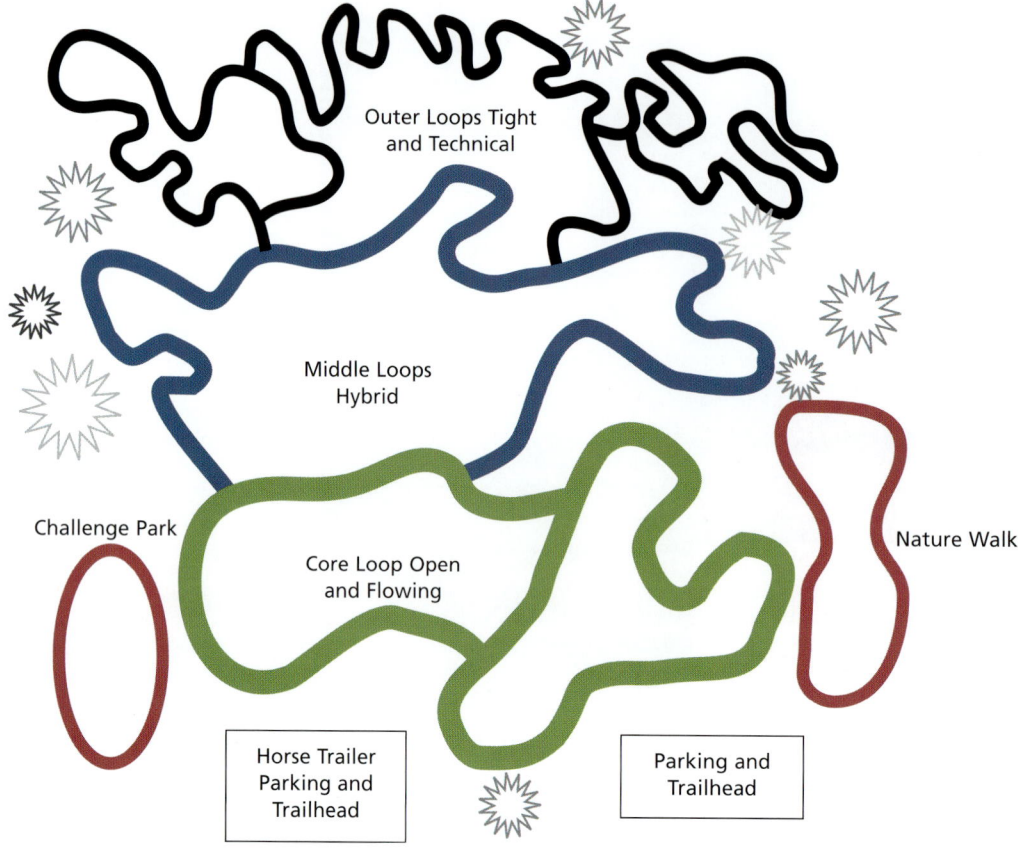

In high-use areas, the core trail leading from the trailhead or parking lot should be wide and smooth to appeal to a variety of users and to allow visitors to travel side by side and socialize at the start. Because a core trail accesses the rest of the system, it receives the most use. The loops that branch from it may be longer, narrower, and more challenging as they get farther from the trailhead and the core trails, because users seeking difficult or remote experiences are usually willing to travel farther.

There are instances when stacked loops are not feasible. The existing trail may be a point-to-point route or the landscape may not accommodate a series of loops. In either case, it is still important to consider how the trail you are proposing fits into a larger trail system. Imagine, for instance, that there are three small parks in a given region, and each park only has room for a single trail. It may be a good idea to create a different style of trail at each location so the three parks create a large, cooperative system of diverse trails.

Step 6: Plan a Contour Route

Here's the point at which all your hard work identifying control points really produces results. Planning a preliminary contour route is basically a process of plotting each control point on a **topographic (topo) map** and connecting the dots. It's helpful to use green for positive points and red for negative ones. When sketching your trail on a topographic map, remember to route the trail along the map's contour lines to help ensure that the grade of your trail will be sustainable. This planning work with a map is just for initial route selection and will not indicate the precise trail location. You'll need to spend time in the field with surveying flags and a clinometer for that. (See page 57 for essential advice on designing a contour trail, and page 70 for help using your clinometer.)

Building Better Trails

Step 7: Determine Type of Trail Flow

Trail users are defined by their means of travel (e.g., foot, horse, bicycle), but this is just one distinguishing characteristic. Speed is important, too. For example, a mountain biker and a runner probably have a more similar trail experience than a runner and a walker, because their speeds are nearly the same.

A trail designed for fast travelers will have a different kind of rhythm or **flow** than a trail designed primarily for slower travelers. Understanding flow can reduce erosion and user conflict. It is important to remember that a contour trail's appropriate flow is often dictated by the landscape.

Contour trail designs can have three basic types of flow:

Open and flowing trails are relatively gentle. They have long sightlines, gradual turns and few technical challenges. They appeal to less-skilled cyclists as well as people who enjoy traveling fast. Open and flowing trails need long sightlines because they invite higher speeds and are attractive to motorized users.

Tight and technical trails have sharper turns and twists, rougher surfaces, a narrower tread, and natural obstacles. They provide challenges and thrills for mountain bikers while keeping speed down, which in turn may reduce user conflict. Tight and technical trails may frustrate hikers or destination-oriented hikers, and shortcutting may result.

Hybrid trails successfully blend open flowing with tight and technical. Hybrid trails are often a good choice for urban areas. These trails may be wider, yet twisty with a rocky or technical tread. Brush and other obstacles very close to the trail should be below eye level, allowing for longer sightlines to help reduce user conflict. Slightly wider trails allow users to pass each other, while technical challenges reduce speed and add variety.

Proper transitions are essential when open and flowing sections are combined with tight and technical sections. Transitions should occur gradually or be located atop hills, so that they are approached slowly. Abrupt transitions are likely to make cyclists brake hard and skid, resulting in braking bumps, trail widening, and, in extreme cases, users being forced off trail.

Trail Flow

Open and Flowing

Tight and Technical

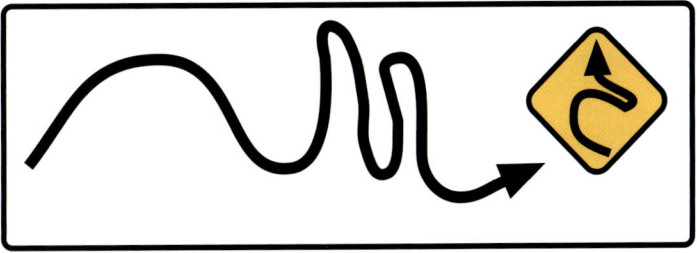

Poor flow—abrupt transitions from one type of flow to another.

Part Four: The Trail Design Process

Open and flowing trails have long sightlines, gradual turns, and few technical challenges. Location: Durango, Colorado. Photo by Dean Howard.

Tight and technical trails have sharper turns and twists, rougher surfaces, a narrower tread, and natural obstacles. Location: Virginia. Photo by Bryan Moody.

Bright Idea

Surf the Contour. When designing a trail across a featureless hillside, include twists and turns to avoid long straightaways. Subtle curves will create gentle ups and downs that add interest and control rider speed.

Building Better Trails

Surf the contour with smooth turns, ups, and downs to add fun and improve drainage. Location: Coed y Brenin, Wales.

Good flow is particularly prized by cyclists. Mountain bikers love the rhythm of a trail where one turn blends into the next, and every descent leads to another rise. A trail with good flow helps minimize erosion, user conflict, and safety concerns.

When you think about flow, the genius of the stacked loop system becomes clear. In a single area, you can create a series of trails with different kinds of flow, which will appeal to a wide range of visitors. Shorter, beginner trails located close to the trailhead, for instance, would ideally be open and flowing, whereas longer, more advanced trails on the periphery of the stacked loop system would feature a tight and technical flow.

Don't Make the Mistake of...

Going Against the Flow. Bad flow, especially fast sections that lead into sudden, sharp turns, is a primary cause of user conflict and trail damage. All trails should incorporate smooth transitions. When you are building, think flow—the key to an enjoyable trail.

Part Four: The Trail Design Process

Step 8: Walk and Flag the Corridor

After the preliminary work is done, use flagging tape to mark the path or space through which your trail will pass—the "trail corridor." Your trail corridor should be wider than the trail tread. The corridor's height, or **ceiling**, should be at least 8 feet high; if equestrians will be using the trail consider a ceiling of 10 feet. Flagging tape is ideal for marking corridors, as it can be tied to high points (such as tree trunks or limbs) to mark the path your trail will take. Once your general layout receives environmental clearance and approval from the land manager, you can establish the course of the trail by inserting pin flags into the ground (see Step 11).

Each pin flag is like a dot. Connecting the dots will help you visualize flow, grades, grade reversals, turns, and all the other key features of trail design.

Building Better Trails

In order to ensure that your trail is built correctly, make your design clear to the construction crew by using plenty of flags.

> ### A Few Flagging Tips
> - Yellow and orange flags don't work well during fall foliage.
> - Green flags won't stand out in forested areas during summer.
> - Fluorescent pink is good in most areas throughout the year.
> - Check with the local land manager to make sure other types of projects aren't being flagged with the color you intend to use.

Step 9: Develop a Construction Plan

This step should involve trail users, land managers, and the work crew. Including the key players in decisions gives everyone a sense of ownership in the project and pride in the trail.

Reach agreement on trail dimensions including corridor width, tread width, and ceiling. Consider how the trail will be built, how long it will take, how much it will cost, and who will provide the labor. Develop a timeline for construction. (See page 187 for tips.)

Step 10: Conduct an Assessment Study

Many land management agencies require studies prior to new trail construction. These may be biological, botanical, cultural, archaeological, or historical. Studies can be expensive and time consuming (so be patient), but sometimes a simple walk-through by the area's naturalist may be sufficient.

Make sure the trail plan you propose is exactly what you want, because changing it after this study has been conducted may require going through the entire process again. Assessment studies usually cover a corridor 50 feet on either side of the flag line.

Step 11: Flag the Final Alignment and Confirm Permission

You've already flagged the dimensions of the corridor and ceiling, now you're ready to stake the exact location of the trail tread. Pin flags work best for marking tread location. Pin flags are reusable, lightweight and can be placed almost anywhere. Short flags are fine for desert or arid areas. Use longer flags when there is vegetation. Identify the obstacles (rock outcroppings, for instance) that will be left in the tread or included in its design. Let natural terrain features guide you.

Walk (or run, if you can) the entire flag line in both directions, making adjustments to improve flow. Avoid long, straight lines. Use natural obstacles to accentuate curves and grade reversals. Be creative to produce an exciting pathway. A well-flagged tread resembles a serpentine line with rounded arcs, and optimal flow comes from consistency in the radius of turns.

Outline the proposed tread by putting pin flags on the inside (uphill) edge, the centerline, or the outside (downhill) edge. The downhill edge is preferable because flags can remain during excavation to help the construction crew envision flow and the depth of the trail. When building a **retaining wall** to raise the trail's downhill edge, place pin flags in the center of the trail to indicate the tread's finished depth. This is important for maintaining the grade.

If construction is going to be done using machinery, then pin flags should be placed on the uphill side of the tread. The flags will be easier for the operator to see and won't get buried in the debris pile.

Run along the flag line to test the trail flow.

102

Building Better Trails

Photo by Seb Rogers.

Part Four: The Trail Design Process

Part Five:
Tools for Trailbuilding

Armed with the right tools, you can move boulders the size of Shetland ponies with ease and stop erosion dead in its tracks. Without the right tools, well, you might as well get rid of that opposable thumb, because you're toiling back in the Stone Age—sweating, swearing, and not getting much of anything done.

Tools are so important to trailbuilding that we could easily devote an entire book to the topic. Of course, if we did that, you'd probably just fall asleep halfway into chapter one and drool all over the pages. Instead, we've dedicated one lean, mean chapter to the nuts and bolts.

In This Part ...

- **Handling Tools Safely** 106
    - Safety Tips 106
- **The Ten Essential Tools** 108
- **Other Useful Hand Tools** 112
- **Mechanized Tools** 121
    - The Upside of Mechanized Tools 121
    - The Downside of Mechanized Tools 122
    - A Short Guide to Mechanized Tools 124
    - Choosing the Right Machine 127
    - Tips for Using Mechanized Tools 129
    - Other Useful Mechanized Tools 132

Handling Tools Safely

When handled properly, tools make child's play of otherwise strenuous labor. When handled improperly, they can cause serious injuries. Crew leaders should know the location of the closest medical facility and who will go for help. Time is critical when accidents happen in the field. Create an emergency plan prior to your trailwork day. Make sure everyone knows his or her responsibility during an emergency. Start each workday with reminders about tool safety and the emergency plan.

Safety Tips

Cover the following points with all your volunteers before beginning any trailwork:

Safety begins with a good grip.

Don't underestimate the importance of quality gloves. They can protect your hands from blisters and other injuries, and they'll help insure that you maintain a safe grip on your tools. Wet or muddy gloves can cause a tool to slip from your hands, striking you or someone near you.

Make sure you have a clear area in which to swing.

Watch for overhead or side hazards. A hazard is anything that can interfere with the complete swing of your tool, knocking it from your hands or down onto any part of your body. (For instance, overhanging branches can be hazards.) Keep your tool in front of you at all times; you rarely need to swing a tool over your head. If you do have to make an overhead swing, stop and give your coworkers a "heads up" before you begin. Remember that some tools (particularly McLeods) are not designed to withstand the force of an overhead swing.

Be alert for hazardous footing.

Make sure you have a firm, balanced, and comfortable stance before starting your work. Clear tree limbs, sticks, loose rocks, and other debris from your footing area. Make sure your feet are spaced well away from your target area—particularly when using striking tools.

Choose the right tool for the job.

The wrong tool can force you to work in an awkward position or exert more force than is necessary—wearing out your tools *and* you. Choose the right tool.

Beware of...

The "Circle of Death." If you are within tool-length distance of another worker who is swinging a tool, you are in danger of being gravely injured. We've dubbed this space, "the circle of death," but it is no joke. Always stay well out of range of other workers, and be sure no one else is in your circle of death before swinging your own tool.

Trail Solutions

Make sure the tool is sharp.

This may seem counter-intuitive, but a dull tool can be very dangerous, particularly if it bounces or glances off of whatever it should be cutting and into something it shouldn't. A sharp tool will cut faster, is less tiring to use, and is safer because it's more accurate. Sharpen tools at least once a week; some even require daily attention.

Carry the tool properly.

Always carry tools in your hands, and hold them down at your side. Don't carry more than one tool in each hand, and when you are carrying only one tool, hold it in the downhill hand. Keep the sharpest side of the tool facing the ground, and use blade guards whenever possible. Resist the temptation to act like a lumberjack, as carrying tools over your shoulder is a great way to get hurt or to hurt someone else. Hold the business end of the tool in front of you.

Travel safely.

All trailworkers should stay at least 10 feet apart on the hike in and out from the work site when carrying tools. When moving along a trail that's under construction, announce your presence to workers with tools in their hands, and make eye contact before passing them.

This volunteer has taken trailwork safety to an impressive level by strapping on his bike helmet for extra protection.

Stay alert.

Stay alert for environmental hazards such as poison ivy and oak, stinging insects, and venomous creatures. Also watch for symptoms of sunstroke, altitude sickness, dehydration, and hypothermia in yourself and your fellow workers.

Part Five: Tools for Trailbuilding

The Ten Essential Tools

Clinometer

The grade or steepness of a trail is one of the most important factors in determining whether a trail will last for years or fall to pieces in months. Clinometers enable you to read the percent grade between two points. Clinometers are particularly important during the design stage of trailbuilding. See page 70 for a detailed explanation of how to use a clinometer.

Flagging (Ribbon/Pin Flag)

Flagging, in the form of a roll of *ribbon* or a *wire-pin* flag, is used to highlight an area for trail alignment, construction, and maintenance. Flagging comes in a variety of colors and shapes and should be chosen so that it is easily identifiable. This is one of the few times that you *don't* want your work to blend in with the surrounding terrain. Ribbon flagging is ideal for identifying trail corridors and pin flagging is best suited to marking your trail tread. All flagging materials should be removed once trail work is complete.

Pulaski

Pulaskis have an axe blade on one side and a grub hoe on the other. This tool is preferred by many trail crews for loosening dirt, cutting through roots, grubbing brush, and sculpting because it is widely available and more efficient than single-purpose tools. Unlike grub hoes or mattocks, the Pulaski is a narrower, sharp-edged tool, and should not be used in rocky soil. With the bit and adz keenly honed, a Pulaski is an excellent woodworking tool for shaping the notches and joints of turnpikes, bridges, and other timber projects.

Safety tip: Work with the Pulaski in front of you, and never swing it above your shoulder.

The versatile Pulaski is a popular trailbuilding tool.

Trail Solutions

McLeod

The McLeod is the ultimate tool for finishing your trail tread. It has a flat, square-shaped blade with a cutting edge on one side and a rake with widely spaced tines on the other. The McLeod is useful for removing slough and berm from a trail and for tamping or compacting tread. It can also be used to shape a trail's backslope. The head of a McLeod is not made to withstand serious pounding, so use it for shaping, not swinging.

Safety tip: Because of its shape, the McLeod is awkward to transport and store. Carry it with the tines pointing toward the ground—ideally with a sheath over the cutting edge.

Rockbar (Pry Bar)

Rockbars are made for prying heavy boulders and logs from the ground. The ideal rockbar is 4-feet long, weighs about 18 pounds, and features a beveled end. The key to using a rockbar is leverage. Slip the beveled end under the object and apply basic physics to ease the object toward its destination. Rockbars require coordinated teamwork. Make sure everyone understands each step of a move before it begins. A rockbar can also be used as a drop hammer to break rock or open a crack.

Safety tip: Keep toes and fingers clear of places where they can be pinched.

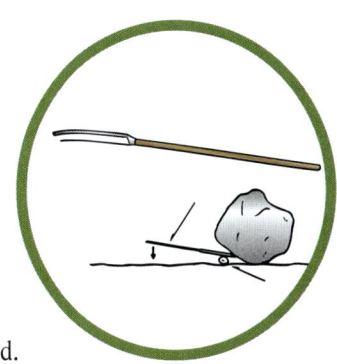

Tape Measure

Trailwork requires accurate measurements. A tape measure is light, compact, and it gets the job done. You'll undoubtedly wind up setting yours down on the trail, so opt for a durable model made of lightweight polystyrene in a highly visible color such as blaze orange or yellow.

Digital Level

Trails must be properly outsloped to shed water and prevent erosion. A digital level is useful for determining whether your trail tread is outsloped and to what degree. Professional trailbuilders use the SmartTool Electronic Level, which is available in 2- and 4-foot sizes. Digital levels may seem like overkill, but they're worth the extra expense. Thrifty and creative trailbuilders mark traditional levels to indicate 3 to 7 percent as an alternative.

A digital level is useful for fine-tuning trail tread outslope.

Part Five: Tools for Trailbuilding

Hand Pruners/Loppers/Folding Saw

Hand pruners and loppers can be used to remove small branches encroaching on the trail. They're also useful for cutting protruding roots that pose as tripping hazards. A brush saw can also be used to handle branches.

Shovel

Shovels are available in various blade shapes and handle lengths. Flat shovels are great for moving large quantities of dirt and for shaping tread and drainages. Fire shovels and round-point shovels are most common for trailwork and are used to move loosened dirt, dig holes and trenches, and remove weeds. They can also be used for cleaning grade dips, culvert outlets, and diversion ditches. Two models are particularly good for trailwork. The *long-handled shovel,* best for digging holes, is generally 48 inches in length. The *D-handled shovel,* best for moving soil or digging in confined spaces, is generally 27 inches in length.

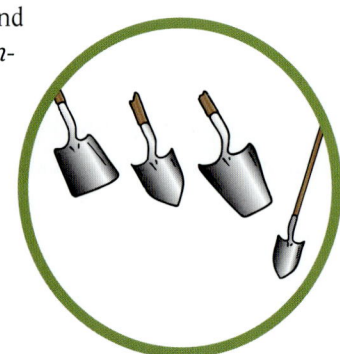

Safety tip: The most common injuries associated with shovels are back injuries. Remember to bend from the knees instead of the waist, and lift with your legs not your back. Shovels shouldn't be used as a lever to pry rocks.

Sledgehammer

There are two basic types of sledgehammer: the *stone sledge* and the *driving sledge*. A stone sledge can be used to crush rock into gravel for trail repair and is helpful for setting rocks into an armored section of trail or a retaining wall. A driving sledge is used to drive spikes or pins and isn't needed in average trailbuilding situations. Because of differences in tempering, the stone and driving sledges are not interchangeable. A sledgehammer with a 6- to 8-pound head and a 3-foot-long handle is a very handy tool. Before swinging, always make sure no one else is in your strike zone and that your feet are firmly planted and spread shoulder-width apart. Of all the hand tools, the sledge holds the greatest potential for serious injury because it is heavy and awkward. Use only short, controlled swings and never use all your might when wielding a sledgehammer.

Safety tip: Sledgehammers can cause stone chips to fly. Protect yourself by wearing a hardhat, eye protection, long pants, and boots.

Trail Solutions

7 Important Items Trailbuilders Often Forget

These items may seem trivial, but once on the trail you'll realize how important they really are.

1 First Aid Kit
A standard first aid kit should contain the basic components to handle minor injuries such as blisters, splinters, small cuts, etc.

2 Gloves
Work gloves protect your hands from blisters, thorny brush, and poison oak or ivy. They also help you grip slippery tools.

3 Safety Glasses
Glasses should be worn when using power tools, breaking rock, or anywhere flying debris is present.

4 Two-Way Radio/Cell Phone
In remote backcountry areas, a two-way radio or cell phone can save you in an emergency. Radios should be assigned to crew leaders or agency personnel, as determined by the number of crews, remoteness of the work site, and accessibility to emergency facilities.

5 Sturdy Footwear
Sturdy shoes or boots protect your feet from glancing tools and improve your footing.

6 Water
All workers should carry adequate water supplies. Crew leaders should curtail the work session if there isn't an adequate supply of drinking water at the worksite.

7 Protective Creams
Insect repellent and sun block are essential. Some creams can be used to treat poison oak or ivy exposure as well as insect bites.

Part Five: Tools for Trailbuilding

Other Useful Hand Tools

You can handle basic trailwork jobs with the hand tools we've listed in the previous sections. If you're going to tackle more complicated work, however, give this section a read.

Clearing Tools

Weed Cutters (Grass Whip/Swizzle Stick/Swing Blade/Weed Whip)

Weed cutters are used to clear trail corridors of succulent vegetation such as grass, light brush, briars, and tree seedlings. This tool is meant to be swung back and forth with both hands. The *L-shaped* weed whip cuts grass and weeds but is unstable for use on larger growth. The *triangular-frame weed* whip cuts briars and woody stems up to a half-inch in diameter. The screws holding the serrated double-edged blade in place can work loose, so check them often.

Safety tip: Avoid the golf swing; never swing a tool higher than your shoulders.

Machete

Machetes are best used to clear the way when surveying new trail routes through dense vegetation. A slightly angled (off-vertical) stroke of the machete is more effective than a low horizontal swing. As it is an effective but crude cutter, the machete should not be used to hack branches from trailside trees.

Safety tip: Use extreme care when working with machetes near others. This tool should not be used during trailwork days with volunteers.

Swedish Safety Brush Axe (Sandvik)

Also known as a Sandvik, the Swedish Safety Brush Axe is a machete-like tool with a short, replaceable blade. Because of the shorter blade and longer handle (27-inch overall length), the Sandvik may be safer than a machete, and it is faster, easier to control, and safer than an axe or brush hook. The thin, flat, replaceable steel blade cuts easily through springy hardwood stems.

Safety tip: A sharp tool is a safe tool. Replace the blade when it becomes dull or nicked.

Trail Solutions

Brush Hook (Bush Hook/Ditch Blade/Ditch Blade Axe)

For removal of brush too heavy for a weed cutter and too light for an axe, consider either the double- or single-edged brush hook. Swung like an axe, the brush hook's long, 36-inch handle and heavy head give it a powerful cut. The curved blade, however, poses an extra safety hazard. Always maintain a firm grip with both hands on the handle. Cut with a slicing rather than a hacking motion, and pull back on the handle at the end of the swing in order to utilize the 12-inch curved blade. Carry brush hooks with the head forward, like a shovel.

Safety tip: Never use an overhead swing with a brush hook. Keep the blade in front of you at all times.

Loppers (Lopping Shears/Pruning Shears)

Loppers are designed for clearing heavy vegetation from trails. With their long handles, a sturdy pair of loppers has the mechanical advantage to cut cleanly through all sorts of brush and branches (most cut limbs of 1 to 1.75 inches in diameter). If you have a choice, select heavy-duty loppers with fiberglass or metal handles. Cutting heads are either the sliding-blade-and-hook type (known as bypass) or the anvil type. Some have simple pivot actions, while others have compound or gear-driven actions for increased cutting power. Do not try to twist the handles when biting into a resistant branch. This can bend the blade. If the loppers can't cut the branch, use a bow saw.

Safety tip: Carry loppers with the jaws pointed down and away from you and with one hand around both handles.

Sawing and Chopping Tools

Bow Saw

A bow saw with a 16- to 21-inch blade is handy for cutting brush and trimming small branches. Larger bow saws (36 inches or more) are unwieldy for brushing projects. They are better suited for cutting medium-size logs along the trail or cutting firewood. When properly maintained, bow saws will cut quickly and efficiently, however they can bind easily. Bow saws cannot be resharpened due to the hardness of the blade, so when the blade becomes dull, rusty, or bent, it should be replaced. If a saw has no sheath, make one by splitting a piece of old garden hose as long as the blade. Fit the hose around the saw blade and hold it in place with cord or duct tape. A sheathed bow saw can be carried by hand or strapped onto a backpack.

Safety tip: Never use a bow saw to cut overhead branches. Use a pole saw instead.

Part Five: Tools for Trailbuilding

Razor-Tooth Saw (Protooth Saw)

These saws have an extra-thick, extra-wide, razor-tooth blade for rigidity. They are used to cut limbs encroaching on the trail and come in a wide variety of sizes and tooth patterns.

Safety tip: Given its sharp teeth, a razor-tooth saw should be sheathed when not in use.

Folding Saw

Folding saws are smaller alternatives to bow saws. Their diminutive size makes them easy to carry and well suited to getting into tighter places. They are useful for limbing, brushing, and removing small downfall. There are a vast array of blade lengths and styles, and some folding saws have replaceable or interchangeable blades.

Pole Saw with Pole Pruner

A pole saw with pole pruner can be used to trim branches that would otherwise be out of arm's reach above a trail. On some models, the pole can be taken apart or telescoped into the handle, and the blade can be removed for easy carrying. The built-in pruner can be operated from the ground with a rope. When cutting larger limbs with the pole saw, it is best to use a two-step process. Begin by cutting the branch, first from underneath and then from the top, leaving a 4- to 6-inch stub. This prevents you from stripping the bark from the trunk of the tree. Next, cut the stub flush with the trunk.

Safety tip: Never stand right below the branch you are cutting, and be sure that others are clear of the falling branch.

Axe (Ax)

Axes can be used to chop deadfall from trails, shape stakes for turnpikes and waterbars, and cut notches for structures made of timber. Most trail crews use the single-bit axe (one sharp side) versus the *double-bit axe* (two sharp sides), feeling that one sharp blade is safer than two. Although the axe is a traditional woodworking tool, saws are usually recommended for trail work because they are safer and generally more efficient for the average user. The axe is best reserved for cutting jobs too thick for available saws. When not in use, or when carrying the axe, sheathe the blade.

Safety tip: Never use a single-bit axe as a sledgehammer or splitting wedge.

Don't Make the Mistake of...

Using tools that aren't in good shape. Tool handles crack and break all the time. Any tool that has a damaged handle should be condemned from use until a replacement is installed. The same is true for a tool with a loose head or a broken cutting edge. Serious injury can result from faulty tools, so be sure your tools are in good shape before use.

Grubbing and Raking Tools

Mattock

A mattock is a heavy grubbing tool with an adz blade that can be used as a hoe for digging in hard ground. The other blade of a mattock may be a pick (pick mattock) for breaking small rocks or a cutting edge (cutter mattock) for chopping roots. Mattocks may be purchased with head weights ranging from 3 to 6 pounds. For heavy work, use at least a 5-pound head. Handles are generally 36 inches long—a good length for most trailwork. The head should tighten on the handle as the mattock is swung, but sometimes it loosens and slides down the handle.

Safety tip: The handle can be removed for ease in packing.

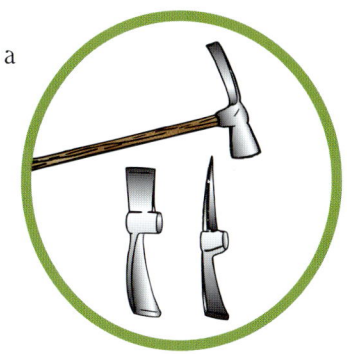

Hoes (Grub Hoe/Adze Hoe/Hazel Hoe)

Grub hoes of various weights are available and are good for building and repairing trail tread. They usually come with a 34-inch handle and a 6-inch-wide blade set at an "adze angle." Hoes are maintained and used like mattocks.

Safety tip: The handle can be removed for ease in packing.

Pick (Pickaxe)

A pick is rarely necessary in trail work, as its job is adequately done by the pick mattock. The standard pick has a narrow chisel blade on one end and pointed tip on the other. The tool can be used to break or pry small rocks, loosen heavy soil and gravel, or to dig a trench or hole. As with any tool used for breaking hard soil or rock, safety glasses should be worn to protect the eyes from flying debris.

Safety tip: Picks should not be used as a lever to pry loose large rock.

Fire Rake (Council Tool)

The fire rake, with its three, tempered-steel blades and 5-foot handle, is traditionally preferred to the McLeod in the eastern states. The triangular tines can be honed with a file. The fire rake is lighter than the McLeod and is better for cutting leaves, mulch, small bushes, and debris from trail corridors than it is for shaping tread or backslopes.

Safety tip: Never carry a fire rake over your shoulder; keep it at your side.

Part Five: Tools for Trailbuilding

Digging and Tamping Tools

Digging-Tamping Bar

A digging-tamping bar is about the same length as a rock bar but much lighter. It has a small blade at one end for loosening compacted or rocky soil and a flattened end for tamping. They are great for digging postholes and tamping the soil around a post once it is set. Some rock moving can also be done using this bar, although it is not quite as rugged or effective as a rock bar.

Safety tip: Never use a tamper to move large rock or logs.

Post-Hole Digger

Used for removing soil from holes for footings or posts, the post-hole digger has clam-like scoops attached to long handles. Soil should be lifted from the hole with leg muscles—not back muscles. The post-hole digger works best at removing loose soil and should not be used to loosen compacted dirt. The scoops bend and break easily if the digger is used as a breaking tool.

Safety tip: Fingers can get pinched when the handles are closed.

Pounding and Hammering Tools

Single Jackhammer

A single jackhammer (3- to 4-pound head with short handle) can be used with a star drill to punch holes in rock. The single jack can also be used to drive bridge spikes and for other jobs that are too demanding for a regular claw hammer but do not require the heavy-duty blows of a sledge.

Safety tip: Wear a hardhat and eye protection at all times.

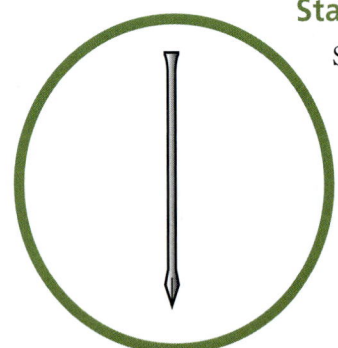

Star Drill

Star drills are usually about a foot long and weigh a pound. They are used with single jackhammers to punch holes in rock or open a seam or crack.

Safety tip: Wear a hardhat, gloves, and eye protection when using a star drill.

Lifting and Hauling Tools

Timber Carrier (Log Carrier)

Timber carriers are used for transporting heavy timber and logs. They look like giant ice tongs with 5-foot-long wooden handles. These handles allow room for two people on each side of the carrier. One carrier can be used to drag the log, and a heavy log can be carried using two or more in order to avoid dragging the log through a fragile area. Timber carriers can also be used to move bridge stringers and are helpful in shelter construction.

Safety tip: A firm tap on the back of the hooks will set the hooks into the log in order to avoid slippage.

Peavey and Cant Hook (Cant Dog/Log Dog)

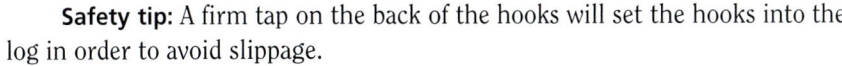

The peavey and the cant hook are used for rolling and positioning logs and timbers. The main difference between these two tools is the shape of the their ends. The Peavey has a straight spike at the end whereas the cant hook has a blunt tip. The spike allows more control over the handling of logs but may cause more damage to the log surface. Peaveys are quicker to reposition when rolling a log or timber some distance while trying to maintain momentum. Cant hooks provide for more precise rotating. When arranged as opposing pairs, both tools can serve as a timber carrier if a true carrier is not available.

Safety tip: Exercise caution so you do not roll logs onto your or someone else's toes.

Griphoist (Cable Winch)

Griphoist is the brand name for a compact, lightweight-rigging tool (cable winch) that can be used to move rock or timber. The machine consists of a metal body with a cable running through it. By cranking the lever, a set of cams clench the cable and pull it a few inches, moving heavy objects with ease. Its biggest advantage is that is a continuous cable puller. In other words, a cable of any length can be used. This allows for long pulls without having to reanchor, which is particularly helpful when pulling from across a stream or ravine. Nylon slings (which weigh less and do less damage than chains) should be used to anchor the winch to a tree and to harness the rock or log. The winch cable should be kept freely suspended (rather than dragging it through dirt or rock) to avoid fraying and deterioration of the cable. Only crews trained in the art of rigging should use the Griphoist.

Safety tip: Always stand clear of stressed lines and out of the load's path of movement.

Come Along

The come along is a simple ratchet-and-pawl cable winch used for pulling, lifting, or stretching. The better models can move substantial loads—large rocks, logs, and stumps—without breaking but are limited by the length of cable that can be wound around the spool (usually about 25 feet). Because of this constraint, hauling material over a considerable distance requires frequent reanchoring of the winch.

Safety tip: Stay out from under the load.

Rigging (Block and Tackle)

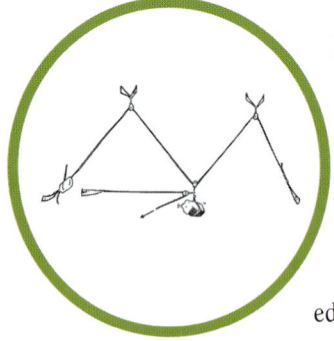

Rigging refers to a system of cables, pulleys, and winches used to suspend and move heavy loads. Rigging systems are most appropriate when there is a considerable amount of work to do at one site, such as when constructing a bridge, a retaining wall, steps, or a shelter.

Safety tip: The setup and use of a rigging system requires sophisticated training or prior experience and should not be attempted without this knowledge. Severe accidents can occur if this system is used improperly.

Wheelbarrow

A wheelbarrow can be used to haul materials and tools. Most wheelbarrows have a metal box and frame, wood or aluminum handles, and solid rubber or pneumatic tires. Pneumatic-tired wheelbarrows are recommended because you can adjust the tire inflation to roll easily on uneven terrain. Lift a loaded wheelbarrow with your legs, not with your back. Another option is to use a two-wheeled cart. They have better balance and can often carry heavier loads; however, they require wider space to maneuver.

Safety tip: Do not overload a wheelbarrow. Several light loads will be easier and safer to manage than one large one. Stay behind the handles, not between them.

Canvas Bags

C. R. Daniels, Inc. and Duluth Trading Post both sell heavy-duty canvas bags ($16 to 20 per bag) that are great for portaging dirt, small rocks, tools, or anything else you want to carry. Originally designed to carry coal, these canvas bags can tote up to 95 pounds of stuff.

B.O.B. or YAK Trailer

The YAK trailer also known as the Beast of Burden (BOB) seems to be the most prevalent single-wheeled trailer used by trail crews. This versatile cargo carrier attaches to the hub of the rear wheel of a mountain bike by means of a special quick-release skewer. It can be used to carry hand tools, chainsaws, and day gear very well. BOB Trailers (bobtrailers.com) offers a holder that zip-ties to the inside of the trailer for carrying hand tools more securely. For instructions on how to transform your B.O.B. trailer into a lean, mean, tool-holding machine, check out Kurt Loheit's Tool Holder Assembly Instructions on the IMBA website. The web page contains diagrams and easy-to-follow directions.

Bark Peeling Tools

Spud (Bark Spud/Peeling Spud)

Bark spuds remove bark from the green logs that will be used in your trail project, slowing the decay process and giving the wood a longer life. The bark spuds has a 1- to 4-foot-long handle and a dished blade with three cutting edges. All three sides should be sharpened on the top side only. The blade slides between the bark and the wood. The best time of the year for removing bark is in the spring.

Safety tip: Push the cutting edge away from your body and keep hands and feet, as well as other workers, far from the front of the blade.

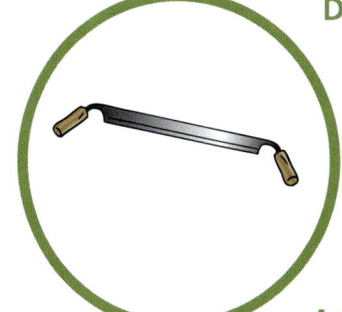

Drawknife

A drawknife is used to strip bark from small-diameter logs or poles. Grasp it by both handles and pull the blade along the log toward yourself. A drawknife has handles at a right angle to the blade whereas a bark knife's handles are in line with the blade. Bark knives are meant only for smoothing rough bark—not removing it.

Safety tip: Drawknives are razor sharp, so use caution.

Adze (Carpenter Adze)

An adze is basically an axe with a curved blade that points inward at a right angle to the handle. It is used to finish (hew) beams and logs to form a flat surface—such as the walking surface of a native log bridge. An adze should be kept very sharp and used only for hewing. It should be handled very carefully, and contact with the ground should be avoided. The blade should always be protected with a sheath.

Safety tip: Exercise caution so as not to cut your feet or shins. When standing on the log being hewed, the toe of your front foot should be elevated so that a glancing blow strikes the bottom of the sole of your boot. Only the back of the heel of the front foot should be resting on the log.

Survey, Layout, and Measuring Tools

GPS Receiver

GPS, or Global Positioning Satellite, is a constellation of satellites around the earth that can be used to identify and store a position anywhere on the earth. A GPS receiver can be used for gathering waypoints along a proposed trail corridor or existing trail. These points will indicate where to build or refurbish a trail and can be superimposed on a map to identify trail alignment or maintenance areas and stored for future reference.

Abney Level

This hand-held instrument has been used for backcountry surveying since the late 1800s. In order to measure or set grade of a trail, set the protractor mounted on the side of the level with the appropriate scale to a fixed gradient. Next, sight through the Abney to a fixed reference (usually another person) until a bubble appears in the crosshair. When the crosshair bisects the bubble, you've reached the preset grade on the Abney. The Abney has been replaced in recent decades by the clinometer, but it's still useful for people who can't use a clinometer due to a lack of binocular vision.

Measuring Wheel

The measuring wheel is used to measure distance on the trail. It records the revolutions of a wheel and hence the distance traveled by the wheel on an existing or proposed trail. Measuring wheels can be used to measure distance for guidebook descriptions and also noted in survey or assessment forms to pinpoint the location of work to be done along the trail.

Miscellaneous Tools

MAX Multi-Purpose Axe

This implement incorporates seven basic hand tools into one compact, versatile unit. A Hudson's Bay–style axe head permanently attached to a 36-inch fiberglass handle is complemented by six quick-attach tools: shovel, mattock, pick, broad pick, fire rake, and hoe. Each component slips into a specially designed socket on the axe head and is secured by either a hitch pin or thumbscrew tightener. All components are drop-forged from high-quality tool steel and fit into a compact canvas case that can be carried on a belt or strapped to a pack. The tool weights only 12.5 pounds.

Files

A 10- to 12-inch flat mill, or a flat, single-cut bastard file is the simplest tool for shaping a bevel or giving a blade a fast edge. Because of the tooth design, files cut in only the forward direction. Dragging on the backstroke quickly dulls the file. If the file becomes clogged with filings, clean it with a wire brush or file card.

> **Safety tip:** Make sure your file has a knuckle guard and a handle. It's also a good idea to wear gloves when using a file.

Trail Solutions

Mechanized Tools

Most traditional trailwork is done with hand tools, which are relatively affordable and easy to transport. Mechanized tools, however, allow you to build and repair trails in much less time. A three-person crew with a walk-behind earthmover can build five to ten times the trail in a single day as a three-person crew using only hand tools. Larger crews using a number of machines can build thousands of linear feet of trail per day.

As time and technology have advanced, machines have become more attractive and accessible to the average trailbuilder. The new breed of earthmover, for example, is powerful, versatile, leaves an extraordinarily light "footprint" on the trail, and is capable of sculpting narrow paths in the most extreme terrain.

The Upside of Mechanized Tools

When it comes to constructing miles of new trail or simply repairing a battered section of an existing one, you can't match the construction speed of a small, earthmoving machine. A trained machine operator can create more consistent trail tread than a group of laborers using hand tools—even full bench tread on steep terrain—and can carve grade reversals that would be difficult to build by hand. Trailbuilding machines also have the power to remove obstacles, such as trees, stumps, and rocks, that would compromise the trail alignment if left intact.

When it comes to building new trail, you can't match the construction speed of an earthmoving machine.

Part Five: Tools for Trailbuilding

It can take years to build a small trail system using volunteers, which can lead to volunteer burnout. Instead of spending years performing excavation, volunteers can be used more effectively to perform finish work, such as smoothing the backslope or fine-tuning outslope. Machines don't replace handwork entirely; they just make it go faster.

The Downside of Mechanized Tools

Mechanized tools are expensive. Earthmovers alone can cost anywhere from $10,000 (used) to $55,000. Moreover, additional vehicle insurance, licensing, and permitting is often required, and you must budget for regular maintenance and repairs. Mechanized tools are also difficult to transport, must be stored safely when not in use, and must be operated by properly trained individuals. Appropriate safety gear, including eye and ear protection, gloves, helmets, knee and shin guards or chaps, and sturdy boots, should be worn when operating or working around mechanized tools.

A tool's impact on the environment is largely dependant on the proficiency of its user. For instance, with a skilled operator at the helm, a small to midsize earthmover can build an immaculate contour trail, while leaving almost no trace of its passage. In the hands of a less-skilled operator, however, earthmovers can cause considerable damage—flattening vegetation and leaving obvious tracks that may be slow to heal.

Despite the user's skill, trailbuilding machines—from earthmovers and jackhammers to chainsaws and drills—are heavy, powerful, and noisy. They can disturb fragile environments and disrupt visitor experiences. For this reason, machinery is not allowed on some public lands. You may find that public land agencies are more willing to approve trail projects that utilize hand tools.

One of the great things about having volunteers build trail is that the hard work generates a greater appreciation for well-built trails. If volunteers are not involved in any phase of the construction, the connection between the community and the trail may be lost. Fortunately, volunteers can still be involved in a trail-building project that uses an earthmover. Volunteers with hand tools can still do finish work—giving your community a better trail and better trail users.

Questions to consider before using mechanized tools:

- Is the environment suitable for mechanized tool use?

- Will you have one or more trailworkers on your team who can safely and skillfully operate each of the mechanized tools required for the job?

- Machines require routine maintenance. Do you have the expertise and money to keep them running during the course of your project?

- Do you have an adequate insurance policy to cover your equipment, and a place to store your equipment safely?

Do Mechanized Tools Create Boring Trails?

Mechanized trailbuilding tools have garnered a bit of a bad rap in recent years. Critics believe that mechanized tools, such as earthmovers, are only capable of creating wide, unappealing dirt highways. Some critics also assert that mechanized tools cause unacceptable damage to the environment.

It is true that some of the larger earthmovers are not capable of building extremely narrow—let's say 12 inch—singletrack treads. This, however, does not mean that an interesting and challenging trail can't be build with a machine. For starters, a narrow tread, in and of itself, does not make a trail challenging. There are a whole slew of other methods to increase the difficulty of a trail. In addition, the 24- to 48-inch-wide tread that an earthmover constructs will often become only 12 to 18 inches wide in just a year or two, as plants grow back and the "active," or well-used, tread is established by visitors.

Mechanized tools are indeed capable of creating beautiful and challenging singletrack trails, and they can do so with very little negative impact on the environment. It all comes down to the type of machine combined with the imagination and skill of the operator. Machines are capable of sculpting 18-to 24-inch-wide singletrack with twists, turns, rocks, and obstacles when the right techniques are employed. In short, successfully building an appealing trail with an earthmover requires a skilled operator familiar with both the operation of the particular machine and the intended trail style.

This beautiful singletrack was built with the pictured excavator in the hands of a very skilled operator.
Location: Afan Argoed, Wales.

Originally developed for landscaping and construction work, walk-behind earthmovers are excellent trailbuilding tools.

A Short Guide to Mechanized Tools

There are three basic types of machines used for trail construction and maintenance: walk-behind earthmovers, ride-on earthmovers, and excavators.

Walk-Behind Earthmovers

Walk-behinds go by several names, including "compact utility loaders." These are essentially small skid-steer bulldozers that you operate while walking behind. They typically weigh about a ton. Toro, Ditch Witch, and Bobcat produce popular models. All accept multiple attachments that enable the operator to perform a variety of construction and maintenance tasks. The two most commonly used attachments are the blade and bucket. The blade is best for new construction, while either the blade or bucket can be used for maintenance. In all, there are more than 60 different quick-change attachments available.

Walk-behinds cost roughly $20,000, which includes one basic attachment. While the price tag is admittedly steep, it's certainly feasible if your organization pools its resources with neighboring groups or receives a grant. A number of IMBA-affiliated clubs have purchased such machines and are reaping the benefits—miles and miles of new trail that could never have been built as quickly with hand tools alone. These types of machines are also available for rent. Visit the Internet for more specific product information.

Ride-On Earth Movers

Sometimes referred to as "mini dozers," these machines also push dirt and rock, but the user rides on the dozer rather than walking behind it. Ride-ons also tend to be more powerful and weigh more than their less-expensive walk-behind cousins. As a result, mini dozers can move more dirt faster. On the downside, ride-ons require more skill to operate than walk-behinds.

The Italian-made Pentamoter Ibex is a unique machine that features a fully articulating blade/bucket and a dumping payload.

The Sutter Equipment SWECO 480 is a very powerful dozer specifically designed for trailwork.

Popular Mini Dozers for Trailwork

The Sutter Equipment SWECO 480 is a very powerful dozer specifically designed and manufactured for trailwork and is arguably the best known ride-on model. The SWECO is expensive at more than $50,000, but it can be rented on a weekly ($1,500) and monthly ($4,900) basis or for about $100/hour with a trained operator. SWECO's have numerous attachments that enable it to perform a variety of construction and maintenance tasks. More information is available at arrowheadtrails.com and alpine-trails.com.

The All Seasons Vehicles Positrack is a compact, rubber-tracked, ride-on machine. The Positrack has an ergonomic setup and a relatively light footprint. The suggested retail price is roughly $25,000. For more information, visit asvi.com.

The Italian-made Pentamoter Ibex is a unique machine that features a fully articulating blade/bucket and a dumping payload. At about $20,000, it is a very versatile machine.

Ditch Witch also produces a ride-on mini dozer that includes an excavator arm on the back, combining two machines in one unit.

Excavators

Many professional trailbuilders prefer excavators to the dozer-style earthmovers described above. Mini excavators, also called "compact excavators" move dirt in a decidedly different fashion: They pull it back toward the machine in a bucket, scoop it up, and then swing the bucket around to deposit the dirt somewhere else. Mini dozers, by contrast, mainly push dirt to create trails. Favorite brands among trailbuilders include Takeuchi, IHI, Bobcat, and Ditch Witch.

Another type of excavator is the "walking" or "spider" excavator most popular in Europe. Larger than mini excavators, they can be used in terrain that is very steep, wet, or difficult to access. Walking excavators typically consist of a platform with two front legs and two swiveling rear wheels.

Mini Dozers vs. Mini Excavators

Mini dozers build trail differently than mini excavators. Dozers push material by driving forward, while excavators use an arm and bucket to move material before driving forward.

Dozers need constant traction and a stable, obstacle-free trail tread on which to work—particularly when turning around. Wet or slippery conditions are problematic. Mini dozers can move lots of material and they build full bench trail relatively quickly.

Many trailbuilders prefer the versatility of mini excavators to dozer-style earthmovers.

Trail Solutions

Mini Dozers

Pros

- Fast travel speed (5 mph)
- Cuts bench relatively quickly
- Simple operation is easy to learn
- Relatively stable
- Capable of off-trail travel, including moderate slopes

Cons

- Can't push debris off the trail's critical point on steep sideslopes
- Limited by slippery conditions
- Can't access material below the trail

Mini Excavators

Pros

- Superior leverage allows a smaller machine to place large rocks
- Easily moves debris away from trail tread on steep slopes
- Can remove organic material before filling holes
- Can access material below trail
- Not severely limited by slippery conditions

Cons

- Slow travel speed (2–3 mph)
- High center of gravity means it can be unstable
- Complicated operation is difficult to learn

Unlike a dozer, an excavator doesn't have to move back and forth in order to push dirt. It can level itself with its small blade and build trail around itself with its arm and bucket. It can use its arm to pull itself over obstacles, work around corners, and reach between tight trees. An excavator can also face backward to fine-tune the trail, reduce the size of the bench, or strategically place obstacles. However, excavators require a lot of skill to operate, and they are relatively slow.

Choosing the Right Machine

No single machine is best for trailbuilding. Just like particular hand tools are better suited to certain trailbuilding projects, various situations require the use of different mechanized tools or combinations of machines. Here are some factors to consider:

Is Hand Labor Available?

A dozer is faster than an excavator at roughing in trails, with the SWECO being the fastest by far. However, a skilled excavator operator can work more precisely, minimizing the hand finishing that all machine-built trails require.

How Steep is the Sideslope?

Excavators or extra-powerful dozers are needed for cutting bench on steep sideslopes due to the large amount of material to remove. Building trail on steep sideslopes also results in very tall backslopes, which can be sculpted better with an excavator than a dozer. A combination of the two machines works well in these situations. The dozer can cut the bench, while the excavator can blend the backslope and broadcast debris.

How is the Traction?

Dozers must drive forward to push dirt, and slippery conditions may result in a stuck machine and trail tread damage. Excavators, on the other hand, can do lots of work from one location and then pull themselves along if their tracks slip.

Excavators are efficient in slippery conditions.

Walk-behind earthmovers with a bucket attachment are great for hauling rocks and other trailbuilding materials.

What is the Desired Trail Width?

The finished width of a machine-built trail is mostly a factor of technique, operator skill, and hand-finishing work. However, some machines are wider than others. Smaller machines can create narrower trail, but they are less stable than larger machines and have less traction due to their smaller ground-contact patch and weight.

Are There Rocks and Roots?

A proposed tread area with embedded rock and large, dense vegetation will require a more powerful machine. Removing stumps larger than 4 inches in diameter or embedded rocks that weigh more than 1,000 pounds are jobs best left to the SWECO or an excavator. A winch can often help with these tasks.

Is There a Thick Organic Layer?

An organic layer deeper than 1 foot or a situation that requires excavation in front of the machine is often best suited to an excavator. Only an excavator can reach in front of and below the machine to remove deep, organic-material-filled holes and to place rocks for walls before backfilling. Dozers may bury this organic material under the trail, possibly resulting in an unstable tread.

Trail Solutions

Using both an excavator and dozer-style earthmover can be a very effective combination.

Tips for Using Mechanized Tools

Learn From a Pro.

Instruction from an experienced machine operator is essential to learning and implementing the specialized techniques needed to build sustainable trails with minimal impact. Expect to spend a few low-production days learning about the machine and the tricks of sculpting singletrack.

Secure the Machine During Transport.

Use two chains and a ratchet binder to securely fasten the machine to the trailer or flatbed during transport. Make sure the chains will not come loose, even if the machine moves in transit. The machine should not be able to leave the trailer even in the event of a crash.

Check Fluids.

Always check hydraulic fluid and engine oil levels before operation. Measure fluids when the machine is warm and level. If renting a machine, check the fluids before you leave the rental shop.

Maintain the Machine.

In addition to keeping an eye on the fluids, keep moving parts well greased, and regularly check the track tension, air filters, and other key elements. Do your maintenance work in a shop rather than on the trail. Diligent maintenance can help avoid a breakdown deep in the woods.

Check Blade Availability.

Many rental walk-behind machines come with buckets instead of blades. A blade is much better for trailbuilding, so check availability before you rent.

Watch the Fuel.

Don't run the machine dry and don't confuse diesel fuel, oil/gas mixtures, and gasoline. Store diesel fuel in yellow containers and gasoline in red containers to avoid confusion. It is easiest to add fuel at the trailhead. Keep fuel away from running machines.

Keep Machine Arms Low.

A low center of gravity equals a stable machine. Raising the arms and the attachment makes the machine less stable. An accidental jerk of the controls can easily tip a machine when the arms are high, especially with a raised bucket full of dirt.

Use Ear Protection.

Screeching hydraulics and roaring engines may damage hearing, so be sure to protect your ears. A hard hat with a face shield is also recommended, especially in forested areas.

Hold the Joystick Low.

The longish joysticks on some machines make subtle machine movements difficult. By holding the stick low and bracing your palm or wrist against the machine, you can improve your control.

Don't try to push too much material. It is better to make repeated passes pushing small loads than to struggle with huge mounds of material.

Trail Solutions

Go Slow and Easy.
Remember: safety first! One accident or stuck machine will ruin the day's productivity—at best.

Push Small Loads and Make Repeated Passes.
Don't try to push too much material. If your tracks slip or the engine strains, you're probably pushing too much dirt. It is better to make repeated passes pushing small loads than to struggle with huge mounds of material.

Float the Blade.
Many dozers feature a "float" setting that allows the blade to automatically track along the ground. Dragging the blade backward in the float setting can be a useful technique for minor grading and removing loose dirt and organic material without digging.

Turn Carefully.
The tracks of skid-steer machines have very little impact when moving in a straight line, especially on thick grass. However, their tracks can dig and churn when turning.

Spread Debris.
Piles of debris next to the trail can be long-lasting eyesores and may impede drainage. Use the machine to push excavated material away from the trail, hiding as much debris as possible. (A machine operator need only spend time spreading debris piles by hand to realize how much effort can be saved by doing this with a machine.)

Decrease Trail Width if Desired.
There are three ways to make narrow machine-built trail. 1) The machine can cut a three-fourths bench tread and then remove the fill, yielding a tread narrower than the machine's tracks. This removal can be done with a smaller machine or by hand. 2) The backslope can be blended into the trail tread. 3) Material can be pulled back onto the tread once the machine has passed.

Keep a Winch Handy.
Eventually the machine will get stuck. Having an appropriate sized winch or come along and similarly sized straps and shackles will enable you to retrieve or right the machine.

Other Useful Mechanized Tools

Motorized Carriers and Power Wheelbarrows

Motorized carriers are useful for extra-heavy or frequent hauling needs. These come in various configurations and typically feature a small engine with a dump body.

All Terrain Vehicles

When working on a long trail, ATVs can be extremely useful. They can carry workers, tools and even haul small loads long distances in a short period. ATVs can also pull a variety of trail-grooming implements—including tine harrows that rake the tread, loosen rocks, and break dirt clods. Their small size means they can be used on relatively narrow trails. If operated with care, ATVs leave little trace.

Chainsaws

Chainsaws with 16-inch bars are adequate for most work. Chain brakes, vibration-damped handles, and high-quality mufflers are key. Leather gloves, ear and eye protection, a hardhat, and saw chaps are required when using a chainsaw.

Safety tip: Chainsaws should only be handled by experienced workers who have been trained and certified in chainsaw use.

Power Weed Cutter (Brush saw)

A power weed cutter with an engine of 35cc to 80cc and bicycle-type handlebars is generally recommended for trailwork. A saw-type or a universal grass-brush blade—not a string cutter, such as those in "weed whacker" models used for lawn trimming—is best. The brush saw is supported by a shoulder harness, but it can still become tiring to use. Be sure to work in a team and switch positions regularly.

Safety tip: The open blade is on the end of a wand, and can snag and swing violently to the side, making it more prone to injuring other workers than the operator. Other workers should stay clear.

DR Field and Brush Mower

This sturdy mower is an excellent choice for cutting heavy grass, weeds, briars, and even small saplings. A DR Field and Brush Mower is simply a walk-behind brush hog that is useful during trail construction and trail maintenance. Models are available with 9, 11, 13, or 17 horsepower. The 17 HP is the best for trail work, as its heavy, 30-inch-wide blade is capable of powering through saplings up to 2 inches thick. It is more useful than a sickle-bar mower because the material is chewed up and often does not need to be removed from the trail.

Safety tip: The mower can throw objects and injure others. Other workers should stay a safe distance from the mower.

Stump Grinder

A gasoline-powered portable stump grinder is handy when you have many stumps to remove. These grinders are powered by a chain-saw motor and have carbide teeth that can be resharpened or replaced.

Rock Drills/Breakers

Single-use or combination rock drill/breakers are available. The drills are used to bore holes in rock or concrete. The breaker can split rock, cut asphalt, drive pipe and signposts, and chip and shape rock. Electric rotary-hammer drills are lower in cost, size, and weight than gas-powered models, and the availability of lightweight gas generators has made it possible to use electric tools at project sites distant from roads.

Hydraulic rock drills and breakers are preferable when you already have a hydraulic attachment on your trail machinery.

Photo by Seb Rogers.

Photo by Chuck Haney.

Trail Solutions

Part Six: Trail Construction

IMBA's mission to improve trail access takes us all over the world. In our travels, we've seen pristine trails that were crafted nearly 2,000 years ago by Roman armies. We've also seen rutted, gullied, and miserably hacked out swaths of mud that were built in the United States less than 12 months ago. Why do some trails last forever, while others fall apart quickly? Much of it comes down to proper construction.

"Build it right, build it once." That's the mantra behind this Part and the simple truth about trailbuilding. A well-built trail that incorporates sound construction techniques will withstand the ravages of time, weather, and trail users of every stripe. What's more, well-built trails need only minor maintenance from season to season. A poorly built trail, on the other hand, can erode and fall apart in months—requiring constant maintenance. Read on to learn how to build trails that visitors will enjoy for years to come.

In This Part ...

- **Clearing the Trail Corridor** **137**
  - How Wide? How High? 137
- **Bench Cut Trails** **140**
  - Building a Full Bench Trail with Hand Tools 142
- **Building Climbing Turns, Switchbacks and Insloped Turns** **149**
  - Climbing Turns 149
  - Switchbacks 151
  - Four Steps for Building a Switchback 153
  - Insloped Turns 154
  - Four Steps for Building an Insloped Turn ... 157
- **Retaining Walls** **159**
  - Key Steps to Building Retaining Walls 159
- **Armoring—Using Rock to Harden Trails** **162**
  - Five Ways to Armor with Rock 163
  - Ten Tips for Rock Armoring 166
  - When Armoring, Always 170
  - Man-Made Soil Hardeners 174
- **Wetlands and Water Crossings** **176**
  - Stream Corridor Function and Dynamics ... 176
  - Five General Guidelines for Water Crossings 177
  - Armored Crossings 179
  - Culverts 180
  - Bridges 183
  - Wetlands 185
- **How Long Will It Take? How Much Will It Cost?** .. **187**

Clearing the Trail Corridor

The first step in building a new trail is to clear the space, or corridor, through which it will pass. At this point, the potential trail corridor is most likely obscured by downed trees, branches, and a hodgepodge of shrubs and bushes. Follow your land manager's guidelines regarding what vegetation you can and cannot cut, when applicable. There are often size and species restrictions.

How Wide? How High?

The width and height of the trail corridor can really make or break the trail experience, yet corridor clearing is often rushed and isn't given proper consideration. A carefully trimmed corridor can accentuate turns, hide nearby trails, prevent trail widening, control speed, and add to the overall ambiance of the trail.

There are several factors to consider when determining corridor width and height:

Vegetation Type and Growth Rate

Some species are more visually appealing and can add to the trail experience. However, plants that grow very fast should be removed or heavily trimmed.

Type of Users

Consider the mix of visitors. Equestrians need a wider corridor and higher trail ceiling (the vertical space above your trail tread). An 8-foot ceiling is generally adequate on most trails. Trails for equestrians, however, should have a 10-foot ceiling.

Speed of Users

A tighter corridor will slow trail users. An open corridor may invite more speed.

A creatively trimmed corridor can add to the trail experience. Location: South Yuba Trail, California.

Trail Corridor

Part Six: Trail Construction

Number of Users
Trails with high anticipated traffic may need a larger corridor to allow for passing and visibility.

Difficulty Level
Corridor size can greatly affect a trail's technical challenge. Narrow openings between trees, low branches, thorny bushes, or cactus close to the trail tread will make for a tight and tricky pathway, adding to the challenge of the trail.

Trail Flow
Are you planning a twisty trail or an open and flowing style? Cut the corridor to match.

Maintenance Frequency
If you know that you can only clear the corridor once a year, trim a little higher and wider.

Sightline Needs
A crowded trail with a mix of runners, dog walkers, and children calls for greater visibility. However, if the tread surface is smooth and the corridor is wide, mountain bikers may be tempted to ride too fast. Creative corridor cutting can help. Keep some vegetation below waist level to control trail width and anchor turns but still allow for clear sightlines. Don't remove trees near the trail tread, just trim their branches for visibility.

Travel Direction
A one-way trail can be trimmed differently than a two-way trail, as sightlines only need to be clear in one direction of travel.

Aesthetics
Determine the desired experience before you begin "beating back the jungle." A trail with a tight corridor can help visitors feel a closer connection with nature. Your goal should always be to minimize your impact on the environment and leave the area looking as natural as possible.

Recommended Tools For Clearing a Trail Corridor
- Loppers
- Brush Cutters
- Folding Saw
- Pole Saw
- Weed Cutters
- Chainsaw
- McLeod

Removing Trees and Brush
When small trees and bushes are growing in the middle of the future tread, don't cut them flush with the ground. They must be dug out, roots and all, or else they'll become dangerous "pungee sticks" when the tread compacts around them. Cutting them at waist level leaves a handle for levering them out. Fill and compact the resulting hole to match the tread.

Trimming Branches

The thickened section of bark just outside the spot where a branch joins its tree is called the "bark collar." When trimming tree branches, always cut to the outside of the bark collar. The resulting nub helps the cut heal more quickly. When removing larger branches, make a partial cut underneath before cutting from the top. This way, when the branch falls it won't strip protective bark. Place felled trees and cut branches at least 10 feet from the corridor, with the butt end pointing away from the trail.

Digging Out Roots

Trees, bushes, stumps, and their root balls must be completely removed from the trail tread. Cutting them at waist level leaves a handle for levering them out.

When trimming tree branches, always cut to the outside of the bark collar.

Part Six: Trail Construction

Building Bench Cut Trails

A bench is a section of tread cut across the side, or contour, of a hill. A **full bench trail** is constructed by cutting the full width of the tread into the hillside. The entire tread is dug down to compacted mineral soil. This design creates a consistent and stable tread, but it takes time and effort, since the organic matter that normally covers mineral soil must be removed. In the end, all this effort pays off in the form of a trail that lasts indefinitely with very little maintenance.

Full Bench Trail

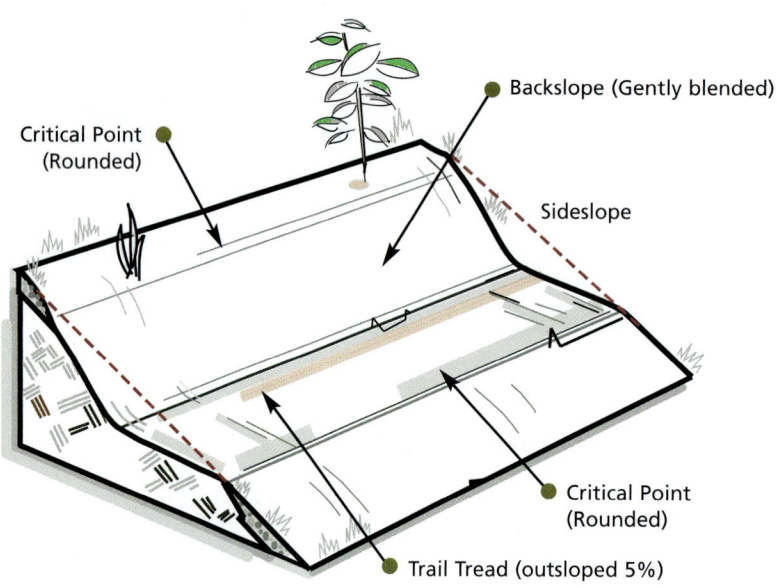

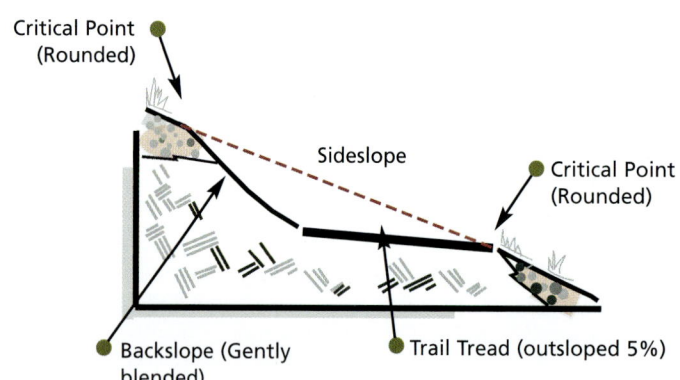

On a **partial bench trail,** only part of the hill is cut away and the soil that has been removed is placed at the lower edge of the trail to try to establish the desired tread width. The main benefit of the partial bench trail is that it requires considerably less digging than the full bench process.

There are serious downsides, however, to the partial bench design. The section of trail tread made of fill soil is soft and rarely compacts consistently. As a result, the fill-soil portion of the trail either gradually slips downhill or it compacts unevenly and creates a berm on the outer edge of the trail, which traps water. Partial bench trails usually aren't sustainable and we rarely recommend this design.

There are a few occasions in which it's simply impossible to build a full bench trail, and you must utilize the partial bench design. It may be impossible, for instance, to dig past tree roots or impenetrable rock in order to place the entire tread on mineral soil. At times like these, you're stuck with the partial bench.

Fortunately, you can improve the durability of a partial bench by reinforcing the downhill side of the tread with a retaining wall. The wall holds soil and stops the tread from slipping downhill. It's important for the top of the retaining wall to be lower than the trail tread so water can still sheet across the trail.

Unfortunately, the construction cost and time of retaining-wall-reinforced tread is usually *at least twice* that of a standard full bench tread. In short, you should aim to build full bench trails whenever possible.

Partial Bench Trail

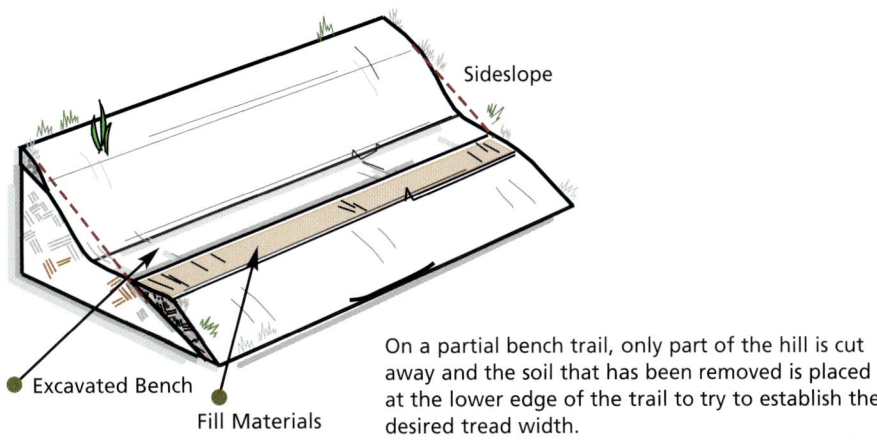

On a partial bench trail, only part of the hill is cut away and the soil that has been removed is placed at the lower edge of the trail to try to establish the desired tread width.

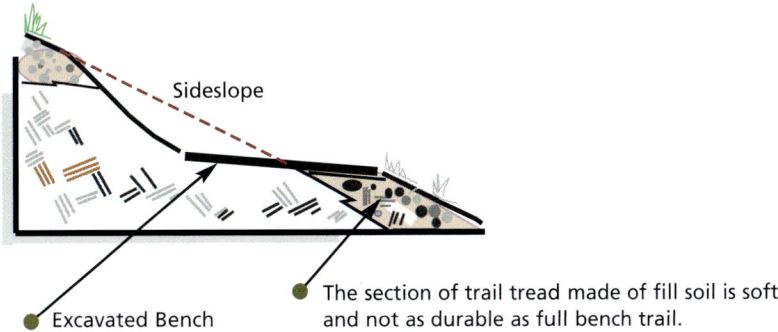

The section of trail tread made of fill soil is soft and not as durable as full bench trail.

Building a Full Bench Trail with Hand Tools

Bench Cut

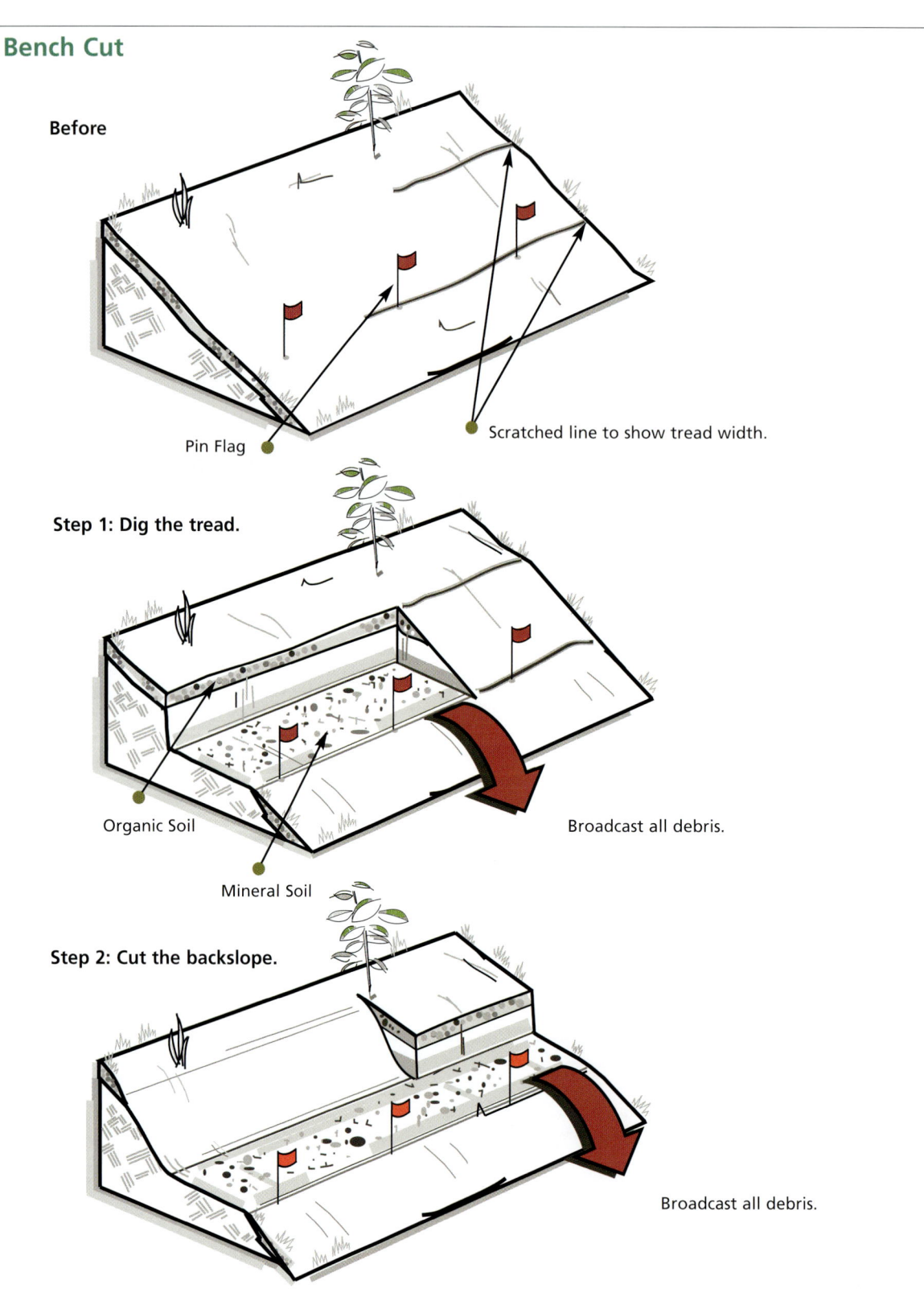

Before

Pin Flag

Scratched line to show tread width.

Step 1: Dig the tread.

Organic Soil

Mineral Soil

Broadcast all debris.

Step 2: Cut the backslope.

Broadcast all debris.

Trail Solutions

Bench Cut

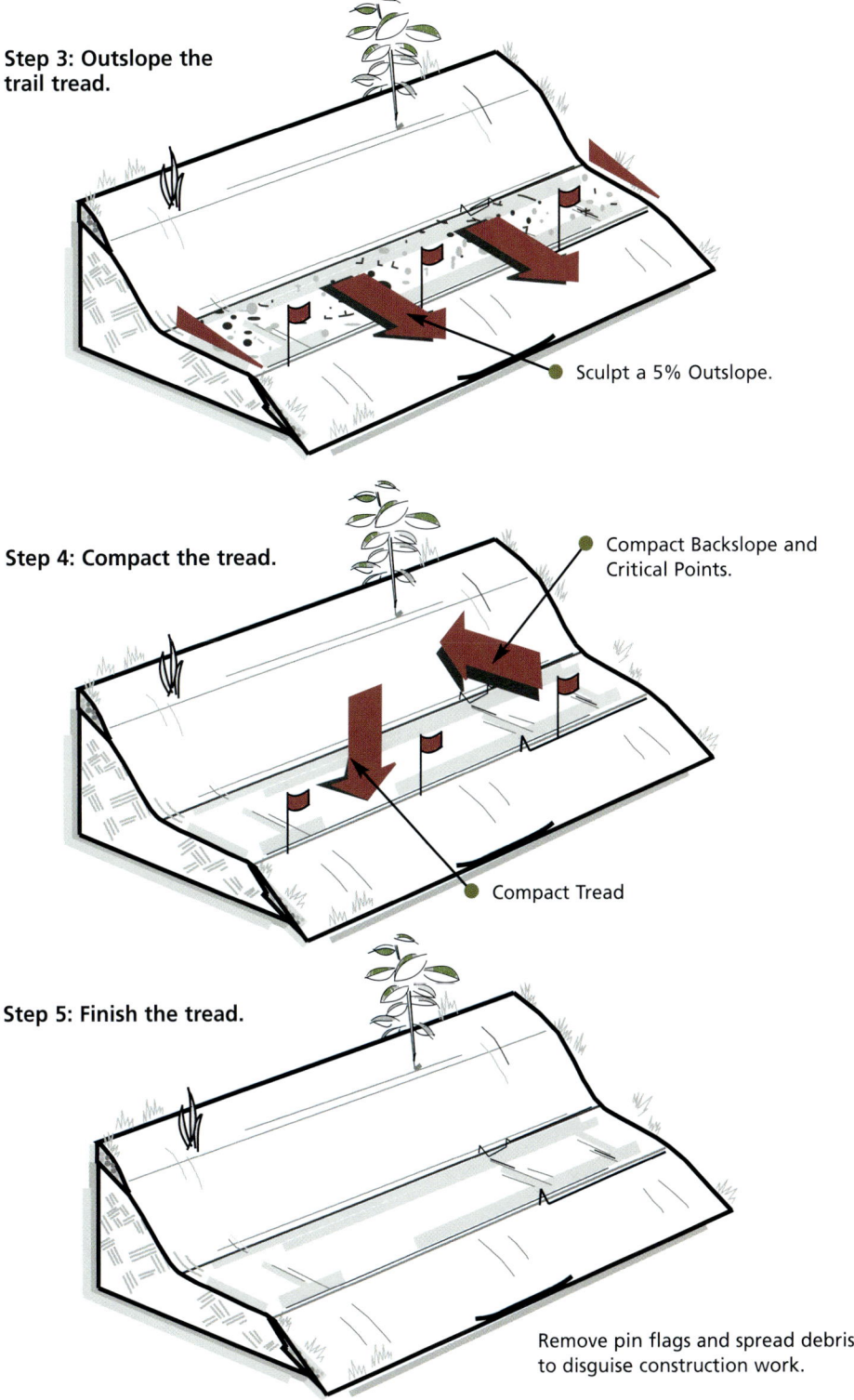

Step 3: Outslope the trail tread.

Sculpt a 5% Outslope.

Step 4: Compact the tread.

Compact Backslope and Critical Points.

Compact Tread

Step 5: Finish the tread.

Remove pin flags and spread debris to disguise construction work.

This is a prime example of full bench construction. Notice the perfectly blended backslope, the firmly compacted tread, and the slight outslope, which will aid in shedding water.

There are five basic steps involved in building a full bench trail.

1   Dig the tread.

2   Cut the backslope.

3   Outslope the tread.

4   Compact the tread.

5   Finish the tread.

Step 1: Dig the Tread.

Let's assume that the trail has been marked with a single row of pin flags and the corridor has been cleared. Start by taking all the loose material lying on the ground (leaves, small branches, etc.) and raking it uphill. Keep this material uphill, as it will be used later in the process.

Now that the line of pin flags is clearly visible, it's time to mark the tread width. Stand below the pin flags and mark a spot, at your desired trail width, uphill from each flag. (If your desired tread width is 18 inches,

Grubbing tools like the Pulaski are best for cutting the bench.

make your marks 18 inches uphill from each pin flag.) Next, connect the dots by scratching a line from pin flag to pin flag and on the marks that you made above each of the pin flags. You have just created a visual marker on the top and on the bottom of the tread. Don't worry about the backcut yet; these marks are only for the tread.

Begin on the downhill edge and use a grubbing tool (such as a Pulaski, hoe, or mattock) to loosen the organic material—decomposing leaves, duff, and humus—working your way down to the mineral soil. A good way to tell the difference: Organic material will burn, mineral soil will not. Remember, there is no need to remove rocks and roots if you are building a technical trail.

Follow the grubbing tools with tools designed to broadcast the loosened soil; shovels, rakes and McLeods are best for this job. Broadcasting is the process of distributing the excavated soil as far downhill and away from the tread as possible.

You may need to make multiple passes as you work toward the top edge of the tread, alternating between the grubbing and broadcasting tools. By removing small amounts of material with each pass, you will prevent the loosened soil from being repacked. Remember to let the tool do the work for you. Once you have created a level surface for the tread, the trail's profile should look like a park bench.

Step 2: Cut the Backslope.

The uphill side of the tread, where it blends into the slope above the trail, is called the **backslope**. Once you've fully excavated the trail tread, the next step is to shape the backslope. If the backslope is left vertical, water may cascade onto the trail or the backslope may erode and collapse onto the tread. It's very important that you nip this problem in the bud by blending the backslope so that it transitions smoothly to the hill above. Blending the backslope lengthens the trail's life by encouraging water to gently sheet across the trail.

Use grubbing tools to blend the backslope into the hillside and broadcasting tools to move the excess soil off the trail tread. Use the bottom of a McLeod to compact and smooth the backcut, and to round the edge where the backcut meets the original hillside. This is called a "critical point" and should be well packed. If the top critical point is not properly packed, water flowing down the sideslope will cut into the backslope and material will slough onto the tread.

Step 3: Outslope the Trail Tread.

Outslope—the subtle, downhill tilt of the trail—is the most important part of the tread, because water won't sheet across the trail properly without it. Use a McLeod to sculpt and carve a 5-percent outslope into the tread. Stand below the trail and scrape the McLeod from the top to the bottom edge of the tread, removing material and broadcasting it down the hillside. You can roughly measure a 5-percent outslope by standing a McLeod on the tread and eyeballing the angle of the handle, which should lean slightly away from the upper hillside. To measure outslope precisely, use a digital level or clinometer.

When creating outslope, remember to broadcast the excavated topsoil several feet downhill, away from the trail. If debris is left near the tread edge, it can settle and become a **berm**, which will interrupt sheet flow, causing water to collect and channel down the trail. The ground beyond the edge of the tread should slope away, if possible. Outslope is difficult to maintain in loose soil conditions, so grade reversals are even more essential under these circumstances.

Outslope

Flat trail tread
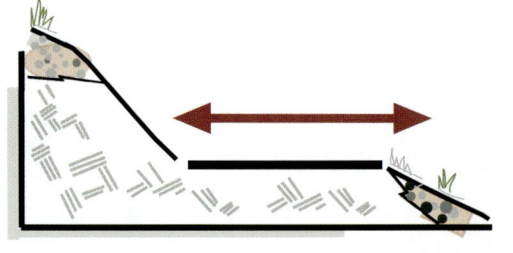

Insloped trail tread
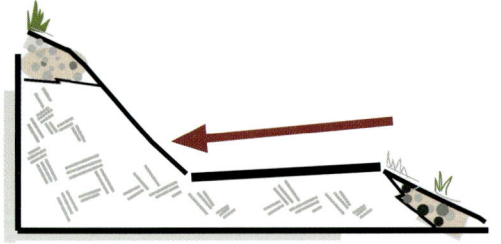

Cupped trail tread
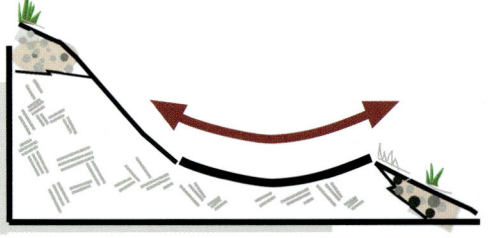

Crowned trail tread
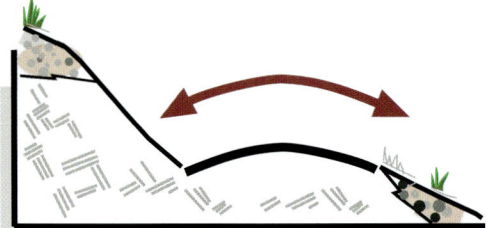

Step 4: Compact the Tread.

Finally, use the flat end of the McLeod to compact your trail tread. Don't leave this step to the trail users. Most trail users travel along the center of the tread, causing loose soil to sink and forming a shallow trench that runs down the middle of the trail. Eventually, water is trapped in this depression and erodes the tread.

Trail compaction may not be possible when working with very loose or dry soil. Under these conditions, it is best to avoid trail grades of more than 10 percent and to exaggerate outslope during construction.

Step 5: Finish the Tread.

Your bench cut trail is almost complete. Remove the pin flags, and use all the material that you initially piled on the topside of the trail to cover that loose soil you broadcasted down the hillside. The leaves, branches, and grasses will help to stabilize the broadcasted soil and will make the trail look more natural. A properly constructed trail looks like it has been there forever.

Why Is Compaction Important?

Compaction is the pressing together of particles to make a denser mass, and it is critical to proper trailbuilding. A fully compacted trail tread makes travel easier because it's smooth, predictable, and, when rocks and other trail obstacles are present, they are firmly planted in the tread. A compacted surface is also more sustainable than a loose one since water is more apt to sheet off of it. In essence, the compacted surface acts as a shield, protecting the trail.

Don't rely solely on trail users to compact the tread for you. If your trail is likely to receive immediate, heavy traffic, you'll need to manually compact the tread during construction. This is particularly true of sections containing fill dirt, such as switchbacks, rolling grade dips, jumps, and partial bench trails.

How do you compact a trail? Moist soil is essential. Compaction can be done by hand, using the end of a McLeod, the tamping end of a rock bar, or a special tamper. Mechanized tampers, however, are more effective. These gas-powered machines come in several different forms, including vibrating plate compactors and "jumping jacks." Either way, it is critical to moisten the dirt before and during compaction for best results.

Smooth or Rough…
What Should Your Finished Trail Look Like?

The look of the finished tread will depend on who the trail's frequent users will be. If the trail will be traveled primarily by advanced users, leave natural obstacles such as rocks and roots that aren't a safety hazard and won't contribute to erosion.

Rocks

On a bench cut trail, remove most rocks from the tread's inner edge. Otherwise, the rocks will force users onto the outside of the tread and could cause it to break down. On the other hand, strategically placed obstacles on the outside edge will keep users in the center of the trail. You don't, however, want to line the outside edge with rocks, as doing so could trap water on the trail.

Large, stable, round rocks are good for the tread surface. So are reasonably square or rectangular rocks. Particularly sharp, pointy rocks, however, tend to force users off the trail. Consider removing these, as well as loose rocks that are likely to work free and create holes. Still not sure which rocks should be moved? If you kick a rock and it's loose, remove it.

Roots

Remove most roots from the trail tread during construction. This is especially necessary for roots running parallel to the tread. Such roots tend to channel water and may force cyclists off the trail. Sometimes large roots that are perpendicular to the tread offer an appealing challenge. Unfortunately, they might also force cyclists to drift to the outside of the trail, causing widening or "tread creep." Consider the style of the trail, and try to determine whether leaving roots exposed will cause significant damage to the tread or tree. Cutting large feeder roots near the downhill side of a tree might kill it. Sometimes it's better to build a small retaining wall and fill over large roots instead of eliminating them.

Building Climbing Turns, Switchbacks, and Insloped Turns

So far, we've told you that rolling contour trails are the most durable and sustainable trails that you can build. We've also told you that the grade of a contour trail should never exceed half of the grade of the sideslope that it's located on (the half rule), and that the average grade should generally be less than 10 percent (the 10 percent average guideline).

If you've added all these rules up in your head, you may be saying to yourself, "Hey, you can't get to the top of a steep and narrow hill on a trail with an average grade of less than 10 percent." You're right. You can't—not if your trail goes in a straight line. Most contour trails, therefore, require direction changes, or turns, to help them gain elevation at a consistent and sustainable grade.

Climbing Turns

When trail users hit the apex of a climbing turn, they'll momentarily ride straight into the fall line. On a trail with a gentle grade, you can get away with this, but on a steeper hill, it would be a recipe for erosion.

A **climbing turn** doesn't have a constructed turning platform or landing. As a result, climbing turns should be used on shallow slopes that don't exceed a grade of about 7 percent. To control cyclists' speeds and prevent skidding, climbing turns should be free-flowing and gentle. Keep the turn radius as wide as possible—ideally 20 feet or more.

The upper and lower legs of a climbing turn are generally joined by a short section of trail (the apex of the turn) that lies directly in the fall line. Climbing turns located on hillsides with a grade of more than 7 percent are erosion prone and should be replaced with well-built switchbacks.

One of the biggest mistakes trailbuilders make is trying to construct climbing turns on sideslopes that are simply too steep. Trail users descending through the turn are automatically forced into the steep fall line. The braking action of their feet, hooves, or tires will loosen soil in this sensitive section of the turn. Gravity and water will remove the loosened soil and create a rutted and damaged surface. This, in turn, will cause users to seek alternative lines and may lead to shortcutting.

It is important to locate a grade reversal just above the turn. The grade reversal diverts water off the trail before it reaches the fall-line section. To reduce user-caused erosion, consider increasing soil durability by armoring the fall-line section of the turn and adding a choke point that slows riders down before they hit the turn.

Part Six: Trail Construction

Climbing Turn

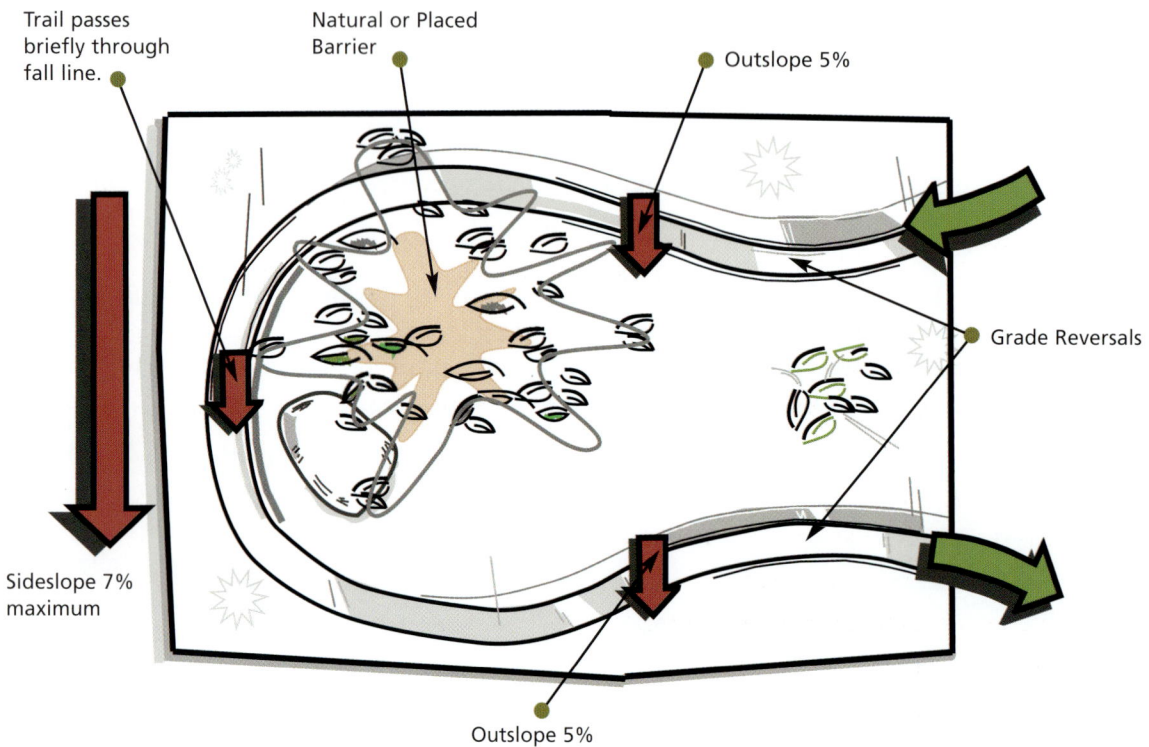

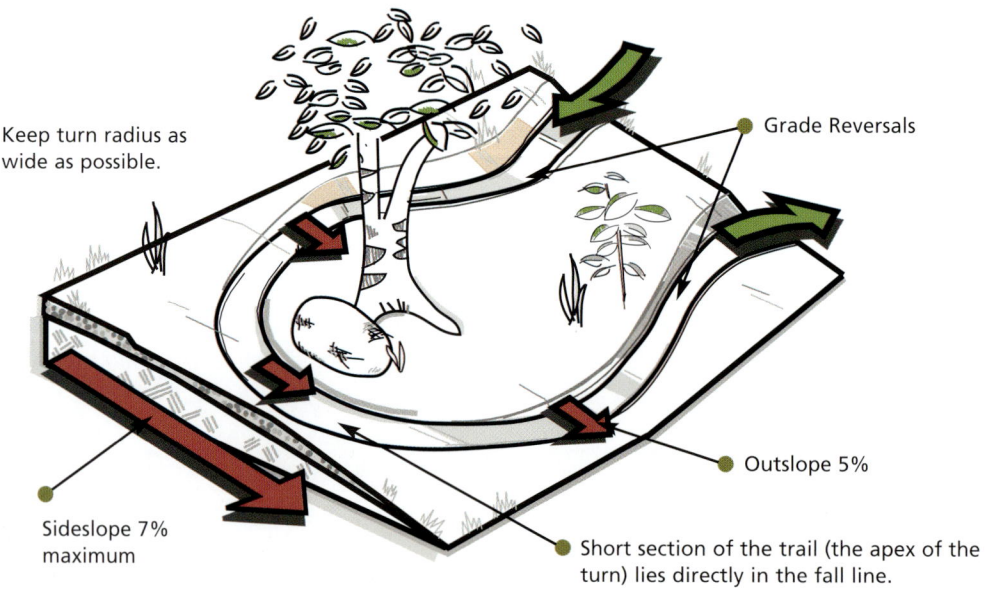

Switchbacks

A **switchback** reverses direction with the help of a relatively level, constructed landing. Switchbacks are difficult to build, but they are much more durable on steep slopes than climbing turns. This is because switchbacks do not force riders into the fall line. Instead, they route the rider onto a level turning platform. We recommend a version called the **rolling crown switchback**. It's carefully engineered for good drainage.

Key Features of a Rolling Crown Switchback

- It's located on a gentle slope (consider potential switchback locations as control points).
- Water drains off all sides of the turn.
- Turns occur on a near-level platform that's slightly crowned (like a pitcher's mound).
- The trail stays on the contour on both approaches.
- Bench cuts and retaining walls are combined as needed.
- Material excavated from the top leg is used to build up the bottom leg behind a retaining wall.
- Retaining walls are carefully built to ensure stability.
- The upper leg is insloped (to help drain water before the turn).
- The lower leg is outsloped.
- Approaches are designed to control user speed.
- Grade reversals in the approaches divert water.
- Switchbacks aren't built directly above one another. They're staggered on a hillside to prevent shortcutting and water accumulation.

Don't Make a Mistake by...

Building a Climbing Turn on a Steep Slope. Climbing turns direct riders into the fall line of the hillside for a short section. This can cause erosion as descending riders hit the brakes to navigate the turn and climbing riders pound the pedals hardest at the turn's apex. You might be able to get away with a heavily armored climbing turn, but most of these fall-line turns will erode badly in no time at all. If you want your climbing turns to endure, build them on sideslopes with no more than a 7-percent grade. Any steeper than that and it's time to build a switchback instead.

Rolling Crown Switchback

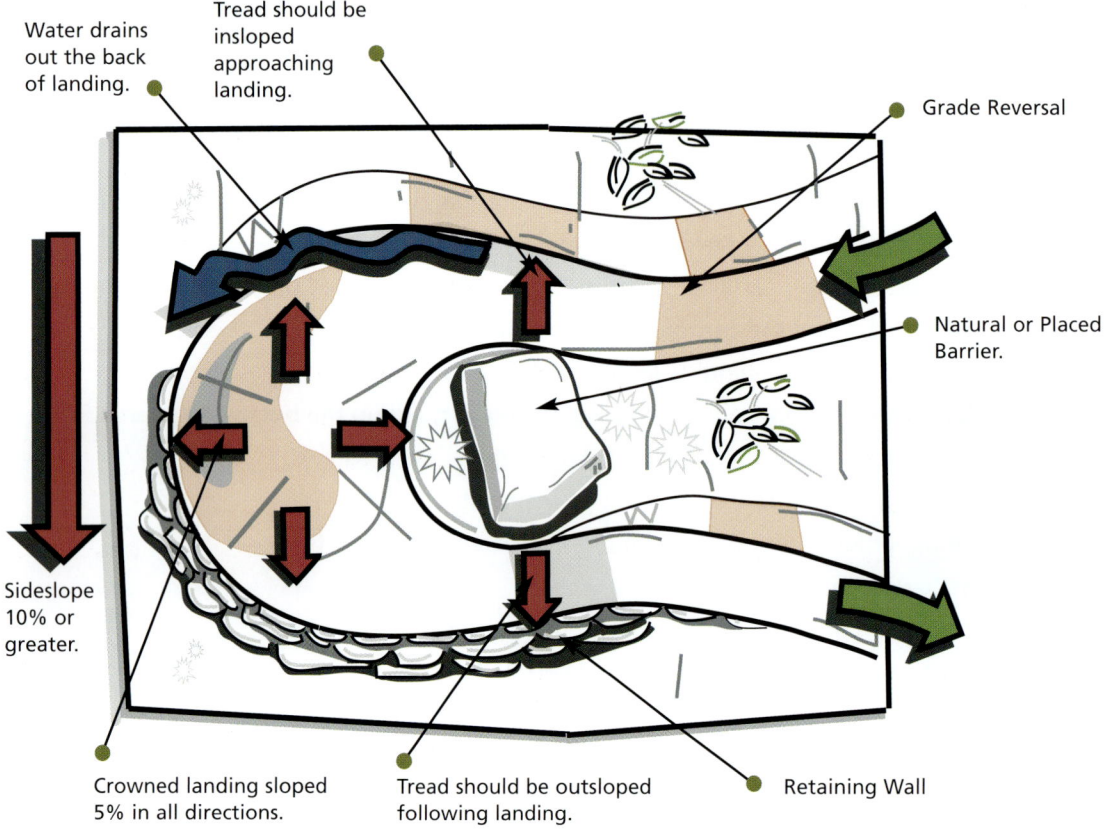

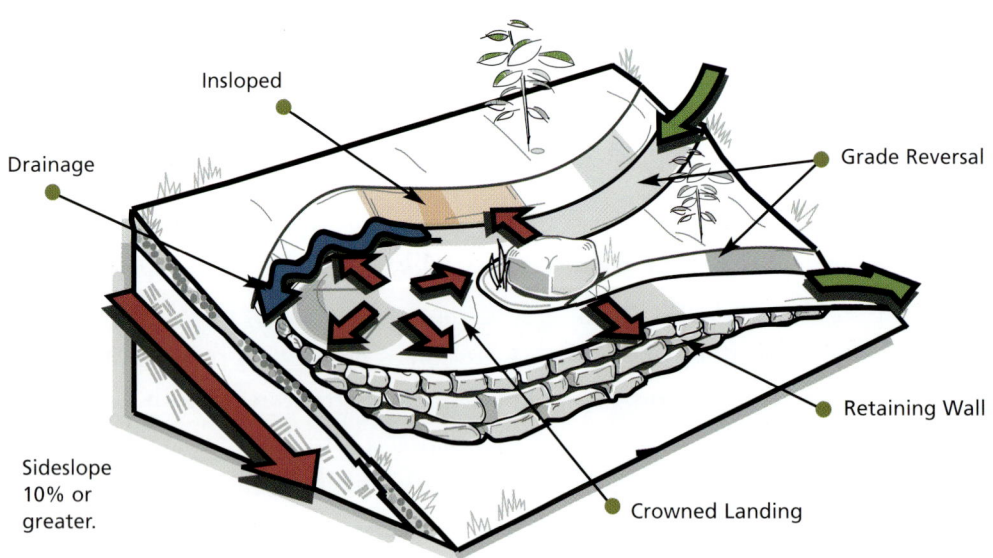

Don't Make the Mistake of. . .

Biting Off More Than You Can Chew. Building a switchback is not a project you want to tackle on a whim; it is one of the largest trail construction endeavors you can undertake. Switchbacks require a small degree of engineering, precise placement, significant hauling of material, and a whole lot of sweat equity. The upside is that a properly built switchback tends to last a long time with little maintenance. Building a rolling crown switchback is a job for about 10 people. (Any more than that and you'll just get in each other's way.) Expect a solid day or two of labor.

Four Steps for Building a Switchback

Step 1: Choose the Location.
The best spot to put a switchback is the flattest area you can find along the desired route of your trail. Building on a steep section of slope will require a colossal retaining wall. Ridges and sun-facing slopes are also ideal. Whenever possible, the switchback should wrap around an obstacle—a tree or menacing boulder will do nicely—to discourage users from shortcutting the switchback. Lay out the turn and mark the lower and upper legs using pin flags.

Step 2: Build the Turning Platform and Retaining Wall.
The first things you'll need to build are the retaining wall and turning platform. The turning platform on a shared-use trail should have a radius of at least 6 feet.

Typically, for every 8 to 10 percent of sideslope, a foot of elevation is needed on the retaining wall. Thus, a switchback built on a sideslope with a 40-percent grade would need a retaining wall between 4 and 5 feet high. Constructing the retaining wall is one of the most time-consuming aspects of building a switchback.

Retaining walls can be made from wood and rock. Large rocks are the preferred material since they do not rot and their sheer weight lends greater strength to the retaining wall. If you have to use wood, select a durable kind or commercially treated lumber.

If rock is used in your retaining wall, make sure it is stacked so that the wall leans into the slope. Use the biggest, flattest rocks you can find. (For more on retaining walls, see page 159.)

After each layer of the retaining wall is built, add a layer of fill behind it to gradually create the turning platform. Place the dirt in thin layers and compact as you go. Thorough compaction is essential to prevent excessive settling of the turning platform over time.

Step 3: Build the Upper Leg.

Excavate the upper leg and the upper section of the turning platform. Completely remove all organic matter; it shouldn't be used as fill material because it will quickly rot and settle, leaving an unstable trail. Excavated mineral soil and small rocks from the upper leg can be added to the larger rocks in the retaining wall and turning platform. The upper leg should be insloped at 5 percent and should create a drain extending well beyond the platform. Insloping begins about 30 feet above the turning platform and can be initiated with a grade dip. The trail grade of this upper leg should be no greater than 5 to 10 percent.

Step 4: Complete the Lower Leg.

Complete the switchback by extending the retaining wall down along the lower leg of the turn. You want to taper this wall so that it blends into the trail beyond the turn. Resume regular, full bench tread at the end of the retaining wall. The lower leg should be outsloped at 5 percent for proper drainage.

Insloped Turns

So far, we've focused on two types of turns for gaining or losing elevation: the climbing turn and the rolling crown switchback. Both turns work well and, when built properly, withstand the test of time. A third type of turn, the insloped turn, is another option. A well-built insloped turn is sustainable, improves trail flow, and adds an element of fun.

Rolling crown switchbacks drain water like a dream but tend to interrupt the flow of a trail and thus can be awkward to negotiate. While this isn't an issue for hikers and horseback riders who are traveling relatively slowly, users who are traveling faster (such as mountain bikers, runners, or motorcyclists) would prefer to maintain their speed and flow through the turn. One way to help this is to inslope the turn, creating a banked or bermed turn.

Insloped turns have been getting recent attention from trailbuilders, but they are not a new invention. If you look closely at the roads you drive in your car, you'll notice that the surface of the road is typically sloped to the inside through corners, directing cars around the bend. This helps vehicles maintain a smooth speed without sliding out of the turn. We can create an insloped turn on the trail as well. The key is to engineer the turn carefully so that it will drain water and withstand the impact of trail users.

An insloped turn can do more than just improve a trail user's experience. It can also make the tread last longer. By improving trail flow, insloped turns can reduce skidding, trail widening, and lateral soil displacement that sometimes occurs on flat or outsloped turns.

Note: It can be very difficult to achieve proper drainage on an insloped turn. Building this type of structure requires a high level of trailbuilding experience and a keen understanding of water flow. Insloped turns may also require extra maintenance.

Insloped turns can improve trail flow and are fun to ride. Just be sure to design them with adequate drainage.

Are Insloped Turns Appropriate for Every Trail?

Insloped turns are most appropriate when trail users are causing (or are predicted to cause) lateral displacement of tread material. Another way to think about it is this: Will the trail flow and user speed cause the rider or runner to "drift" outward in the turn? Will users be required to slow dramatically to negotiate the corner smoothly?

Insloped turns can be used on either single-use or shared-use trails. While hikers and equestrians don't *need* the inslope to maintain their speed, they can easily use this type of turn by traveling along the inside and avoiding the insloped berm. The higher speeds that are possible for riders and runners, however, mean that good sightlines and/or choke points are necessary to help reduce the likelihood of startling other trail users.

Insloped Turn

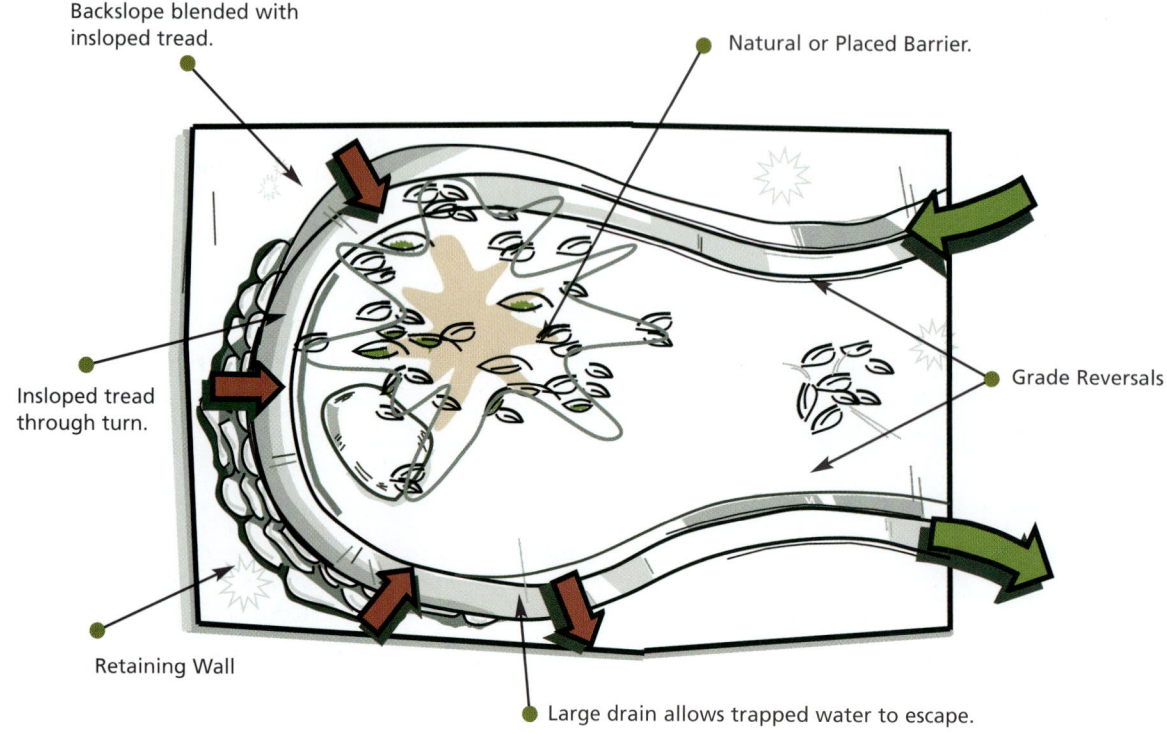

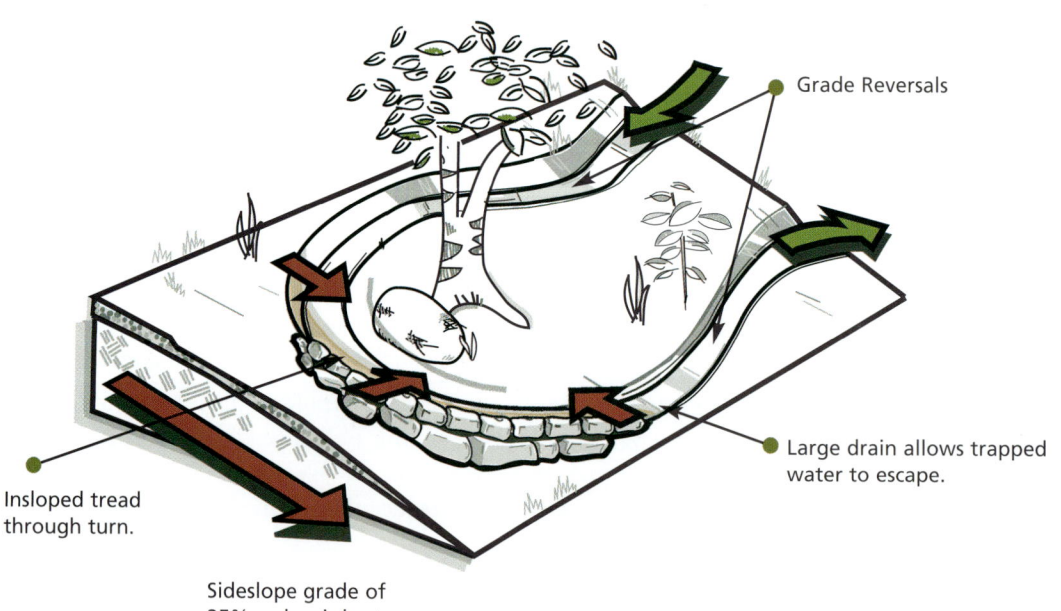

Trail Solutions

Four Steps for Building an Insloped Turn

Step 1: Choose the Location

As with climbing turns and switchbacks, correct placement of the insloped turn is crucial. There are several things to consider.

Sideslope Grade

Gentle sideslopes are best. On steep sideslopes, you may have to build a turning platform, or deck, similar to that built for a switchback. Otherwise, the fall-line section of the turn may be too steep to withstand the forces of gravity and trail users. A general rule of thumb: It is easiest to build an insloped turn on sideslope grades below 25 percent. On steeper slopes, consider building a retaining wall and turning platform to lessen the grade of the turn.

Approach

Orientation of the insloped turn should be like that of a climbing turn: The upper and lower legs run along the contour, with the trail turning quickly and evenly through the fall line. By building the insloped portion of the turn on the fall line, water is not trapped or otherwise impeded as it flows downhill. An insloped turn should include a choke point and a grade reversal on the upper leg of the turn. The choke point will help to slow user speed, and the grade reversal will divert water off the tread before it hits the fall-line portion of the turn, where it is likely to do the most damage.

Turn Radius

The radius of an insloped turn should range between 10 and 15 feet, enabling the rider to move through the turn without a significant change in speed. Tighter turns must be navigated at slower speeds and therefore they don't require a bank or berm. Wider turns include a lengthy fall-line section that is less sustainable and can lead to higher-than-desired speeds.

Natural Obstacles

Position the turn around a low-lying natural obstacle to prevent people from shortcutting. Large rocks and low bushes work well. Since an insloped turn forces the rider to lean into the corner, avoid placing the turn too close to large obstacles, such as trees, where riders might hit their heads or shoulders. Also, remember to keep sightlines open. Since the potential for speed is greater than in other turns, make sure the riders can see what, or who, is around the bend.

Step 2: Build a Turning Platform and Retaining Walls.

On steep sideslopes you may need to construct a turning platform to lessen the grade of the turn. On slopes steeper than 25 percent, consider raising the lower section of the turning platform. A general guideline is that for every 10 percent of sideslope steeper than 25 percent, raise the lower side of the turning platform 1 foot. (For example, on a 35-percent sideslope, you would raise the lower edge of the turning platform 1 foot.)

If you need to construct a turning platform, the lower portion of the platform should be reinforced with a retaining wall. A retaining wall may also be needed to hold longer banks or berms in place and to withstand the forces the riders apply as they push their bikes thru the turn. The wall should start after the grade reversal on the top leg of the turn and continue around the outside of the turn until it meets the lower leg. See page 159 for tips on building retaining walls.

Step 3: Build the Insloped Turning Area.

There is no standard height or recommended inslope angle to the bank. Just remember that the steeper the sideslope, the higher and steeper you'll want the bank to be. In general, very little inslope is required to make your turn flow smoothly, and as little as a 7-percent tilt toward the inside of the turn will make a difference in the feel of your trail. When building the bank, make sure that you're creating a consistent slope from top to bottom.

Construct the bank with small rocks and mineral soil. Add a small amount of material at a time and be sure to compact each layer. The top layers should consist of mineral soil only. You will need to use soil that is cohesive and compacts well; sand will not work. In areas where the clay content is minimal, consider importing some clay-based fill to mix with the natural soil. Remember, if the bank is short, it can stand alone, but taller banks will need to be constructed against a retaining wall.

Step 4: Fine-Tune the Turn.

Stand back. Look at the entrance and the exit of your turn. Are the transitions smooth? Visualize riding it, and run it in both directions. Is the inslope too much, not enough, or just right? Are there any lumps or bumps that need to be leveled? Tweak the grade reversals before and after the turn for drainage, and make sure the flow is smooth. Are the sightlines open? Trim back the vegetation in the center of the turn if necessary. Strategically place rocks or native plants on the sides of the tread to create choke points, which will help keep people where you want them.

> ### How Does Water Stay Off an Insloped Turn?
> Water trickling down the trail should be diverted by a strategically placed grade reversal. Water flowing down the sideslope, headed toward the turn, is diverted by the constructed bank, so it doesn't reach the small section of fall-line trail at the apex of the turn. The only water on this stretch of trail falls directly from the sky, and this minimal amount will run down the trail only to be dumped immediately by another grade reversal on the lower leg.

This insloped turn has great flow but would benefit from a better grade reversal on the upper leg.

Trail Solutions

Retaining Walls

Retaining walls are used frequently in trailbuilding. They can support turning platforms on switchbacks, shore up trails across rough terrain, or reinforce the outer edge of a partial bench. Building large retaining walls is difficult, so enlist the help of someone who has experience.

Key Steps for Building a Retaining Wall

Step 1: Choose Rocks or Wood.
Large rocks are the preferred material for retaining walls since they do not rot and their sheer weight lends greater strength to the structure. If wood must be used, construction of **crib walls** is usually necessary to achieve strength and stability. The same key steps apply regardless of building material.

Step 2: Use Appropriate Rocks.
If possible, select angular rocks that have flat sides and square edges (shaped like a microwave oven) as round rocks are difficult to work with. It is better to use large rocks (at least 50 pounds, ideally 150) than small ones. If you can lift the rock by yourself, it's probably not big enough. Try to use local stone so your work will look natural. Importing rock may spread invasive plant matter.

Partial Bench Trail with Retaining Wall

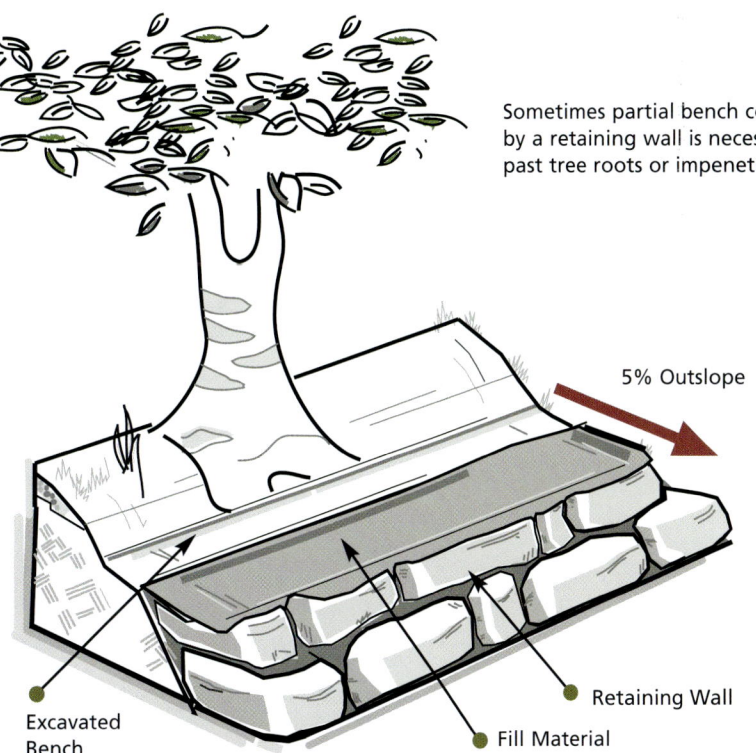

Sometimes partial bench construction supported by a retaining wall is necessary to route a trail past tree roots or impenetrable rock.

- 5% Outslope
- Excavated Bench
- Fill Material
- Retaining Wall

It's important for the top of the retaining wall to be lower than the trail tread so water can still sheet across the trail.

Part Six: Trail Construction

Rock Retaining Wall

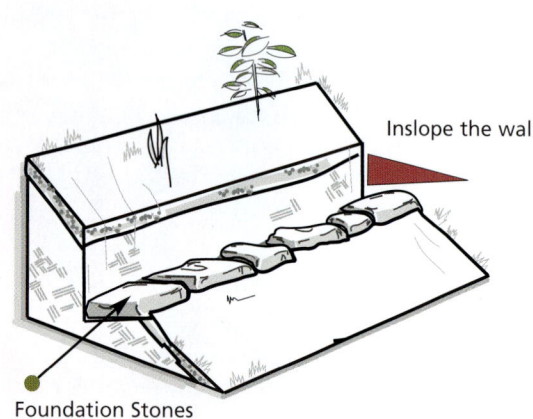

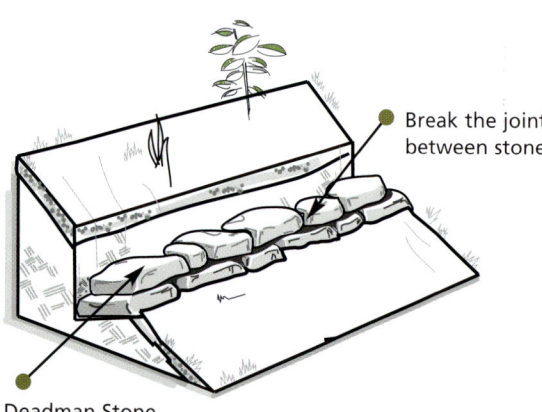

Step 3: Lay a Foundation.
The first rocks in a retaining wall play a crucial role in anchoring everything else in place. Excavate a footing, then place large, well-anchored rocks to form a base layer. The foundation rocks must be immobile once they are set in place.

Step 4: Build a Wall.
Once you have a solid foundation, place more rocks in tiers to form the wall. Ensure that all rocks touch one another and everything is locked in place. This process is a lot like building a jigsaw puzzle. You'll need to move rocks around to find the best fit. If a rock wobbles under foot, reposition it. Use smaller angular rocks as wedges to fill gaps. Without mortar, friction and gravity must hold your wall together.

Step 5: Break the Joints.
Place each rock so that it spans the gap between the adjacent rocks. Like building a brick wall, you must avoid directly aligning joints because they will weaken the structure. Each course of stone should overlap the cracks in the preceding row.

Step 6: Use Headers.
Every 4 to 6 feet, try to place a **deadman** or **header**—a piece of heavy timber or a large rock used as an anchor—that extends into the bank behind the retaining wall. This helps lock everything together.

Step 7: Inslope the Wall.
The wall should tilt into the slope. This angle is described as the wall's batter. **Batter** should never be shallower than 4:1, (an inward tilt of 1 foot for every 4 feet of height). A 2:1 batter is better.

Trail Solutions

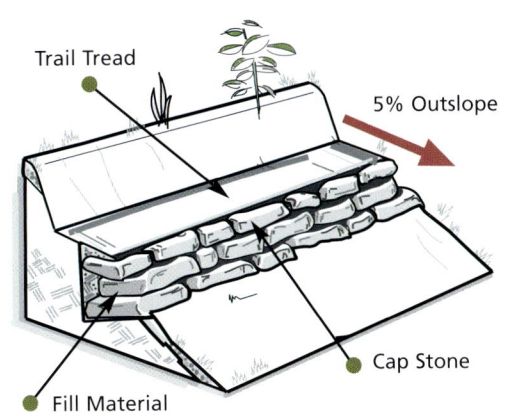

Step 8: Back Fill.

After each layer of the retaining wall is built, add a layer of small rock and mineral soil (nothing organic) to fill the space behind the wall. Compact the fill material in layers while it is slightly wet to prevent uneven settling. A mechanical compactor is the best tool for this key step.

Step 9: Place Capstones.

Use large, flat rocks for the top layer. Their weight and size will help hold everything together. When you are finished, the top of the retaining wall should be slightly lower than the surface of the trail to insure proper drainage.

Wooden Retaining Walls

A retaining wall of logs is often called a crib wall and achieves strength by using headers or deadmen that have most of their length buried in the hillside. These deadmen are connected to the logs at the face of the wall using notched log-cabin construction, sometimes reinforced with spikes or pins. Be sure to use large rot-resistant logs or timbers or commercially treated wood.

Armoring—
Using Rock to Harden Trails

Armoring is a method of using large rocks to "pave" a trail and prevent erosion. Armoring is primarily useful in two situations. First, an elevated trail tread can be created *above* especially soft or wet terrain when no alternate route is available. Second, armoring can be used to harden the trail tread against user-caused erosion.

It is important to distinguish between user-caused erosion and water-caused erosion. It would be foolish to spend the time to armor a trail if water drainage issues haven't been effectively addressed. Water will destroy armoring by flowing under the rocks and undermining the foundation or by frost-heaving the rocks out of position.

Armoring is a centuries-old method of using large rocks to harden the surface of roads and trails, like this ancient path in Wales.

Trail Solutions

Armoring Can Benefit a Trail by:

1. Hardening a contour trail in extremely rainy climates.
2. Stabilizing steep sections of contour trail with grades from 20 to 45 percent.
3. Reinforcing stream crossings.
4. Crossing a low-lying muddy or sandy area when a reroute isn't possible.
5. Hardening landing areas following jumps or drop-offs.
6. Toughening the trail surface on high-traffic routes to withstand user-caused erosion.

5 Ways to Armor with Rock

There are five basic armoring techniques, and each method has its strengths and weaknesses.

1 Flagstone Paving

Large, flat-faced stones are placed directly on a mineral soil base or an aggregate foundation (a mixture composed of sand, gravel, pebbles, and small rocks, which is devoid of organic material). Each stone's largest and smoothest face is placed up, at grade, to form the tread surface. This is the most common and simple armoring technique.

Flagstone Paving

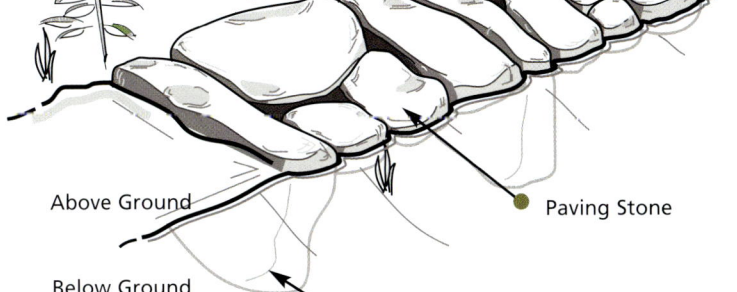

Above Ground

Below Ground

Paving Stone

Anchor Stone

Part Six: Trail Construction

2 Stone Pitching

This is an ancient road-building technique in which medium-sized rocks are set on end, or "pitched" up on their side. The stones are hand-fitted tightly together, with aggregate packed into the gaps to tighten the construction. Think of a book in a bookshelf—only the spine is showing and the rest of the book is hidden. Modern trailbuilders in soggy Wales have revived and perfected stone pitching as a means of elevating the trail above the year-round mud in their country. It seems like a tough job, but stone pitching can often be more efficient than flagstone paving, depending on your rock selection.

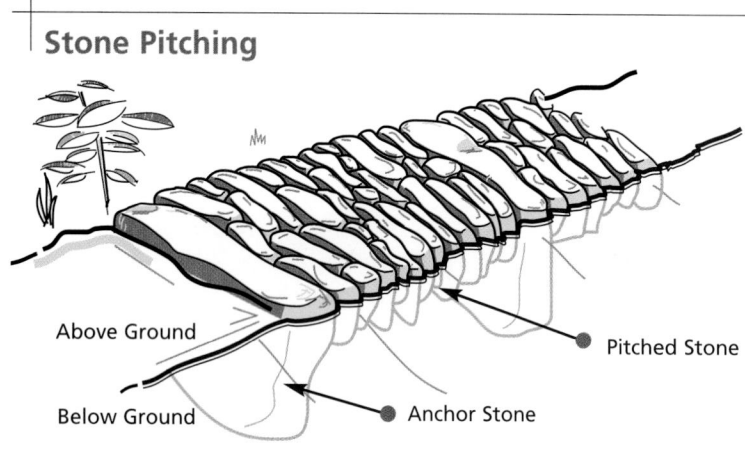

Stone Pitching

3 Raised Tread Construction

Rocks can be used to elevate the tread above especially soft or wet terrain. First, a foundation of large rocks is embedded in the tread. Medium rocks follow and are locked into position. The tread is capped by aggregate, or inch-to-dust stone material. In essence, this is a turnpike made of stone. Trailbuilders in Wales use the term "raised camber construction" to describe the crowned tread designed to shed water. Make sure your rock turnpike drains and does not function like a dam, raising water levels on one side of your structure.

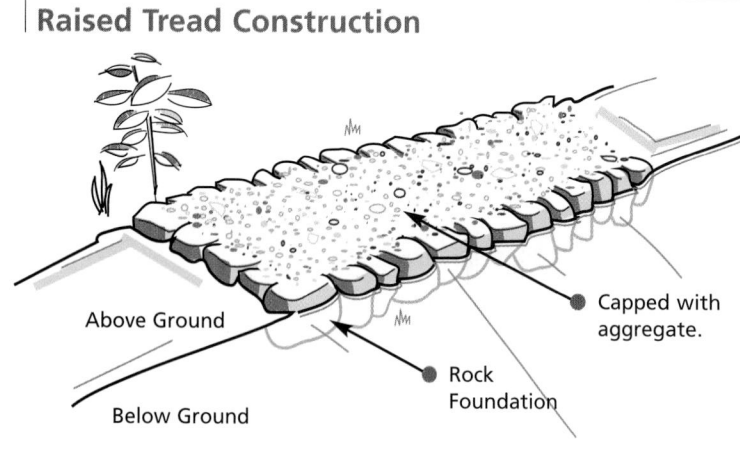

Raised Tread Construction

4 Boulder Causeway

Giant boulders and rock slabs can serve nicely as trail tread. Boulder causeways are essentially super-sized versions of the flagstone paving technique.

Boulder Causeway

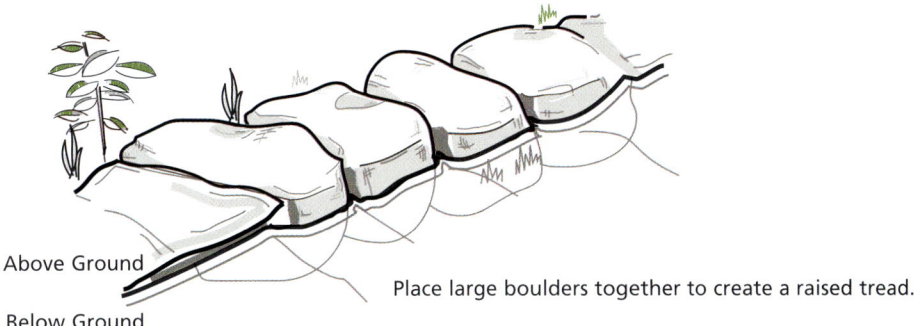

Above Ground

Below Ground

Place large boulders together to create a raised tread.

5 Natural Rock Outcroppings

Routing the trail over existing, exposed rock is an excellent way to create highly challenging freeride trails, because the exposed rock can support fall-line trail sections.

Routing the trail over existing, exposed rock is an excellent way to add challenge and durability.

Part Six: Trail Construction

10 Tips for Rock Armoring

1 Remove Organic Material First.
As with all trailbuilding, it is important to excavate down to mineral soil if practical. You want to lay your rock on a firm foundation, so remove the organic material from the tread before placing your stones.

2 Start at the Bottom.
If you're working on a slope, start at the bottom and work upslope. The weight of the rocks will hold your work together.

3 Drop the Anchor.
The first **keystone** in an armored trail section plays a crucial role in anchoring everything else in place. The anchor rock must be large and immobile once it is properly placed, and at least two-thirds buried. Remember that angular rocks are better for this purpose than round. Place additional solid anchors every couple of yards.

4 Lay the Tread.
Once a solid anchor rock is placed, follow by placing more rocks to form the trail tread. Ensure that all rocks touch one another and everything is locked in place. This process is a lot like building a jigsaw puzzle. You'll need to move rocks around to find the best fit. If a rock wobbles under foot, reposition it. Use smaller, angular rocks as wedges to fill gaps. Without mortar, friction and gravity must hold the rocks together.

5 Break the Joints.
Place each rock so that it spans the gap between the adjacent rocks. Like building a brick wall, you must avoid directly aligning joints or they will weaken the structure. Try to minimize lengthwise gaps that run parallel to the trail if these gaps might catch a bicycle wheel.

6 Use Tie Stones.
Every 4 to 6 feet, place a header or keystone that spans the breadth of the trail tread. Like the anchor, a tie stone helps lock everything together.

7 Fill the Gaps.
Filling the gaps between large rocks with small rock, stone dust, gravel, or sand is a key step. Pack the fill material tightly, using hand tools. "Inch-to-dust" is a term used to describe small quarry waste, also known as **crusher fines**. This broken stone is the best fill material because it contains natural cements present in the parent stone. Scottish trailbuilders call it "magic dust."

8. Compact the Tread.

It is best to compact any surfacing material in layers while it is slightly wet. A mechanical compactor is the best tool for this important step.

9. Corral the Trail.

Include something to define the sides of the armoring. Large ominous "gargoyle" rocks, logs, trees, or other obstacles staggered on either side of the trail serve as physical and visual barriers to keep riders on the armored section of trail. Make sure your barriers flow naturally with the trail, or users might find them annoying instead of interesting, and create new routes around them.

10. Consider Trail Flow.

Smooth flow is vital on trails for cyclists. Mountain bikers love the rhythm of a trail where one turn blends into the next, and the trail surface is somewhat predictable. A trail with good flow helps minimize erosion, user conflict, and safety concerns. Strive for a subtle transition into the armored section.

Bright Idea

Use Your Brain to Transport Stone. This isn't the time to prove your He-man status by hand-carrying 120-pound rocks. Use some sort of mechanical aid or use gravity. A wheelbarrow is the most common method for moving stone. You can lay it on its side, slide a big stone in, stand it up, and wheel to your worksite. For longer distances and heavier loads, a variety of power wheelbarrows are available. Ropes, cables, pulleys, and other rigging hardware can also be useful. Trained, experienced experts must supervise rigging.

Corral the route with objects to define the sides of the armoring and keep visitors on the trail. Location: Coed y Brenin, Wales.

Trail Solutions

Appalachian Armoring

There are some locations where rock is scarce and traditional rock armoring is simply not an option. Fortunately, there are other means of armoring your trails. Concrete blocks, garden pavers, slabs of salvaged concrete, and rot-resistant woods have all been used with good results. Remember, drainage problems must be addressed in addition to armoring the tread, as flowing water will ruin armoring.

Appalachian Armoring is a method that blends broken concrete with rot-resistant locust logs. IMBA leader and professional trailbuilder, Woody Keen, developed Appalachian Armoring to halt erosion in North Carolina's Dupont State Forest.

The key to Appalachian Armoring is deadmen logs, which lock slabs of concrete into place. The logs are partially buried, and rebar is driven through the ends to make sure they stay in place. Do not use soft wood like pine, which will quickly rot.

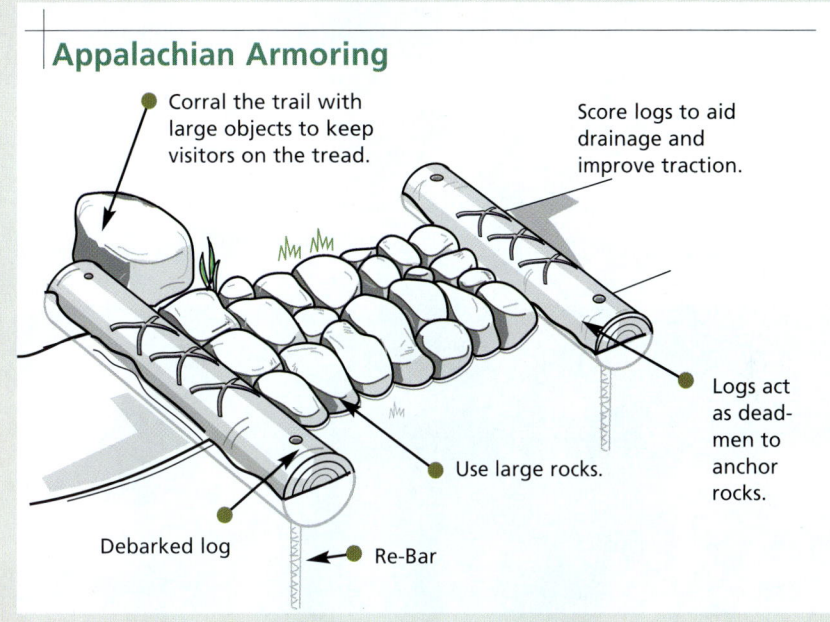

Appalachian Armoring
- Corral the trail with large objects to keep visitors on the tread.
- Score logs to aid drainage and improve traction.
- Use large rocks.
- Logs act as deadmen to anchor rocks.
- Debarked log
- Re-Bar

The steeper the trail the more often you need to place a log as a deadman—every 4 feet on steep slopes. Less steep slopes might call for a log every 5 to 6 feet.

Once the logs are in place, the concrete can be positioned using flagstone paving and stone pitching techniques. Concrete is a great material because broken slabs of it are often available at no cost. If suitable stone is available, by all means use it.

When Armoring, Always...

Be Safe.
- A hardhat, eye protection, gloves, and steel-toed boots are necessities.
- Don't hurry.
- Learn the mechanics of lifting without injury.
- Communicate with people around you.
- Keep hands away from any rock being shifted by pry bars or other means.
- Skid a rock in a controlled manner rather than rolling it. Rolling rocks rarely stop where you want them to. . .

The impressive foundation of this raised tread in soggy Wales will be capped with aggregate or gravel.

Use Proper Tools.
- At least three heavy-duty pry bars are essential for moving rock.
- Pick mattocks and Pulaskis are useful for digging, prying, and positioning rock.
- A heavy sledgehammer will help to break rocks and coax them into a tight fit.
- Rock hammers and chisels allow you to shape stones.

Be Considerate When Locating Material.
- It is best to use local stone, when available, so your work will look natural. Importing rock may spread invasive plant matter.
- Try to use rocks that are out of sight of the trail and uphill of your project location.
- Don't move rocks that will damage vegetation or sensitive areas.
- Restore any significant disruption caused by rock quarrying.

Note: Sometimes you'll need to import rock or transport it long distances. British trailbuilders truck stone from commercial rock quarries and transport huge quantities with power wheelbarrows.

Choose the Right Shape and Size.
- If possible, select angular rocks that have flat sides and square edges. The best are rectangular, shaped like a toaster; round rocks are difficult to work with.
- The exact size and shape will depend on the armoring technique.

Flagstone paving is the most common and simple armoring technique.

Part Six: Trail Construction

Some Final Thoughts on Rock Armoring

Even though you are using rock to armor a trail tread, all of the principles of sustainable trails still apply. It is essential to follow the half rule and incorporate grade reversals because the key to long-lasting stone armoring is to prevent water from flowing down or under that section of trail. Well-built stonework can withstand years of traffic, but it will fail rapidly if attacked by gravity-powered water.

Stone pitching calls for rocks to be set on end, or "pitched" up on their side.

Trail Solutions

This boulder causeway raises the trail above wet terrain. Location: Dalbeattie, Scotland.

Part Six: Trail Construction

Man-Made Soil Hardeners

There are a range of commercial products designed to reduce erosion and stabilize soil. For the purpose of this discussion, we'll simply call them "man-made soil hardeners." These products can be grouped into three categories: chemical binders, physical binders, and geosynthetics.

This subject could easily consume 100 pages. For brevity's sake, however, we'll just provide an overview. One word of caution: Man-made soil hardeners are typically more costly than natural materials and won't stand the test of time on trail grades of more than 5 percent.

Chemical Binders

There are several liquid stabilizers on the market that, when mixed with water and soil, help increase the moisture resistance, density, and weight-bearing strength of otherwise unstable soils. Although the concept seems to be a good one, these stabilizers have been given mixed reviews when applied to trails. Some products failed to firm up the soil, while others made the soil's surface extraordinarily slick and potentially hazardous to users. Others can be harmful to the environment. Always consult the land manager before using chemical binders on a trail.

More research needs to be done before we can come to any strong conclusions about the worthiness of chemical binders. In the meantime, it's safe to say that armoring a trail with rock is a more proven approach.

Physical Binders

When trailbuilding, you want to avoid soil that is either extremely fine or extremely coarse. Finely textured soils such as silt and clay drain poorly while coarsely textured soils such as sand don't bind well and are easily displaced by heavy traffic. Of course, sometimes you'll need to build trail in these less-than-ideal conditions. That's where physical binders come into play. Physical binders are materials that enable trailbuilders to bring balance to their one-sided (so to speak) soils. We've seen a wide range of materials used as physical binders—everything from clay-based kitty litter to oyster shells to high-tech soil additives. In some cases, physical binders can be quite effective. It's all a question of finding the right additive for your particular type of unstable soil.

Geosynthetics are man-made sheets, nets, and honeycomb grids designed to stabilize soil. When used with high-quality fill material, geosynthetics can help improve trails that cross soft, water-saturated soils.

Geotextile Sheets (geosheets for short) are commonly used in turnpikes to separate and support fill material from the underlying saturated soils. Let's say, for instance, that you've decided to spread crushed rock over a section of continually boggy trail. (We're assuming that the trail could not be rerouted, which should be your first choice.) Without the use of geotextiles, trail traffic will eventually mix the imported rock with the wet, fine-grain soil. In short, you will have gone from a simple bog to an expensive, chunky bog—not much of an improvement. With a geosheet placed between the rock and the boggy soil, the materials are kept from mixing. The geotextile sheet also allows water to drain through, which ensures that the rock tread stays high and dry. Geotextile sheets last indefinitely if kept out of the sun, but they degrade rapidly when exposed to UV rays.

Geonets are composed of a polyethylene drainage core sandwiched between two geotextile sheets. Geonets can be used to separate trail materials, reinforce trail, and enhance drainage. Since they have a bit more bulk and structure to them, they tend to reinforce trail better than a single-layer geosheet.

Geocells are a honeycombed grid that helps hold fill soil in place over saturated soils. Trailbuilders typically cover soggy ground with a single layer of geosheet, and then place the geocell grid on top of that. Each cell in the honeycomb is then packed with fill soil. Finally, the entire honeycomb is covered with an additional cap of fill soil—typically about 2 inches deep. Geocell results are mixed. The cap soil tends to erode away (particularly on steep inclines) which, in turn, exposes the honeycomb and poses a hazard to trail users.

The Geosynthetic Research Institute at Drexel University is a focal point for research and development into all aspects of geosynthetics. Details: www.drexel.edu/gri

The U.S. Forest Service publication Geosynthetics for Trails in Wet Areas describes geosynthetic products and specific trail applications. Details: www.fhwa.dot.gov/environment/fspubs/index.htm

Wetlands and Water Crossings

Encountering water is almost inevitable when building trails, especially on contour routes that cross hillsides and their many natural drainages. Water crossings can be challenging to design, labor-intensive to build and maintain, and most important, they can be devastating to aquatic ecosystems.

A poorly designed trail can dump sediment into wetlands and streams, damaging fragile habitat. Trailbuilders need basic knowledge of wetland ecosystems, stream dynamics, and aquatic habitat to construct sustainable crossings that minimize impact on these important ecosystems.

Stream Corridor Function and Dynamics

Stream corridors, which consist of the channel, adjacent floodplain, and riparian vegetation, perform a number of critical watershed functions. They serve as conduits for water, sediment, organic material, and aquatic organisms. They act as sponges by moderating flood flows, augmenting summer flows, and filtering runoff. They provide shade, cover, and food to the stream ecosystem. Most terrestrial and avian biota depend upon stream corridors for at least part of their habitat needs. Watershed health depends upon maintenance of the ecological connectivity provided by streams and their associated corridors. Trail crossings, when done poorly, can disrupt this connectivity and impair stream corridor functions.

Stream channels are highly variable in shape and naturally dynamic. Properly functioning streams will adjust their shape to accommodate small changes in flow and sediment transport. They also evolve over time. For example, a meandering stream will typically migrate across its floodplain, changing its location incrementally while maintaining the same cross section and slope. After a significant disturbance, streams will undergo a series of changes to reestablish stability, sometimes at a different base elevation or channel slope. These changes will spread upstream and downstream to maintain continuity. Anchoring streams with stationary trail crossings can disrupt this evolutionary process—with cascading consequences.

> The U.S. Forest Service's Stream Systems Technology Center in Fort Collins, Colorado, provides more information on this subject at: www.stream.fs.fed.us.

Water crossings should be avoided whenever possible. However, when you have no alternative to crossing a drainage, your priorities should be:

1. Minimize the impacts to the stream channel.
2. Minimize the impacts to the streamside environment.
3. Create a safe and sustainable passage for trail users.
4. Minimize the number of crossings.

Trails must be carefully designed and constructed to minimize impacts to rivers and wetlands. Location: Nevada City, California. Photo by Steven Wilde.

5 General Guidelines for Water Crossings

1 Consult with Land Managers.

The land management agency should have specific data on the stream corridor, including seasonal flow volumes, frequency of flood events, fish habitats, and water quality records. This information may help you determine the type of crossing required to minimize impacts.

2 Identify Water Crossings as Key Control Points.

A water crossing is an important control point during the design phase. Certain terrain and stream features dictate where crossings are acceptable. Stream crossings should be located at riffle areas instead of at pools or meanders, as riffles are relatively stable, have the coarsest substrate, and can best accommodate a crossing.

3 Carefully Design Crossing Approaches.

The trail should descend into and climb out of the steam crossing, preventing stream water from flowing down the trail. Be careful, however, to keep the crossing on a gentle grade. In general, your trail should descend and climb out of the stream at no more than an 8-percent grade. If the trail enters and exits the stream on a fall line, it will dump water and debris into the stream. Look for gradually sloping stream banks on which to locate the crossing to avoid the impact of full bench tread excavation.

4   Include Grade Reversals.

Grade reversals should be designed on both sides of the stream-crossing approach. This will prevent large volumes of water and sediment from flowing down the trail into the stream.

5   Mimic the Stream.

The crossing should maintain the stream's cross section, slope, alignment, and substrate, thereby mitigating challenges to aquatic life. Habitat fragmentation is incremental and cumulative; even a small crossing, when poorly done, contributes to loss of ecologic function. Mimic the stream by giving your crossing a natural bottom and maintaining the slope and width of the waterway.

Proper Drainage Crossing

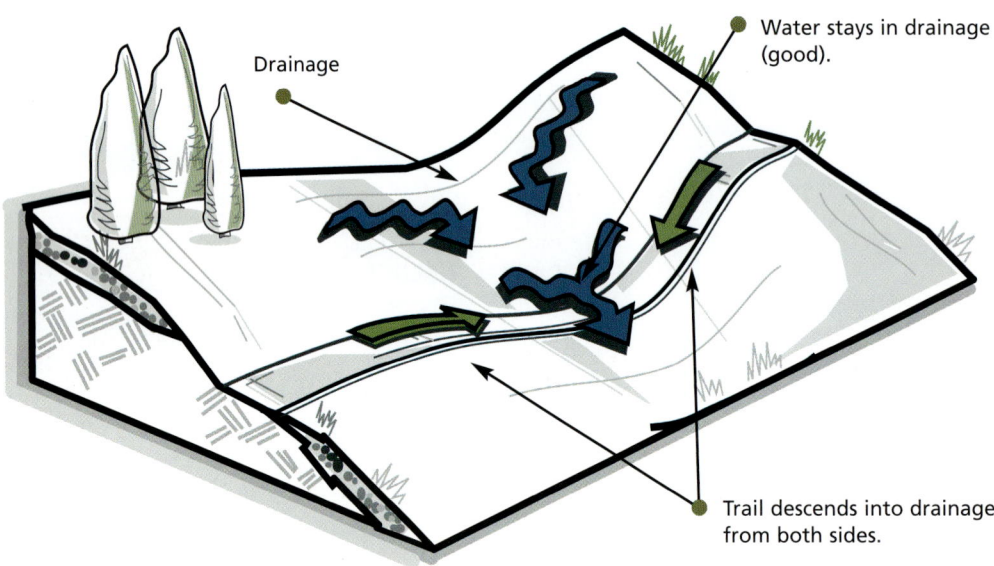

Improper Drainage Crossing

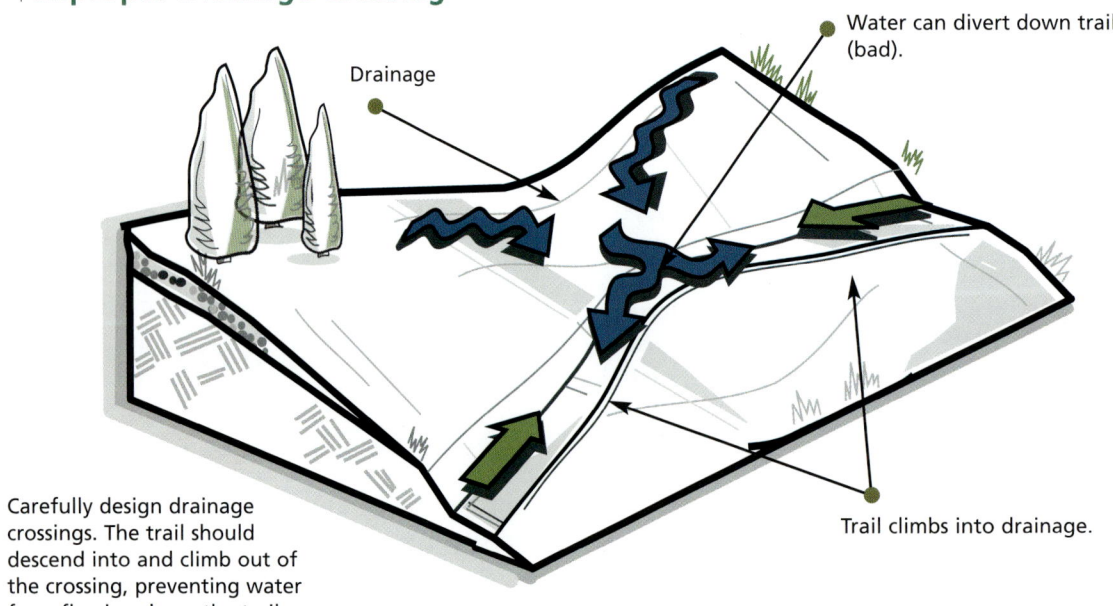

Carefully design drainage crossings. The trail should descend into and climb out of the crossing, preventing water from flowing down the trail.

Trail Solutions

Armored Crossings

Armored crossings, or fords, are a simple and inexpensive means of allowing trail users to pass through water while minimizing sedimentation. You should only consider building armored fords in a stream with slow water velocities and a depth of less than 3 feet during high flows. Fords should be constructed in shallow riffle sections of stream. Low banks are important criteria to minimize excavation on the approaches. Be sure to select a section with stable bed and banks.

Armored Crossings Construction and Installation

Armoring a stream crossing is much like armoring a wet section of trail (see page 162). Stones are sunk into the ground at grade to make both the streambed and the approaches more durable. It is essential to armor both the entry and exit of the crossing—at least one bike length on either side—to prevent sediment from being carried into the stream and to harden the trail and stream banks against splashing and floods. The new, hardened surface will protect the banks, the stream, and the trail.

Stone-pitched armoring is the most durable form. Be sure to use large stones that won't be dislodged by floods. To properly size the stones, you need to know the stream's scour depth at flood. On larger streams, heavy equipment may be needed. The stream's normal sediment load will fill the cracks and move freely over the larger rocks, thereby maintaining channel shape and sediment continuity. In clay, silt, or sand-bedded streams, it may be necessary to underlay larger stones with gravel, cobble, or geotextile to prevent excessive settling. Construct the ford with the same cross section and at the same slope as the adjacent channel (remember: mimic the stream) to avoid potential under-cutting and sedimentation. Some flattening of the bank may be necessary to allow travel, and some ponding of flow will likely occur in these areas.

Although armored fords are one of the least invasive means of crossing a stream, it is still important to consult the land manager before disturbing any creek or streambed to fully understand seasonal flows, habitat issues, and permit requirements.

An armored ford is a durable, simple, and relatively uninvasive means of crossing a stream.

Part Six: Trail Construction

Armored Crossings Pros and Cons

Pros:

Armored Crossings...

- Do not interfere with the movement of water, sediment, aquatic life, or woody debris when they are properly constructed.
- Are long-lasting.
- Maintain a natural look in backcountry settings.
- Can be constructed by hand with volunteer labor, if the stream is small enough.

Cons:

Armored Crossings...

- May adversely affect water quality if inadequately constructed or if built in areas with heavy traffic.
- Cause constant disturbance of substrate, which may affect macroinvertebrates and fisheries.
- May require periodic maintenance if ponding and silt accumulation occurs.

Culverts

Before you think about installing a culvert, consider the consequences to the stream!

A culvert is a conduit—usually metal or plastic pipe—that allows water to flow beneath the trail. Culverts are ideal for crossing small drainages with minimal flow volumes and small, predictable flood peaks. They can be appealing solutions due to their low cost and easy installation. However, culvert crossings on larger streams are frequently problematic.

Of the three types of crossings, culverts have the highest potential for damaging streams. They are often undersized, usually due to cost concerns. They are frequently installed incorrectly—too high or too low in elevation, too steep or too shallow in slope, or with an incorrect alignment to the channel. Improper installation frequently results in flow constrictions, headcutting, upstream sedimentation, downstream scour, debris blockage, and excessive velocities within the pipe. These effects create barriers to fish and macroinvertebrates, destroy stream habitats, and interrupt ecological connectivity. Incorrectly sized or improperly installed culverts commonly fail, causing significant damage to the watershed through channel abandonment, gullying, and inundation of streambeds with silt. Sometimes when culverts fail, the stream will flood onto the trail and may even adopt it as a new channel, damaging both trail and stream.

Even a properly constructed culvert crossing can have negative, incremental impacts by reducing the amount or quality of wildlife habitat, and forcing flood flows into a small area, rather than allowing them to

Don't Forget...
The Stream Crossing Code

1. Stay out of streams and wetlands.
2. If a crossing is essential, build above the water with bridges and boardwalks.
3. If a bridge is not feasible, armor the crossing well.

spread across the floodplain where silt and woody material can settle. Culverts usually require regular maintenance in order to keep them free of debris.

Culvert Construction and Installation

Culverts should be sized to handle the largest floods expected. Work with the land manager to determine flood frequencies and magnitudes. If no data is available, make a field estimate of flood flows by examining the stream's banks. Indicators include a break in bank slope, a change in the size of sediment particles on the bank, the inside height of undercut banks, water stains on boulders, and changes in vegetation. Look for signs of higher flows, such as flood debris, and size the culvert appropriately.

Culverts should be "invisible" to the stream, with no change in channel width, slope, or substrate. They should span at least the entire width of the creek. (Even for the smallest of creeks, a minimum 24-inch culvert is recommended). Even better, and particularly for longer culverts, use a culvert a couple of feet wider than the stream to allow a narrow flood fringe to develop, improving habitat and debris movement through the culvert. Pipe arches or half culverts can be useful in these situations. Align the culvert so there are no sharp bends as the stream enters and exits. Sink the culvert into the streambed to allow a natural bed surface to form inside the pipe.

If a smaller culvert is used due to cost, it must be carefully designed so that flows stay within acceptable limits of velocity and depth. This will ensure that the target species and age class of fish will be able to pass through the culvert unharmed. Resting pools may be needed at either end of the culvert if it is particularly long. After reading this info, you may be thinking, "Wow, this is complicated!" That's why professional help from a hydrologist, engineer, or biologist will likely be necessary to properly design a culvert crossing.

This super-durable rock culvert maintains a natural streambed.

Given the frequency with which culverts fail, *plan for failure* by anticipating what will happen if the culvert is inundated in an exceptionally large flood or due to sediment buildup or a debris jam. Build the crossing so that flows can overtop the culvert without damage or diversion from the stream channel. Locate the culvert in a low spot, with the trail rising significantly on both approaches, allowing the topography to work for you. Minimize fill, and use coarse material when necessary, as it will be more resistant to erosion. Armor around the culvert with large rock to provide additional protection if necessary.

Cover the culvert with at least 12 inches of soil. Plastic culverts are lighter and easier to cut than their metal brethren, making them more managable for jobs that take place far from trailheads.

> "Culverts are hard on fish," notes Forester Phil Wolff of the Tahuya National Forest in Washington state. "If a culvert blows out, there is a huge sediment load delivered to the stream." Also, water generally flows too fast through a culvert. Instead, for stream crossings, Wolff recommends either bridges or hardened crossings. Another option is a half-pipe culvert: The steel tube is cut in half and laid in place as the roof of a tunnel, leaving the bottom as a natural stream course.

Think about culvert maintenance before installation. The longer the culvert, the more likely it is to clog with silt, branches, and debris. Longer culverts are also harder to clear once clogged.

Culvert Pros and Cons

Pros:

Culverts. . .
- Are drier than fords.
- Are cheaper than bridges.

Cons:

Culverts. . .
- Have the highest potential for damage to streams.
- Are often sized and installed incorrectly in a stream, adversely effecting stream habitat and the free movement of water, organisms, sediment, and woody debris.
- Often fail, causing damage—sometimes major damage—to stream ecosystems.
- Are bulky and difficult to transport to backcountry locations.
- Have high maintenance requirements. When they become blocked, they back up water and cause trail damage.
- Are not natural and remind everyone using the trails they are near civilization.

Trail Solutions

Bridges

Building a bridge is one of the biggest trailbuilding challenges. It requires a strong understanding of engineering and hydrological principles. Bridges are labor intensive, expensive and, like other water crossings, frequently require permits. However, if the stream you wish to cross is large, or has particularly variable hydrology with large flood peaks, a bridge is the best means of crossing. By putting the trail above the water, you will minimize the impact each has on the other. There is a wide range of bridge designs—from simple one-log-and-a-handrail versions to expensive, factory-built, steel models. Land management agencies typically have standards for bridges on their land. Know these guidelines before investing money and time in bridge construction. Choose materials that meet your needs and budget.

Tips for Successful Bridge Building

- Make the bridge high enough so that the approach is on a gentle grade (if not level). Proper height also helps avoid flood damage. Design your bridge with the 100-year flood in mind. Bridge crossings should be built at the riffle reaches of a river or stream.

- Extend approach ramps well onto the trail.

- Bridges and their approaches should not have sharp turns. A tight turn onto a bridge deck is very dangerous when it's wet or icy.

- Design the bridge so that travelers on either end can see each other and slow or yield before meeting abruptly in the middle.

- Design bridges with their users in mind. For example, an equestrian crossing may have specific railing and decking requirements for safe passage.

- For wooden bridges, use screws and bolts instead of nails.

Bridges are labor intensive and expensive to build, but by putting the trail above the water, you will minimize trail/stream impacts. Avoid stair-steps on shared-use trails if possible. Photo by Chuck Haney.

Part Six: Trail Construction

- Avoid letting bridge stringers (the structural supports that span the stream and support the bridge decking) touch the ground. Stringers that rest on the ground may rot and collapse. Sit stringers on sills of stone or replaceable wood.

- When building with unfinished wood from the bridge site, use only naturally rot-resistant species such as cedar, cypress, hemlock, locust, redwood, or tamarack. In eastern North America, locust is by far the most rot-resistant wood.

- Bark must be stripped off the logs you use or the wood will rot and suffer insect damage.

- Before beginning work, consult an experienced bridge builder or at least check with the land management agency for its construction guides.

> We could easily dedicate a book to building bridges. Instead, we've just provided a few important guidelines. There are several in-depth sources of bridge info.
> The U.S. Forest Service's Trail Bridge Catalog is available at: www.fs.fed.us/na/wit/WITPages/bridgecatalog/
> The Federal Highway Administration's Recreational Trails Program website provides numerous resources at: www.fhwa.dot.gov/environment/rectrails/index.htm

Bridge Pros and Cons

Pros:

Bridges...
- Cause minimal impacts to stream function if properly placed (at a riffle reach and above the flood width of the channel).
- Can be a beautifully engineered trail attraction.
- May eliminate or minimize long grade approaches to the crossing, reducing trail erosion into stream.
- Make installation easier with pre-fabricated versions.

Cons:

Bridges...
- Are expensive.
- Can require labor-intensive construction.
- May necessitate engineering and design plans, raising project costs.
- May anchor a stream by not allowing it to migrate in the floodplain.

Wetland crossings should be avoided whenever possible. When there is no other option, an elevated boardwalk will minimize impacts.

Raised tread construction like this turnpike is useful for crossing seasonally wet areas or soggy ground.

Wetlands

Wetlands are among the most vital and fragile ecosystems on this planet. They come in many forms—from lowland swamps and marshes to alpine bogs fed by springs and snowmelt—and perform important functions, including regulating water flow, retaining run-off, and purifying water. Wetlands also host diverse and often rare species of plants and animals. For all of these reasons, it is important to tread lightly through wetland ecosystems, and to avoid routing your trail through wetlands whenever possible.

General Guidelines for Building Trails Through Wetlands

The general guidelines for water crossings also apply to wetland crossings: They should be identified as key control points, and users should be directed away from them. However, if you must route the trail across a wetland environment, consult the land manager for permission (an environmental assessment study and permitting may be necessary) and to help you determine the best approach for low-impact trail construction.

There are several types of trail structures used to cross wetlands. The traditional names for these structures are somewhat complex—turnpike, causeway, punchon, gadbury, bog bridge—and explaining the ins and outs of each one would be beyond the scope of this book. We've simplified things here by dividing wetland trail structures into two general categories. **Raised Tread** is constructed directly on the ground. (Includes turnpike, causeway, raised camber, and some types of armoring.) **Boardwalks** are raised above the ground. (Includes puncheons, bog bridges, ladder bridges and gadburys.)

Constructing both raised tread and boardwalks in fragile wetland ecosystems requires careful planning and execution. The U.S. Forest Service publication, *Wetland Trail Design and Construction* is an excellent resource and should consulted for any wetland trailwork. It is free of charge and available online at www.fhwa.dot.gov/environment/fspubs.

"Students in the Watershed" Tahuya State Forest, Washington

The 23,000-acre Tahuya State Forest sits 15 miles northwest of Tacoma, Washington. The many streams flowing through the Tahuya provide the gravel spawning beds, fresh water, and shelter needed by salmon. On the same plot of land, 180 miles of trails host motorcyclists, mountain bikers, hikers, and equestrians. These trails cross the streams in about 100 places.

Early in 1994, managers from Washington's Department of Natural Resources (DNR) recognized that these recreational trails could be harming water quality and fish habitat, so they began conducting soil and hydrology assessments of the trail system. The managers also began discussions with trail users and experiments in erosion-control measures. The results provided scientific data on trail erosion and excellent information on trail design and tread hardening.

To gather more detailed measurements, the scientists enlisted the aid of students from the nearby North Mason High School. The students measured silt caught in sediment traps, soil loss on trail surfaces, rainfall, and numbers of trail users.

The results of the "Students in the Watershed" project produced four main conclusions:

- Roughly 150 metric tons of sediment would have eroded into streams each year from the 180 miles of trails, if not for erosion-control measures.
- The steepness of trail segments significantly increases the potential for surface drainage, trail rutting, and sediment delivery to streams. Trails with grades of more than 20 percent cause much more erosion than trails with gentler grades.
- Heavy trail use during wet periods significantly increases erosion, but armoring can greatly reduce erosion caused by trail users.
- Long stretches of trail without water diversions will cause more erosion. Well-designed, well-located, and well-constructed water diversions can effectively minimize rutting and erosion at low cost.

During three years of study, the students and scientists were able to create scientifically credible charts that clearly demonstrate the effects of rainfall, trail steepness, and trail design on erosion and the subsequent health of Tahuya's streams.

How Long Will It Take? How Much Will It Cost?

The following factors contribute to trailbuilding time and cost.

Type of Trail

The trail style and the mix of anticipated trail users plays a fundamental role in trailbuilding time and cost. The primary access trail in an urban trail system may need extensive construction work to achieve the necessary wide and smooth tread. On the other hand, a 12-inch-wide, singletrack trail could be built with less resources.

Type of Terrain

Time and effort increase drastically as soil gets harder, roots and rocks increase, vegetation gets thicker, and the grade gets steeper.

Location of Trail

The proximity of the work site to vehicles, materials, tools, and trail workers will affect both cost and time.

Hand or Mechanized Tools

Mechanized tools can reduce construction time and cost. A three-person crew using a mini dozer can build 500 to 700 feet or more of finished trail per day. A three-person crew using only hand tools, by contrast, may only build 200 feet on a good day. The average laborer building a trail by hand earns $15 to $25 per hour, whereas the average trailbuilder using mechanized tools earns $30 to $60 (the higher rate reflects the skill involved in operating the machinery as well as machinery maintenance and transportation costs). Initially, it may appear that hand laborers are a comparative bargain. In most cases, however, machine-built trails are actually less expensive to construct, since mechanized tools significantly cut labor hours and the overall cost of the project. (See Part Five for more information on tools.)

Professional or Volunteer Labor

On average, one experienced pro using conventional hand tools can build 10 feet of bench cut trail per hour, or 80 feet per day. In steep, rocky, or heavily forested conditions, that average can drop to as little as 1 foot per hour or 8 feet of finished trail in a single day. If you use volunteers, construction costs are much lower, but the work takes much, much more time.

Trail Structures

Construction time and costs are also determined by the number of labor-intensive features on your trail. Switchbacks and bridges, for instance, will quickly raise the price of your project. Every switchback adds between $300 and $1,000, or many hours of volunteer time, and large-scale bridges can cost as much as $50,000 or even $80,000.

Note: If your goal is to build several miles of trail, consider hiring a professional or renting/buying a machine such as a mini dozer. Part Five covers mechanized tools in much greater detail, and Appendix C lists IMBA-affiliated professional trailbuilders.

Here are some estimates we gathered after polling several professional contractors early in 2004. If you are using all volunteer time, you can use these estimates to put a dollar value on the work.

PROJECT	COST
Trail Construction by Machine	Easy conditions: $1 per foot/$5,000 per mile Typical conditions: $2.50 per foot/$13,000 per mile Hard conditions: $5 per foot/$26,000 per mile
Trail Construction by Hand	Easy conditions: $1 per foot/$5,000 per mile Typical conditions: $5 per foot/$26,000 per mile Hard conditions: $10 per foot/$52,000 per mile
Switchback Construction	$300 to $1,000 per switchback
Wooden Bridge	$20 to $25 per square foot of decking
Metal Bridge	$50 and up per square foot of decking
Trailhead Facilities	Restrooms: $15,000 to $20,000 apiece Gravel Parking Lot: $15,000 to $25,000
Trailhead Kiosk	$2,000 to $3,000
Trail Markers	$5 to $20 apiece
SWECO Rental	$485 per day/$4,500 per month
Walk-Behind Mini Dozer Rental	$120 per day/$500 per week

Securing Grant Money—
Gas Taxes Fund New Trail Projects

Building a new trail can be a huge challenge. In addition to red tape, there's usually the question of cash. When trail construction companies and land managers said, "Show me the money," one IMBA-affiliate, the Georgia-based Southern Off-Road Bicycle Association (SORBA), did just that. Their bankroll? The Recreational Trails Program (RTP).

The RTP provides federal funding for trail projects nationwide. Managed by the Federal Highway Administration, the RTP has helped communities build and repair thousand of miles of trails involving 5,000 projects in all 50 states.

Between 1995 and 2002, SORBA earned more than a dozen RTP grants ranging from $35,000 to $125,000—more than $750,000 in total. The funds have helped pay for hundreds of trailwork tools, five, fully equipped trailwork trailers, a Toro Dingo, and even a John Deere Trail Gator. SORBA also used RTP funds to hire former Subaru/IMBA Trail Care Crew leader Mike Riter to serve as Trail Education Specialist for SORBA and Gainesville College.

IMBA board member and SORBA leader Jay Franklin attributes SORBA's success to great land management partners and a professional approach. He advises other volunteer organizations to dedicate at least one member to chasing RTP grants. "Know the guidelines upfront and make sure your application is professional. The process can be cumbersome, but the rewards are worth it," said Franklin.

Bright Idea

Trails Can Be Expensive To Build. Know all the potential sources of funding for trailbuilding in your area. Recreational Trails Program (RTP) funds, state trails programs, and local economic development programs can help bridge the funding gaps and get a proposed trail project off the ground (or *on* the ground). Contact your state's RTP administrator, state park system, or chamber of commerce to inquire about available funds. You can also visit the IMBA website for info on trail grants and funding.

Location: Canmore, Alberta. Photo by Steven Wilde.

Part Seven: Trail Maintenance

Location: South Downs, Brighton, England. Photo by Seb Rogers.

All trails benefit from routine maintenance. Foresight, care, and hard work—everything that you put into building a new trail—should also go into maintaining an existing one. Thousands of trails around the world are in desperate need of repair. The following sections offer solutions for maintaining perfect tread and problem trails alike, so you can keep trails in good shape and visitors happy.

In This Part …

- **Assessing the Condition of the Trail** 192
- **Maintaining the Trail Corridor** 195
- **Identifying Trail Problems** 197
  User-Caused Erosion Problems and
  How to Solve Them 197
  Water-Caused Erosion Problems
  and How to Solve Them 200
- **Drainage Solutions** 201
  Deberming and Maintaining the Outslope . . 201
  Knicks 203
  Rolling Grade Dips 204
  Waterbars: Good Intentions, Bad Results . . . 206
  Armoring 207
- **Special Conditions: Wet, Flat, and Sandy** 208
  Wet Areas 209
  Flat Areas 209
  Sandy Areas 210
- **Rerouting and Reclaiming Damaged Trails** 211
  Time to Reroute? 211
  Ten Tips for Rerouting and
  Reclaiming a Trail 211

Assessing the Condition of the Trail

Resist the temptation to rush onto the trail, tools in hand, to try to refurbish it. After all, you need to know what the problems are before you can repair them. The following four steps will help you assess your trail's needs.

Step 1: Create a Trail Assessment and Repair Sheet.

Repairing a trail all by yourself is tough work, but you can use a trail assessment sheet to direct other people to perform the repair work with you. Trail assessment sheets (like the sample) give you a means of identifying maintenance projects, their locations, the nature of the problems, and a strategy for resolving each situation. You can even list the tools needed and assign a particular work crew and crew leader to tackle each project.

Sure, drawing up an assessment sheet may sound like pen-pusher drudgery, but consider the alternative: You scout a trail, discover several problems that need correcting, and then try to relay that information to your fellow trailworkers without the aid of specific directions...

"*Uh, we need to fix that gully in the first couple miles…you know, over by the really big tree, but I don't mean the gully that looks like Michael Douglas' chin, the one I'm thinking of is a few turns before that, it looks a lot like the scar on Clint Eastwood's neck in* Hang 'Em High—*you know the one I mean? Well, there's also a soggy patch we should fix about 2 miles down the trail—it's right there by the mossy rock….*"

You get the idea.

A trail assessment sheet takes the ambiguity out of maintenance work. Feel free to use this version as a model. It'll take you a couple minutes to create a master and make some photocopies, but when the weekend rolls around and your group of volunteers is standing at the trailhead awaiting orders, your assessment sheets will prevent a lot of confusion.

Trail Solutions

Trail Assessment and Repair Sheet

Site Number:

Location:

Priority:

Crew Leader:

Problem:

Repair:

Sketch Existing Trail:

Sketch Repair:

Crew:

Tools:

Step 2: Walk or Ride the Trail.

Once you've devised an assessment sheet, it's time to hit the trail in search of maintenance projects. Take a pedometer or measuring wheel (if walking) or strap a cyclocomputer onto your bike and start recording your mileage the moment you leave the trailhead.

Whenever you find a spot that needs repair (we'll cover what to look for in a minute), pull out an assessment sheet, record how far the site is from the trailhead, the nature of the problem, and other information you deem necessary. You may also want to record the severity of the problem. Trail assessment is a lot like performing triage in a busy hospital. You can only tackle so many projects on a given day, so identify and fix the most critical problems first. Consider undertaking sections that pose risk to visitors first and then move on to the sites that will degrade quickly if not corrected immediately.

Step 3: Confer with the Land Manager.

Meet your land manager, if applicable, and discuss trail projects well in advance of scheduling a work day. Here's where your trail assessment sheets come in handy. They'll help you accurately explain the problems on the trail and how you plan on resolving them. Save copies of all your assessment sheets so that you can develop a track record of everything you have done to maintain and protect the trail. This is key if you ever need to prove your group's stewardship credentials.

Step 4: Assign Work Crews.

Assign a leader and work crew of two to five people to each maintenance project. With your assessment sheet in hand, the work crew should be able to answer the following questions:

- Who is on the crew and who is the leader?
- Where is the work site (in miles or feet from the trailhead)?
- What tools do we need?
- What is the problem?
- How should we go about repairing the problem?

Trail Solutions

Maintaining the Trail Corridor

Bushes grow, trees fall, and branches have an uncanny way of thrusting themselves onto the trail—precisely at eye level. Thus, your first order of business is to make sure that the trail corridor is still passable and that the sightlines are acceptable. Scout the trail with an eye for unwieldy vegetation and tree branches in the trail corridor, trees that have fallen and blocked the trail, loose rocks on the tread, and exposed roots that could pose a danger to users. Then, follow the four steps below to remedy these problems.

Step 1: Trim Vegetation.

Keeping the corridor maintained helps keep people on the trail. For example, cutting back vegetation helps visitors stay on the center of the tread. Most forested areas require two corridor-clearing projects per year, and sometimes more. Early spring is an ideal time to clear downed trees, and fall is the best season to clear overgrowth.

Creative pruning along alternate sides of a trail accentuates curves to keep a twisty trail twisty. Don't trim more than necessary. Over-trimming tends to make a trail too straight, inviting speed. Remember to match the corridor height and width to the desired trail style, and be sure to maintain a high ceiling (about 10 feet) on trails used by equestrians. (Of course, many desert trails and paths through open terrain don't need trimming.)

You can remove overgrown grass and light brush from the corridor with a weed whip. Loppers will come in handy for bushes and small branches. Be sure to cut branches outside of the bark collar. Completely remove stumps from the trail tread so they don't pose a tripping hazard. See page 137 for corridor clearing details.

Trimming vegetation helps visitors stay on the center of the tread.

Part Seven: Trail Maintenance

Step 2: Cut and Move Downed Trees.

Remove blow-downs and deadfall from the trail tread, especially if the trees in question force visitors off the trail or trap water. Logs are generally removed from beginner and intermediate shared-use trails. On advanced-level singletrack, however, downed logs can be considered desirable obstacles, as they help keep speed down and provide experienced users with a challenge. In that case, the log can be partially moved so that novice riders can pass it easily while more experienced riders can ride over it. See page 226 for details.

Step 3: Remove Loose Rocks.

Trails that feature deeply embedded rocks can be a technical wonderland for advanced users. Loose rocks, on the other hand, are generally a hazard on beginner and intermediate trails. They are eventually torn from the tread, leaving holes that can trip trail users. Fill such holes and be sure to moisten and compact the fill soil.

Step 4: Examine Exposed Roots.

Yes, some mountain bikers like the challenge of riding over roots, but masses of exposed roots often indicate a larger erosion problem on the trail, requiring attention. Consider removing a solitary root from the trail tread if it poses a hazard. If you can catch your foot beneath the root, it should probably be removed. Roots that run perpendicular to the trail are usually less hazardous to users than irregular roots running the length of the trail.

Photo by Seb Rogers.

Identifying Trail Problems

Every user group impacts the trail. They skid their feet or tires, they skirt puddles, they travel off trail to avoid mud, and so on. Water causes impacts, too. Trailbuilders know that most trail problems can't be categorized as either user- or water-caused. Both often join together and wreak havoc on the trail.

In this section, we've listed the most common indicators of user- and water-caused erosion and proposed solutions for each.

User-Caused Erosion Problems and How to Solve Them

Boots, Hoofs, and Tires

If you can recognize the brand of boot used by a recent hiker, you have a serious problem on your trail.

Problem: The trail is too steep and exceeds a maximum sustainable grade (see page 59).

Solution: Maximum sustainable grades are site-specific and fluctuate based on soil properties, types of users, and the length of the section. You can either reroute the trail to incorporate sustainable grades, or if it is a short steep section, you can armor the trail to protect against user-caused erosion.

Problem: The trail is in a wet location.

Solution: If the trail is on low-lying terrain and not on a slope, reroute the trail onto a sloped hillside. If your trail is built on the sideslope, but is still holding water, chances are you have don't have adequate outslope. Build a knick to enhance drainage or retrofit grade reversals into your trail. In exceptionally rainy environments and areas with high water tables, even well-built trails located on slopes can be persistently wet. The only solution in these cases is a raised trail tread (see page 162 for more advice on raised tread construction).

This muddy trail in low-lying terrain would benefit from a reroute onto a drier hillside.

Part Seven: Trail Maintenance

This fall-line situation illustrates tread creep. Several different treads are visible because trail users have created a new path whenever the existing path becomes gullied.

Trail Widening, Trail Braiding, Tread Creep

When there are problems with the design or the function of your trail, users may drift from the tread and/or create their own routes. This practice is unsustainable, harmful to the environment, and can even be unsafe.

Problem: Obstacles are forcing users off the trail.

Solution: If the trail is in the flats, nothing can stop users from choosing their own adventures. If you have sideslope, use it. This is the best way to keep users from straying off trail. If users are going around an obstacle, remove the obstacle and/or corral users on the trail. Consider trimming vegetation that may be causing users to leave the center of the tread.

Problem: The trail is always wet and muddy.

Solution: Water sitting on your trail maybe the source of the problem, but your users exacerbate the issue. See Boots, Hoofs, and Tires on the previous page.

Trail Solutions

Problem: The trail intersection is not well designed.

Solution: Monitor the flow of traffic at trail intersections by installing choke points on either side. Try to minimize speeds at intersections not only for safety, but also to keep users from drifting off of the tread. If possible, it is always better to have users climb to an intersection.

Washboard and Braking Bumps

Trails develop braking bumps when mountain bikers are suddenly forced to hit the brakes. The repeated hard braking creates a choppy, washboarded trail surface. The main culprit here is a flawed design.

Problem: Abrupt flow transitions or turns force users to brake excessively in one spot.

Solution: Slow users down before sharp turns and flow transitions. If you go from open and flowing to tight and technical, add some challenge and choke points to create a transition.

The Development of Social Trails

Social trails usually form because trail users notice a point of interest that they cannot reach while traveling on the original trail.

Problem: The trail bypasses a potentially positive control point.

Solution: Reroute the trail to include the scenic overlook, rock outcropping, or lake access to keep your users on the trail.

Problem: The trail comes within view of a potentially negative control point.

Solution: Reroute the trail to obliterate sightlines to trash dumps, sensitive ecological and archaeological areas, and other places that are out of bounds so the users aren't tempted to investigate.

Problem: Users feel that they are not getting the experience they seek.

Solution: Know the users!

Both flowing water and trail users have eroded and widened this fall-line trail. The best remedy would be to construct a sustainable, rolling contour reroute.

Water-Caused Erosion Problems and How to Solve Them

Eroded Trail

Gullies and washed-out tread indicate a drainage problem. Water is not sheeting off the trail. Instead, it's flowing down the trail and carving those gullies. The longer water is allowed to travel down your trail, the greater its erosive force.

Problem: The trail is on the fall line (remember the half rule and maximum sustainable grade).

Solution: A fall-line trail is a maintenance nightmare; water will always win the game. The best option is to reroute the trail so that it incorporates rolling contour design and full bench construction. If this is not an option (i.e. endangered species on both sides), you may need to implement some armoring techniques.

Problem: The trail lacks outslope, and water is not sheeting off the trail gently.

Solution: Restore the outslope of the trail. The slight tilt of the trail tread will encourage water to sheet across and off the trail instead of funneling down the center. It is common for trails to lose their outslope over time. In addition to removing the water-trapping berms on the trail, make sure that your trail also incorporates grade reversals as a defense against water.

This trail lacks grade reversals and outslope. Water is channeling down the tread and will erode the trail over time. A possible remedy would be to construct a rolling grade dip and reestablish outslope.

Problem: The trail lacks grade reversals.

Solution: Retrofit grade reversals into your trail if possible. If your trail has conservative grades, this should not be a problem. If you cannot incorporate grade reversals, several water-diversion techniques can be utilized. A complete discussion of rolling grade dips and knicks is on page 202.

Trail Solutions

Drainage Solutions

IMBA recommends several techniques for diverting water from an existing trail.

Deberming and Maintaining the Outslope

Even well-built trails with proper outslope can lose their tilt over time and begin trapping and funneling erosive water.

There are two reasons for this:

1. The center of the trail may become compacted with use, resulting in a U-shaped tread that traps water.

2. Loose material can collect on the outer edge of the tread, forming a berm that traps water.

Fortunately, the remedy is straightforward. **Deberm** the trail by scraping the mounded dirt off the tread's edge, and reestablish a 5-percent outslope. This is a frequent maintenance job on most trail systems.

Note: Outslope is difficult to maintain in loose soil conditions. Loose soil lacks cohesion and is easily displaced to the sides of the trail by tires, feet, and hooves. Grade reversals are essential to insure proper drainage in these situations.

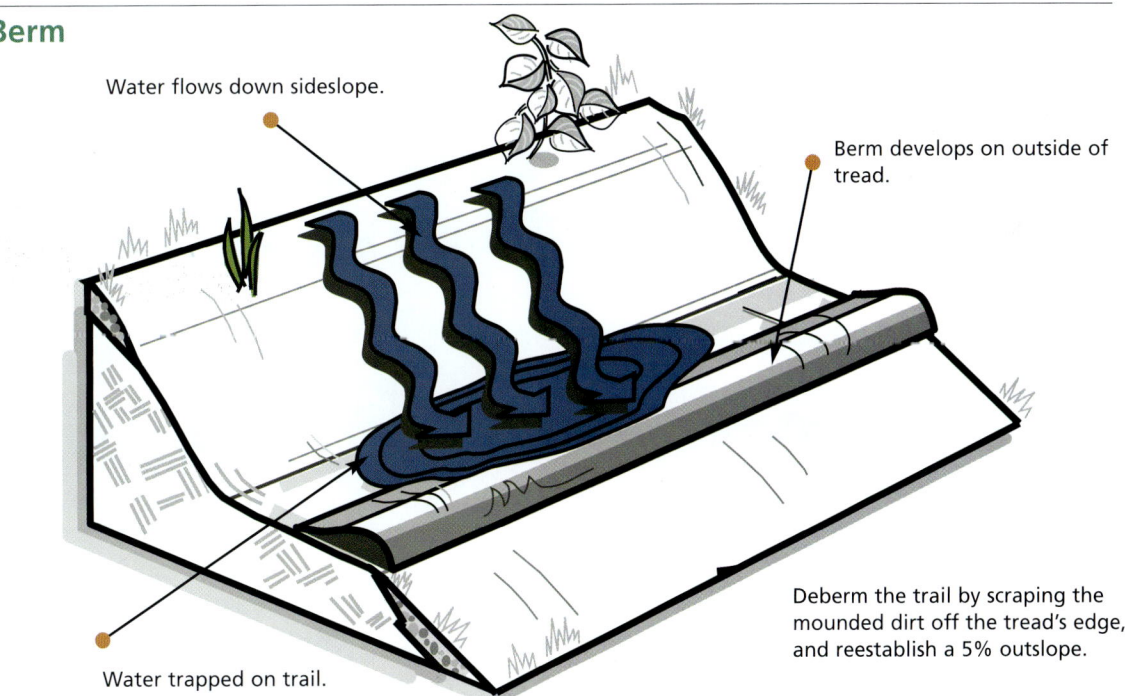

Berm

Water flows down sideslope.

Berm develops on outside of tread.

Water trapped on trail.

Deberm the trail by scraping the mounded dirt off the tread's edge, and reestablish a 5% outslope.

Part Seven: Trail Maintenance

Knicks and Rolling Grade Dips

Grade reversals should appear in your trail as frequently as possible. If a trail wasn't designed with enough grade reversals to shed water, artificial ones can be added. We recommend two types: **Knicks** and **Rolling Grade Dips**.

Puddles often indicate an appropriate place to construct a knick.

Don't Make the Mistake of. . .

Building a "Path to Grandma's House." This is what we call some trailbuilders' obsession with lining trails with logs. A properly constructed trail doesn't need them. In fact, lining a trail with logs or rocks traps water on the tread and increases erosion.

Trail Solutions

Knicks

A knick is a semi-circular, shaved-down section of trail, about 10 feet in diameter, that is canted to the outside. A knick is smooth and subtle; many visitors won't even notice its presence. The center of the knick is outsloped at about 15 percent, which is what draws water off the trail. For a knick to be effective, there must be lower ground next to the trail tread so that water will have a place to drain. Knicks are typically built on gentle sections of trail where water tends to puddle. Knicks also work well on noncohesive soils such as sand, pumice, and decomposed granite.

Knick

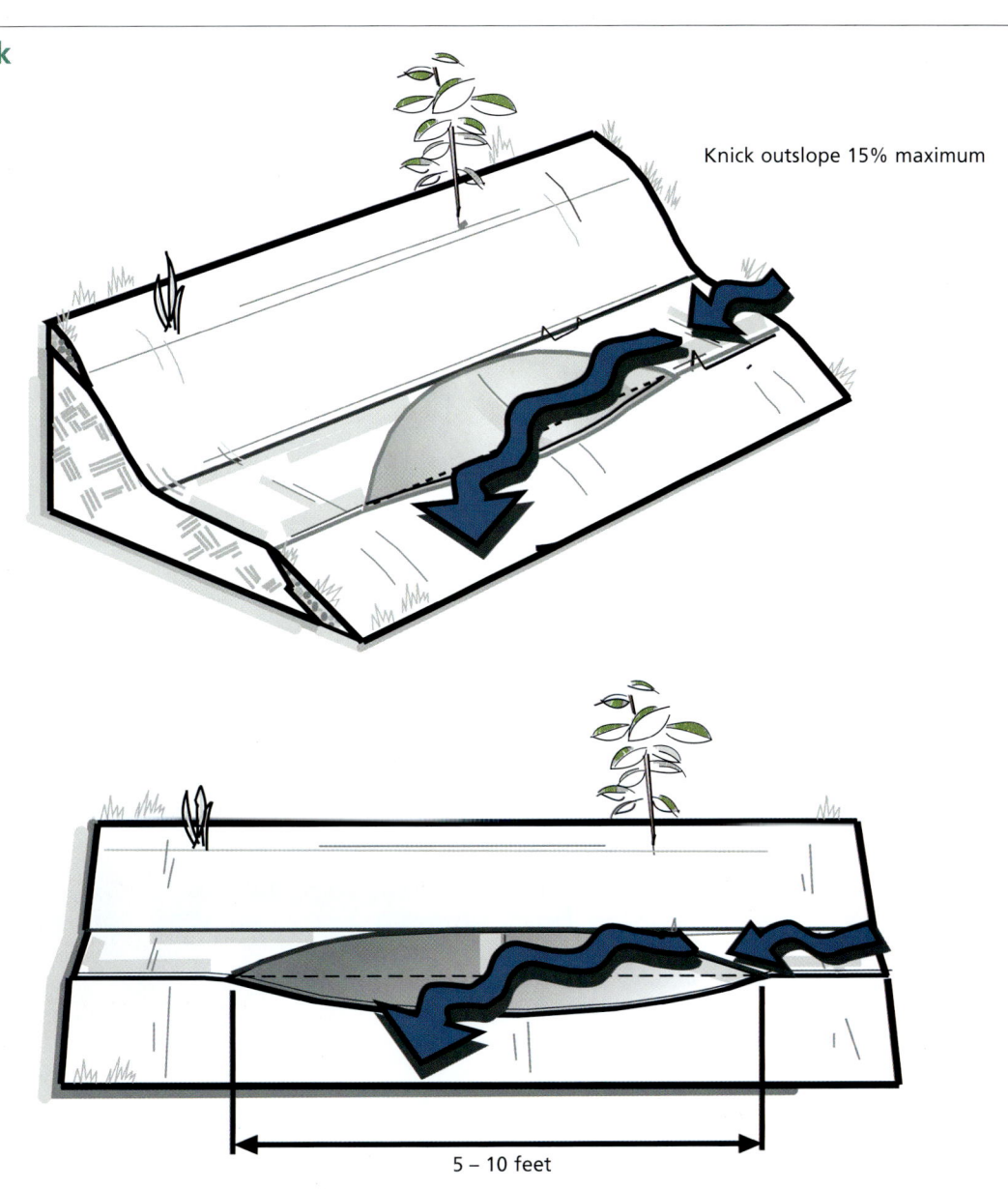

Knick outslope 15% maximum

5 – 10 feet

Part Seven: Trail Maintenance

Rolling Grade Dips

A Rolling Grade Dip (RGD) builds on the knick device. It features a similar outsloped depression in the tread, followed by a long, gentle dirt ramp. RGDs are sometimes described as a soup spoon lying on the trail; the scoop of the spoon is the dip in the trail, and the handle of the spoon is a gentle dirt ramp that follows. The dip should be longer than a bike (about 9 feet). The excavated soils from the dip are used to create the backup ramp that fortifies the dip. This ramp is long, 10 to 20 feet from tip to tail (depending on the steepness of the tread), and outsloped at 5 percent like normal tread. The total length of an RGD varies widely depending on the steepness of the trail tread, but most are somewhere between 15 to 30 feet.

Proper placement of RGDs is crucial. Look for a natural roll or change in trail grade that can be accentuated. On steep trails, several RGDs may be needed. Fall-line trails may have to be rerouted if water is a constant problem, since it is impossible to convince the water to travel off the trail if the trail is the most direct way down. Don't place RGDs in turns.

Certain soil types like decomposed granite and sand don't bond well and won't hold together to form a good ramp. Remove and disperse your excavated materials in this case, and carve the entire RGD out of the trail tread.

When built properly, RGDs and knicks require only minor maintenance; each season you'll need to remove the leaves and silt that occasionally collect in dips and knicks. If left unattended, both designs will clog over time and become ineffective.

These volunteers have nearly completed a grade dip that will be almost invisible to trail users and need very little maintenance.

Trail Solutions

Rolling Grade Dip

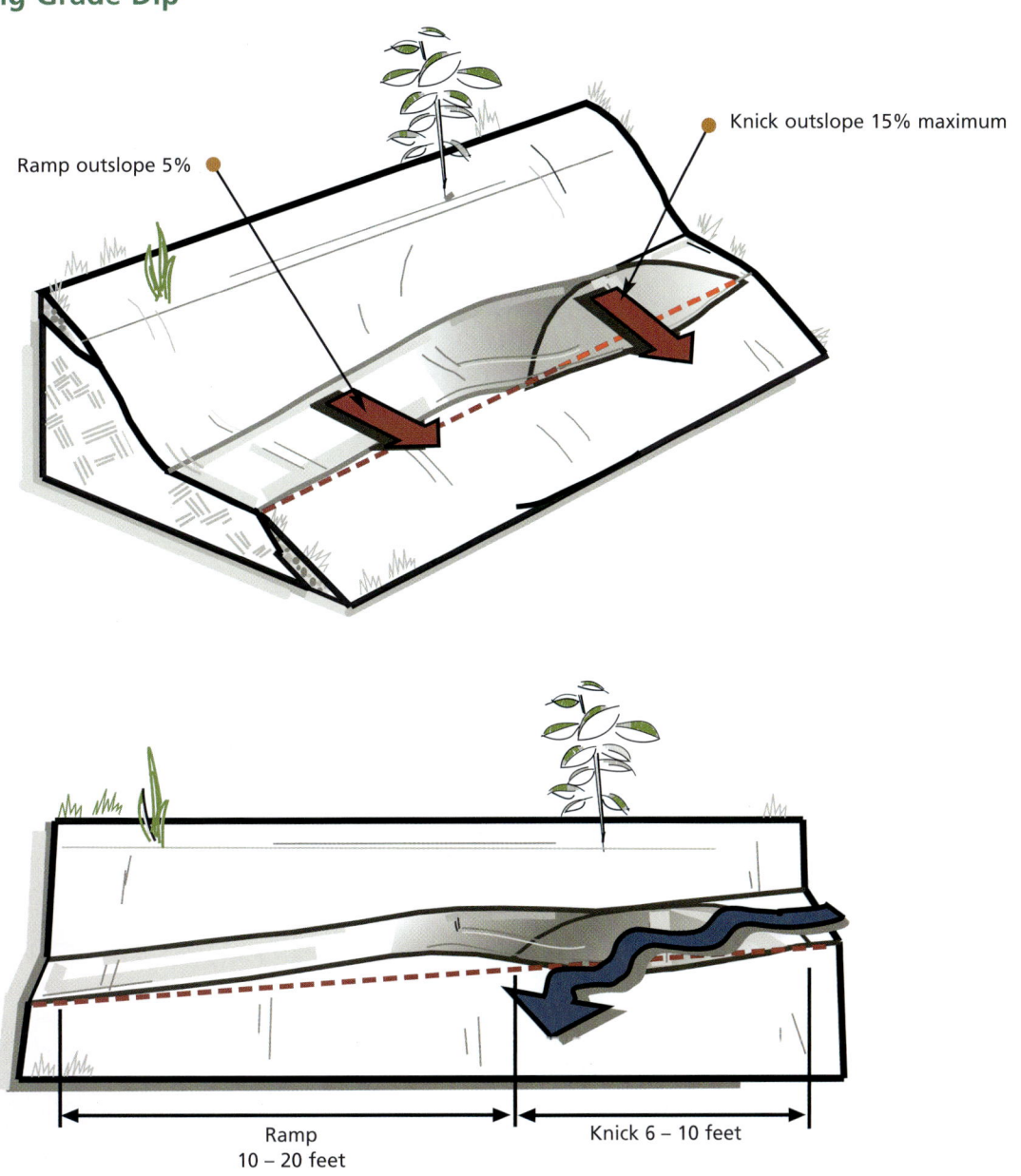

The Difference Between Knicks and Rolling Grade Dips

A knick is smaller than a RGD. Knicks are also more steeply outsloped (about 15 percent at its center), and they don't feature a ramp. RGDs can be used on relatively steep sections of trail, whereas knicks are typically employed on gentle sections of trail where water tends to puddle.

This newly built knick will help drain water trapped on the trail tread.

Waterbars: Good Intentions, Bad Results

Many trails lack enough grade reversals to properly divert water from the tread, and once erosion begins, many trailbuilders install drainage structures to halt the problem. Waterbars are one of the most popular—but least effective—drainage structures employed. By installing rock, rubber or wood barriers across the trail, builders hope to divert water. Unfortunately waterbars suffer from the following problems:

- They require frequent maintenance.
- They clog with sediment quickly.
- Heavy water flows wash over the top.
- Visitors tend to go around the bars, widening the tread.

In short, waterbars are not the most effective means of stopping erosion. At best, they are a temporary Band Aid. Again, we recommend designing grade reversals (see page 67) or adding knicks and rolling grade dips to help shed water and prevent erosion.

Trail Solutions

Bright Idea

Replace Waterbars with Rolling Grade Dips. A Rolling Grade Dip (RGD) is a shaved-down section of trail followed by a gentle dirt ramp that helps collect and draw water off the trail. RGDs are longer and subtler than traditional waterbars. They are also more effective than waterbars because they're large and durable, yet smooth enough to be negotiated by all users. They're a particularly good drainage device for trails used by mountain bikers. Unlike waterbars, RGDs don't entice cyclists to ride off trail to get around them. And since a properly built RGD is very subtle, cyclists won't impact the tread by braking hard as they approach.

Armoring

Whether or not your trail can endure frequent traffic is largely dependent on the soil's wetness, texture, structure, and depth. In an ideal world we'd all be building our trails on loamy soil.

Of course, we don't live in an ideal world and not all dirt is created equal. Thus, many of us are stuck building trail on a thin layer of soil that drains poorly, packs up when it's wet, or simply falls apart under traffic. If you've designed your trail properly and are still grappling with soil problems, you may need to harden your soil. There are two main ways to accomplish this: You can armor the tread with natural rock, or you can harden the soil with manmade materials such as soil binders and geosynthetics. (See page 162 for a thorough discussion on armoring.)

Trail users have avoided this rubber water bar and widened the trail. A rolling grade dip would be more effective here.

Part Seven: Trail Maintenance

Special Conditions: Wet, Flat, and Sandy

While it's never prudent to route a trail through flat areas, wetlands, or extremely sandy terrain, there are times when you have no choice: You must work on a trail that's been built in such conditions. Here are some guidelines for maintaining trails in challenging conditions.

Trails in low-lying terrain often become muddy quagmires because water has no place to drain. Try to locate trails in places where the tread is slightly higher than the adjacent terrain.

Trail Solutions

Wet Areas

Trails that cross marshes, swamps, and other moist spots make land managers frown (think worn trails). It's hard to walk or ride a trail and not to leave a mark when the tread is consistently wet. Here are a few tips for dealing with soggy terrain.

Find the High Spot.

Keep the trail high. Microtopographic changes are common in low-lying wet areas. Just a few feet in elevation can often mean the difference between a 30-foot slog through the mud and a dry, flowing trail. Using a clinometer during the leafless period of the year really helps in finding these small hummocks and ridges. The highest area near rivers of considerable size is usually on the levee closest to the channel or at the base of the flood plain.

No High Spot? Try Building One.

When the landscape still won't cooperate with your plans, create topography by raising your trail. You can use rock to raise the trail above a spring or seasonal wet area, build a turnpike to cross a wet meadow, or construct wooden decking to clear moving or perennial water. (See pages 162 and 176 for tips.) Just remember that drainage must accompany turnpikes and raised treads to avoid blocking water flow.

Flat Areas

Flat terrain lures many trailbuilders. Initially, it seems that miles of trails can be built without having to excavate tread on a sideslope. Once the trail is built, however, difficult problems arise.

Multiple trail treads often result, as users can easily deviate from the original tread and create new, unauthorized trails. Persistent wet spots develop as the tread compacts and assumes the profile of a rain gutter. This concave tread gets wet fast and dries slower than the surrounding area, which further encourages trail users to bypass wet spots and widen the trail. Finally, if the flat area transitions into a down slope, all the water from the gullied tread is focused on one narrow stretch of trail, which accelerates erosion.

In truth, flat terrain is oftentimes the most difficult topography on which to develop sustainable trails.

Work the Bumps.

Microtopography (small bumps and rises) is your trailbuilding weapon against the perils of flat terrain. You can utilize small changes in elevation—even a mere foot or two—to build a small bench and an outsloped tread that sheds water.

Build Smooth Turns and Build 'em High.

Proper flow is critical to the health of all trails, but is particularly important on flat terrain. If you combine fast straightaways with tight corners, riders will hit their brakes and erode the trail. You can avoid this problem by designing smooth turns that can be safely navigated at a consistent speed.

You can also help slow riders before they enter the turn by routing the trail between chokes—large trees, rocks, or thick vegetation that slow users before the turn. The location of your turns is also important. Avoid constructing turns in the lowest areas where water is bound to collect. Whenever possible, turns should be located on the highest microtopography of the area.

Sandy Areas

Deep sand can be the trailbuilder's pit of despair. Some users try to avoid loose, sandy stretches of trail by skirting them, while others simply churn through with extra power. In almost no time, 10-foot long, sandy sections become 100-foot long sand traps. Sand simply does not create a firm trail bed because it does not stick together.

Don't Make it Steep or Tight.

The first step in this process is to refrain from pushing the grade. A 5- to 7-percent tread may be as steep as you can go in very sandy soils. When built correctly, rolling, fast trail in a sandy area can feel like floating—somewhat like skiing in powder. Think of broad, sweeping turns rather than tight, twisty trail.

Make it Sticky.

You can alter the sand to make it stick together. Clay-based soil binders will balance the texture. Organic material gathered nearby or imported mulch can also help. When cutting a new trail in sandy areas, reserve all the organic material upslope of the bench cut. When the trail tread is complete, add the duff back onto the tread and tamp it into the sand. This will improve the texture of your soil.

Think "Inside Turns."

There are two types of turns that can be built along a variable sideslope, or a hillside with protrusions and indentations. Inside turns are concave, meaning the hillside helps keep the rider on the trail by providing a berm. Outside turns are convex and more difficult to ride because they feel like they're off-camber and centrifugal force pulls the rider outside and away from the trail. Try to create inside turns in sandy areas rather than outside turns so that the force of the bike is pushing sand into the hill rather than off of it. To maintain these turns over time, periodically add organic matter to the trail bed, which will help solidify the tread.

Try Armoring.

As with wet spots, sandy areas benefit from armoring. Remember to use large rocks in your armoring. In sandy areas there is little to hold the rocks in place so they need to be big, or stone pitched, to hold over time.

Rerouting and Reclaiming Damaged Trails

Too many trails are hastily designed and become maintenance nightmares. Stand back and look at the big picture. Sometimes the best solution for eroded trails isn't aggressive maintenance. Sometimes you simply need to replace the problem trail altogether with a sustainable reroute. Designing and building a reroute may be time-consuming, but having to return every few months to fix a fundamentally flawed trail? Now, *that* is definitely a waste of time. Rerouting a trail may actually be easier and quicker in the long run than trying to fix the existing problem.

Time to Reroute?

Consider rerouting when the trail. . .

- Is consistently wet despite being properly outsloped.
- Grade exceeds 15 percent and erosion problems are evident.
- Is located in marshes, meadows, and other flatlands and isn't draining properly.
- Is damaging surrounding natural resources.
- Features poorly designed flow, which leads to user conflict or user-caused erosion.
- Contains sections that are bypassed by users because they are so rutted, muddy, or otherwise damaged.

10 Tips for Rerouting and Reclaiming a Trail

Here are some elements to bear in mind as you consider closing, rerouting, and reclaiming a trail. Remember that closing a trail can be as, if not more, time consuming as opening a new one.

1 Talk Before Rerouting.

Get permission from the land manager to reroute a section of trail, and do the proper studies before you start digging. Plant removal or passage through a particular habitat may cause concern when proposing a reroute and could require an environmental assessment. Your land manager will be able to tell you if this is the case.

2 Educate Trail Users.

Most conflict surrounding trail closures can be avoided if people understand why a route must be closed. All your hard work will be wasted if trail users continue to use the old route. Make sure to spread the word about what you are doing and why. Post signs to let people know what changes will be taking place. Ask for public feedback and recruit volunteers for the trailwork. Once work is complete, consider posting maps showing the new trail and explaining why the old trail is closed. Be positive and focus on the benefits of the reroute.

Before and after. On the top is the original trail.
Shown below is a new rolling contour reroute with the old trail completely reclaimed.

3 Design a Sustainable and More Enjoyable Trail.

A trail that's viewed by one person as an eroded maintenance nightmare might be someone else's favorite challenge. When rerouting around steep sections, look for special features that make the new route challenging while keeping grades sustainable. Make the reroute more appealing than the one it replaces. The best way to ensure that a closed trail will remain closed is to create a more attractive replacement.

4 Design a Smooth Intersection.

Create a natural, seamless transition onto the new section. Trail users shouldn't be able to recognize where the reroute begins.

5 Break Up Old Tread.

The old, compacted soil in the retired trail tread should be tilled or scarified so that new plants can seed themselves and grow. Don't skimp on this key step: Till deeply—at least 2 inches beneath the surface. Use Pulaskis, pick mattocks, or even a rototiller.

6 Control Erosion on the Closed Trail.

It is essential to stop water from flowing down the old route so that erosion does not continue. If the old trail was steep, you might need to install check dams to hold sediment and minimize the erosion. **Check dams** are easy-to-build structures, typically made of logs, rocks, or straw bales fixed across the trail to trap soil. Be sure check dams are tall so that they trap the soil and well secured so they won't wash away. If the trail you're closing is especially rocky, and little soil remains on the surface, try using burlap bags filled with dirt as your check dams. Cut an "X" into the top of a moist bag and transplant a local shrub.

7 Transplant Vegetation.

Starting plants on the old trail is the best way to restore the landscape. Disturbed soil often provides an opportunity for invasive plant species to take hold. Combat these invasives by planting native species. Completely cover and camouflage the old trail with the topsoil, plants, grasses, and small trees taken from your new route construction. Use proper transplanting techniques to reduce plant shock.

8 Disguise the Corridor.

A basic way to keep people off the closed trail is to make it look like it was never there. Your goal is to eliminate the visual corridor, including the airspace above the old trail tread. Drag logs and branches across the tread. "Plant" deadfall in the ground vertically to block the corridor at eye level. Finally, rake leaves and other organic matter over the tread to complete the disguise and encourage new plants to grow.

9 Redirect Trail Users.

Be sure to adjust signage so that it no longer directs trail users onto the closed route. Signs should now direct users onto the new trail.

10 Your Last Resort: Block the Corridor.

As a last resort you can block the beginning and end of the trail with a fence and signs. The fence will look out of place and could draw more attention to the closure, which may cause controversy. Answer expected questions by posting signage on or near the fence, explaining the reason for the closure. When the trail has been closed for a while the fence can be removed.

Trail Closure and Reclamation

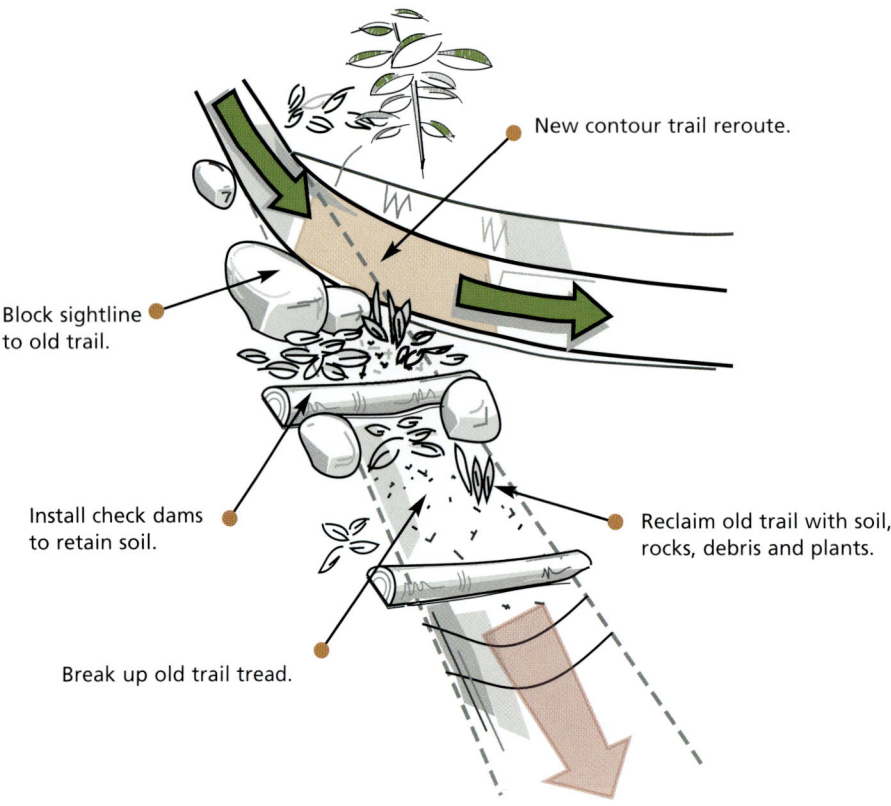

Create a smooth transition onto new trail.

New contour trail reroute.

Block sightline to old trail.

Install check dams to retain soil.

Reclaim old trail with soil, rocks, debris and plants.

Break up old trail tread.

Old fall-line trail, eroded and gullied.

Don't Make the Mistake of...

Failing to Disguise a Closed Trail. If you fail to disguise the old trail, it will continue to attract visitors and it will continue to erode. Always reclaim eroded areas with proper erosion-control techniques and reclaim all closed trails with transplanted native vegetation that conceals the old corridor.

Trail Solutions

Photo by Seb Rogers.

Part Seven: Trail Maintenance

Photo by Sterling Lorence.

Part 8: Building Challenging Trails

Throughout this book, we've discussed the fundamentals of designing and building sustainable trails. Using those principles and techniques as a foundation, you can add challenging elements to trails that will provide exhilarating experiences for mountain bikers who want to push themselves to new limits.

Whether you're constructing stunts, such as rock drops or ladder bridges, or designing a trail for downhillers, the following sections will guide you through the basics of building technical features, so that you can increase the challenge on a trail as safely and responsibly as possible.

One last important disclaimer: The dimensions we've supplied in the following sections are just starting points. You can make the trail features outlined in these sections more or less challenging by varying the dimensions. It's up to you how big, how tall, and how challenging you want to go. . .

In This Part...

- **Freeriding** 218
    - The Ups and Downs of Freeriding 218
    - Freeriding: Hype or Reality 219
    - IMBA Freeriding Position 221
- **Freeriding and Risk Management:**
  Fifteen Steps to Success 222
- **Technical Trail Features** 231
    - Three Ways to Create a Challenging Trail . . . 231
    - Using Existing Natural Trail Features 233
    - How to Design a Drop-Off 234
    - Construction Guidelines for
      Wooden Technical Features 235
    - Ten Tips for Building a Ladder Bridge 239
- **Downhill Trails** 242
    - Fifteen Tips for Building Excellent
      Downhill Trails 242

Freeriding

The Ups and Downs of Freeriding

When a freerider falls while attempting a jump in the Utah desert, does anyone hear it? If the answer is "yes," how does that person react?

IMBA has had to consider the ups and downs of freeriding since this brand of cycling took root late in the 1990s. First we had to define it, because freeriding means different things to different people. Then we had to decide if freeriding was fundamentally an asset or a challenge to our sport and our core mission.

Several years and countless meetings later, we have some answers. IMBA has defined freeriding as "a style of mountain biking that celebrates the challenges and spirit of technical riding and downhilling." We have committed staff time and resources to creating strategies that make it work.

The Buzz

There's no denying that freeriding continues to create a positive buzz in the mountain biking world, almost like snowboarding and telemarking sparked a stale ski industry. Freeriding is inspiring a new era of suspension technology and customer excitement.

Freeriding is pulling ski resorts back into the mountain bike–tourism game. Facilities that were once underutilized in warm-weather months are proving to be ideal settings for freeride parks, technical downhill trails, and dirt jumps that attract visitors, keeping staff employed year round.

Freeriding resonates with a new generation of riders. Whether soaring off jumps, teetering on high-rise stunts, or just balancing on log rides, they're passionate about riding bikes. They are—at least in part—the future of mountain biking.

The Bust

The downside of freeriding continues to threaten our sport. Coupled with the explosion of X Games–style events and their appearance in the media, freeriding has caught the eye of the general public and advertising agencies. Ask a random person on a sidewalk to describe mountain biking and there's a good chance the answer will include big-air crazy riding. In a litigious society, this isn't a positive association, particularly as it bounces through the mind of a risk-averse trail manager.

Cross-country riding on singletrack trails has already been hurt by unauthorized trailbuilding fueled by freeriding. Land managers revile illegal trail construction, particularly when the clandestine work includes rickety, wooden structures. In some locations, they've reacted by imposing a moratorium on new trails—or even worse, banning bikes altogether. We have no viable defense for riding practices that destroy plants or otherwise damage the environment. When this type of reckless behavior is linked to mountain biking, we can only lose ground.

Additionally, the speed and on-the-edge elements of freeriding don't mix well with hiking, horseback riding, or even cross-country mountain biking. Providing single-use trails for many user groups is expensive and often impossible because of land limitations. As a result, support for new, separate, freeriding trails is hard to find.

Still, at the end of the day, freeriding is basically just advanced-level mountain biking. When viewed in this way and managed appropriately, it's unquestionably positive for our sport and it deserves to thrive. That's why IMBA is committed to making freeriding work.

IMBA has defined freeriding as "a style of mountain biking that celebrates the challenges and spirit of technical riding and downhilling." Photo by Sterling Lorence.

Freeriding: Hype or Reality?

Shimano, the largest bicycle component manufacturer in the world, recently unveiled a new gruppo designed specifically for freeriding, called Saint. They heralded Saint's debut with a bold, multi-media marketing campaign.

When a company the size of Shimano invests massive resources to address a new segment of our sport, it's significant. And Shimano isn't the only bike company focusing on freeriding. Almost every bike supplier has at least one freeride bike in their product line, with some companies giving it much more attention.

A quick thumb through any mountain bike magazine shows that freeriding clearly has the focus of the bicycling media. Mountain biking films feature freeriding almost exclusively.

Perhaps even more telling is the prevalence of freeriding in mainstream media. Freeriders are shown in advertising for everything from cars to credit cards and chocolate milk. There's even a PlayStation 2 video game, "Downhill Domination," in which players can select a choice of big-hit, full-suspension bikes and joystick their way over a simulated downhill course with huge cliff drops, while avoiding trees, forest fires, moose, and other obstacles.

While freeriding has certainly captured a lot of the hype surrounding mountain biking, it's not clear if this interest accurately reflects the way most people ride. According to the Bicycle Product Suppliers Association, 567,119 full-suspension bikes were shipped to dealers in the U.S. in 2003—only 9 percent of all 26-inch-wheel bikes distributed.

The wooden trail features associated with freeriding were first built in British Columbia to raise the trail above the soggy and tangled forest floor. Photo by Sterling Lorence.

In a recent poll of IMBA members, only 3 percent selected freeriding as the type of riding they do most often, compared to 62 percent who ride cross country. However, when asked about their riding skill level, 71 percent of IMBA members said they were advanced or better. While these people may not classify themselves as freeriders, they would likely relish the opportunity and challenge offered by more technical trails.

IMBA membership, however, may not be the best barometer of freeriding's popularity. While the success of freeriding in British Columbia has been well documented, the groundswell of freeriding momentum is not limited to this Canadian province. A number of authorized freeride areas have been built throughout the United States, and IMBA receives daily calls from land managers and mountain bikers looking to establish new places to freeride.

Freeriding is especially appealing to today's X Games–influenced youth. Freeriding looks cool, and kids want to be a part of it. Kids cycling groups are gravitating toward freeriding by offering technical riding instruction.

A key component to increasing freeride opportunities is getting freeriders more involved in advocacy. Although several new freeride-specific advocacy clubs have been formed, this is not the norm. Most freeriders are either unaware of IMBA, or don't care to be a part of it. Simply put, they are more interested in just riding their bikes.

Freeriding is clearly a major part of our sport that is here to stay. It's imperative that existing clubs and IMBA find ways to connect with it to create the next generation of mountain bike advocates and assure the future of our sport.

IMBA's Freeriding Position Statement

1. Freeriding is a style of mountain biking that celebrates the challenges and spirit of technical riding and downhilling.

2. IMBA supports freeriding as long as it's practiced responsibly and in appropriate locations. We are committed to helping develop authorized trails and riding areas that appeal to all mountain bikers. We are continually developing educational tools to help land managers, clubs, and individual riders develop sustainable, appropriate freeriding options.

3. The future of all aspects of mountain biking depends on cooperation with land managers and our collective commitment to protecting the natural environment.

4. Young mountain bikers identify with the challenges and spirit of freeriding. By recognizing and supporting this enthusiasm, IMBA will help insure the future of mountain biking.

5. IMBA supports downhill racing. We develop and recommend sustainable course-construction techniques.

6. IMBA supports off-trail riding only in appropriate, designated special-use areas.

Photo by Photo-John.

Freeriding and Risk Management: Fifteen Steps For Success

The freeride movement went through an awkward adolescence in the 1990s. Early movies and magazine stories gave many people the impression that freeriding was synonymous with riding off-trail and in a reckless fashion. As a result, some land managers cling to the notion that technically challenging trails are fundamentally unsafe. They oppose freeriding out of a fear of potential injuries and lawsuits. The good news is that mountain bikers can responsibly create and ride challenging trails without sparking liability concerns or provoking lawsuits. In this section we present 15 steps to managing freeriding risk.

1 Be Aware of Possible Social Issues.

There are many social and emotional issues surrounding freeriding. Technical riding areas, both natural and constructed, have been opposed by a variety of groups in the past, including land managers, environmentalists, neighbors, other trail users, and even other mountain bikers. If you're planning to develop new freeriding opportunities, you should be aware of some of the social issues that may come into play. These issues can be effectively addressed through open communication and understanding.

2 Build Partnerships and Communicate.

Successful trail projects require close collaboration among freeriders, land managers and local mountain bike clubs. By consulting with freeriders and incorporating their suggestions into trail management decisions, planners can develop trail systems that have broader appeal. This effort will also reduce unauthorized trail construction. Judgmental attitudes and negative stereotypes from either side can undermine successful partnerships.

3 Determine Shared Use or Single Use.

IMBA supports shared-use and single-use trails. However, a trail specifically designated for freeriders will usually be more successful if it is single use. Frequent, technical trail features are unsuitable for equestrians and may not provide an enjoyable experience for hikers. Adding technical trail features to a crowded trail shared by joggers, dog walkers, and inexperienced trail users is rarely a good idea. However, shared-use trails that offer technical challenge are feasible in the right situation. Backcountry trails that experience little traffic and purpose-built trails, where the challenge is located on one side of the trail, can be technical and still host a variety of users.

4. Understand Local Liability Laws.

One of the first things people want to know is, "Will I be held liable if someone gets hurt while riding a trail on my property?" Most states have laws, called Recreational Use Statutes, that protect land managers and property owners from being held liable in the event that someone is injured while recreating on their property.

Recreational Use Statutes vary from place to place, so we recommend that you research the laws governing your own area. You can find a primer on U.S. liability laws and analyses of Recreational Use Statutes for each state at imba.com. Private landowners are rarely at risk of being held liable for injuries incurred on their property unless they charge the public a fee to access their land, or it can be proven that the injury was a clear result of their gross negligence.

It's important to note that while Recreational Use Statutes often prevent landowners from ultimately being held liable, they do *not* prevent lawsuits from being filed in the first place. It takes time and money to mount a defense against a lawsuit, regardless of the outcome. Therefore, the goal is to avoid lawsuits by practicing diligent risk management.

5. Understand Related Case Law.

Case law is based on how the courts have ruled in the past. These previous judgments can help demonstrate that, generally speaking, courts have upheld limiting landowner liability related to trail use. Records show that few lawsuits have been filed that relate to mountain biking incidents caused by trail conditions. Of the suits filed, hardly any were decided against the landowner.

If local government officials are wary of lawsuits, you could research and include specific case law in your trail proposal. Consider enlisting a local attorney/mountain biker to help research case law and overcome liability concerns.

6. Provide for Skills Progression.

It's important to introduce freeriding challenges to users sequentially so they can enhance their skills in a managed environment. Construct a practice area with a wide variety of challenging obstacles, from easy to difficult. The most challenging features should mirror the most difficult obstacles users can expect to encounter on the trail system. Another great idea is to offer regularly scheduled skills clinics. In addition to teaching riding techniques, include tips on responsible trail use.

7. Place Technical Features Appropriately.

There are two suitable locations for technical trail features: in a challenge park and on a trail. The placement of a technical feature on a trail is determined by a number of factors. Is the trail shared use or single use? What are the skill levels of the trail's users? When assessing user abilities, don't forget to consider the varying skill levels of all visitors—not just mountain bikers.

Challenge parks and dirt jumping areas should include a wide variety of challenge, from easy to difficult, to provide for skills progression. Location: Tamarack Resort, Idaho. Photo courtesy Tamarack Resort.

8 Develop an Effective Signage System.

It is important to develop a comprehensive signage system for your trail network. Signs should be placed at the main trailhead, trail intersections, and other key locations. The main trailhead kiosk should describe trail difficulty using a trail rating system. Pay particular attention to signs at the intersections of trails with differing difficulty levels. Also, it's important to sign before very challenging technical trail features, like big drop offs, narrow bridges or other elements of increased risk. When placing signs, consider where you are. Trails with high use should be well signed. Conversely, a technical trail deep in the backcountry should have far fewer signs. Signs can be an intrusion on a visitors outdoor experience—use them with care.

9 Utilize Trail Filters.

A trail filter, sometimes referred to as a gateway or qualifier, is a high-skill-level, low-consequence obstacle that demonstrates the difficulty of the upcoming trail or trail feature. Examples of a filter are a narrow, handlebar-width opening between two trees, a rock garden, or a rock step. Place filters at the beginning of each advanced trail and just before technical features. By making the entrances to technical trails and features difficult, you prevent unprepared riders from overstepping their abilities.

This sign at the Keystone, Colorado, freeride park clearly describes the risks of man-made terrain.

10. Provide Optional Lines.

There should always be an easier, alternate route around a technical feature. On advanced trails, the technical trail feature can be located on the main line, with an easier option to the side. On intermediate or beginner routes, technical trail features should be outside the main trail flow—even disguised from the main trail—so they serve as an option for advanced riders seeking a more challenging line. Optional lines can potentially be in the same corridor as the main trail; for example, a drop-off could vary in height from one side of the trail to the other.

Creating Optional Lines

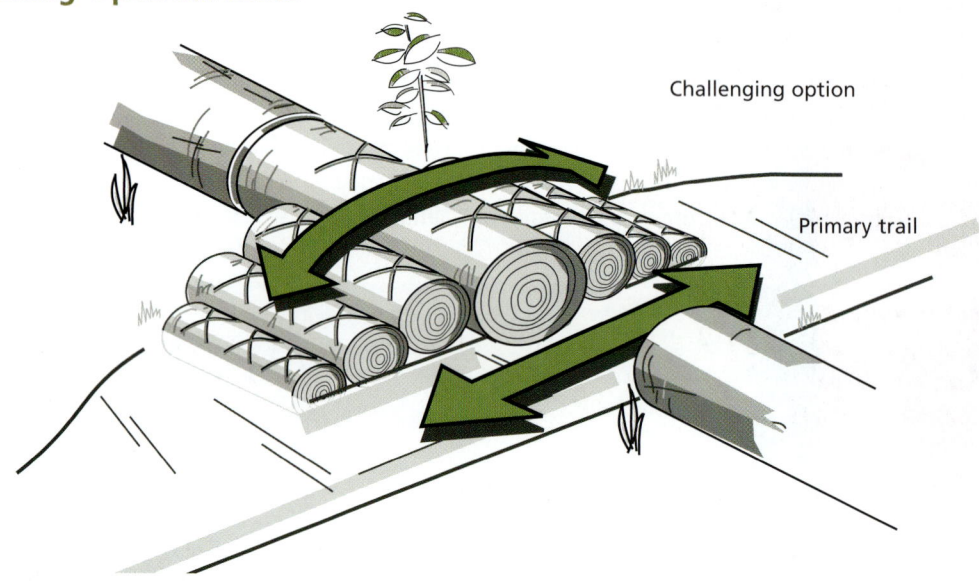

11. Provide Adequate Fall Zones.

A **fall zone** is the area adjacent to a technical trail feature, which provides a clear landing for a rider who has failed to negotiate the obstacle. Fall zones should be located at the bottom of descents, on the outside of corners, on either the side of the trail, and around obstacles. Consider removing branches, stumps, logs, rocks, and other protruding objects that could cause injury if the fall zone is utilized. Another option is to add mulch or dirt to further soften a fall zone.

Fall Zone

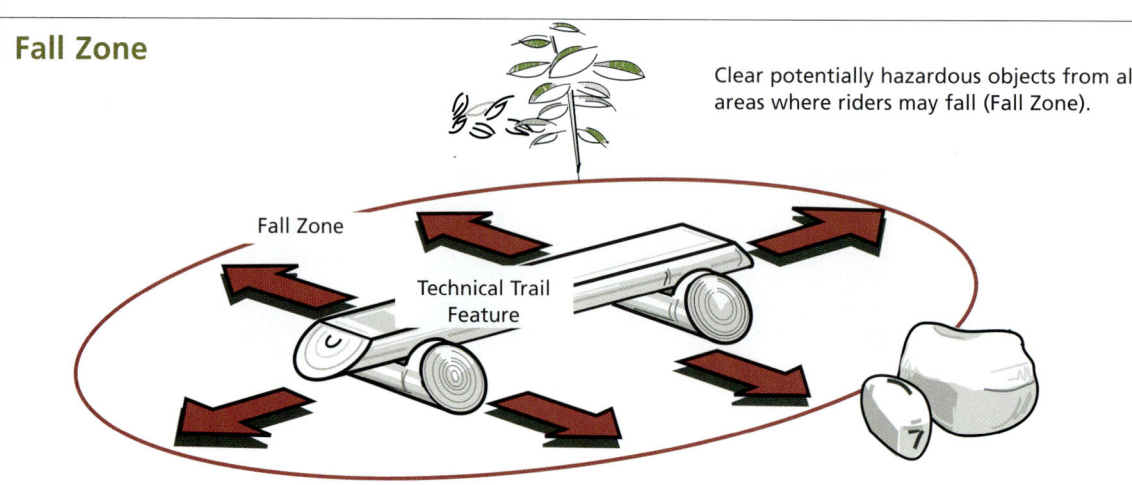

Trail Solutions

12 Follow Construction Guidelines.

Both natural and man-made additions to trails must be durable, predictable, and designed to minimize injuries when trail users fail to negotiate them properly.

13 Develop an Inspection and Maintenance Log.

All trails require consistent inspection and maintenance. Technical trail features should be inspected for durability, predictability, and safety. Consistent maintenance logs should be kept to ensure trails and features are being kept up to standard. Different trails require different levels of maintenance, depending on a variety of factors, including climate, volume of use, and the number and type of trail features. Wooden structures, like bridges and teeter-totters, require routine upkeep. You must be committed to their inspection and maintenance.

14 Designate a Risk Management Coordinator.

Recruit an individual who will be responsible for making sure the risk management techniques outlined here are properly implemented and documented. This person will also evaluate all of your safety measures and will work with the landowner or land manager to create an action plan to follow in case of emergencies on the trail. Assign responsibility to an individual who is known for his or her conscientious behavior and attention to detail. Remember that the risk management coordinator shouldn't be saddled with implementing the 15 Steps alone. Rather, he or she should serve as a point-person for a group of volunteers who will help make the trail a safe and enjoyable place to recreate.

15 The Final Step: Be Prepared to Give Answers.

When seeking to create freeriding opportunities, a written trail proposal may be necessary. When freeride and technical trails are proposed, it is important to address risk management concerns. Consult your land manager to determine what steps need to be taken, and what level of detail is required in a proposal.

Bright Idea

Work with Land Managers to Create Special-Use Challenge Parks. Technical trail features are becoming increasingly popular with mountain bikers. Many land managers are open to the idea of having special-use zones or playgrounds for bikers, similar to skateboard or snowboard parks. Work with your local land manager to create these opportunities.

Freeriding Flies in Florida

Quiet Waters Park is located in southern Florida, near Deerfield Beach. Though there have been mountain bike trails in the park since the 1990s, park managers only recently agreed to devote space for more advanced, freeride-style trails. Club Mud, an IMBA-affiliated mountain bike group, secured approval and built the project. In this interview, Harvey Schneider, a Club Mud director, explains his club's success.

What does Club Mud's expert riding area look like?
Our expert riding area consists of numerous dirt jumps, elevated boardwalks, and drops. It's a separate area in the middle of the trail system with one heavily filtered entrance. It's completely sealed off with fencing made of natural deadfall.

How do you make sure that less-skilled riders don't hurt themselves on the stunts?
There's a 3- by 6-foot canvas banner sign at the entrance that states: "Expert Riding Area. If in doubt, please stay out." We have about 20 signs posted throughout the area warning people of the dangers and assumed risk of riding there. It's very clear.

Were park managers instantly open to the idea of a freeride area?
The initial undertaking was actually a bit of a gamble. We submitted plans to the park and were given the go-ahead with no guarantees that they would ultimately approve it. Basically they wanted to see it built first. It took about eight months to complete and cost a few thousand dollars. We all held our breath for the final inspection, but we passed with flying colors and were commended for the quality of our construction.

It sounds like you had to have a lot of faith in your land manager and vice versa.
The process definitely requires trust from both sides, and that takes time. Club Mud began with a few people simply maintaining trails in two different parks that were not being maintained. We've also appointed one liaison for each park whose job is to promptly respond to inquiries or requests, and to make sure the park manager's concerns are addressed quickly.

A lot of park managers are unfamiliar with the whole concept of freeriding. How did Club Mud go about convincing park managers that a technical skills area would be a good thing for their park?
All recreational activities on public land, from softball to rollerblading and everything in between, come with a degree of risk. Managing that risk is simply a matter of establishing and abiding by reasonable guidelines. Mountain biking is a new territory for many land

managers, so it's important for the local clubs to work with land managers to establish risk management policies regarding mountain biking as well as trail and structure building. We established strict design and construction guidelines for the area trails and the technical trail features. We assured the park managers that these construction guidelines would be strictly adhered to and that the freeride area would not be mistaken for part of the regular trail system.

Most park managers are concerned about risk and liability. How did you persuade them that Club Mud had covered those issues adequately?
Four specific things were done to mitigate liability. We stipulated that the entrance would be built so that riders would have to carry their bike in to the area; we required that a fence be built around the area so that there was only one access point; we posted appropriate signage throughout the area; and we maintained strict guidelines for construction materials. All wood used in the construction was pressure treated, and everything was lag bolted together.

It sounds like your club did a lot of work to get approval. Was it worth it?
Definitely. Now that we've established our credibility, our plans are approved or rejected in advance. We currently have plans pending for a dual speed-trials course and additional dirt jumps, as part of an "Extreme Day" event, and we will soon be submitting plans for phase two of the expert riding area.

The expert riding area in southern Florida's Quiet Waters Park utilizes clear signage to help manage risk.

Part Eight: Building Challenging Trails

The easiest way to add challenge is to utilize existing natural features, like rock slabs. Photo by John Gibson.

Building Technical Trail Features

3 Ways to Create a Challenging Trail

1 Existing Natural Features

The easiest way to build a technically challenging trail is to incorporate existing natural features. Use rock slabs, ledges, rock gardens, and fallen trees as control points as you plan the route and layout of your trail. By including natural features in your design, you also will highlight the landscape and minimize social trails.

2 Enhanced Natural Features

The next approach is to increase the technical challenge of your trail by manipulating natural materials. Use rocks and logs to create drop-offs, rock gardens, boulder rides, log pyramids, and log rides. Building enhanced natural features is a good way to add technical difficulty to trails in areas where challenging terrain is limited.

3 Man-Made Structures

Another way to increase challenge on a trail is to add man-made structures. Ladder bridges, wooden ramps, and teeter-totters are prime examples. These structures often require artificial materials such as processed lumber and fasteners.

Rock vs. Wood: Which is the Better Material for Technical Trails?

When building technical trail features, you have two basic materials to work with: rock and wood. Factors to consider are durability, predictability, maintenance, and aesthetics.

In most cases, rock is the best material to use. Well-built rock structures will withstand decades of trail use, will ride the same day after day, and will rarely require maintenance. Generally, rock blends well into the surrounding environment.

This doesn't mean that you should avoid building wooden technical features. A well-designed and maintained wooden feature can safely stand the test of time on the trail. Careful attention must be paid to construction and maintenance to ensure the durability of wooden features; rot-resistant wood and appropriate fasteners will help your feature last. It's also important to use materials and construction techniques that match the surrounding environment.

This awesome log ride is an example of using enhanced natural materials to add challenge. Location: British Columbia.

Trail Solutions

Using Existing Natural Features

When many people think of technical trail features, the images that come to mind are of wooden "stunts." While we'll explore such devices shortly, let's first talk about incorporating existing natural features into your trail. Such features include rock slabs, ledges, and rock gardens. There is a real benefit to routing your technical trail over such structures, as they require relatively little maintenance and you do not have to move or manipulate them.

Incorporate Natural Drop-Offs.

Incorporate natural ledges and drops into your trail design. Be sure drop-offs fit the overall flow and skill-level of the trail. Transitions are important. A tight turn following a drop-off will cause cyclists to skid or ride off the trail. High drops can offer two lines—one difficult and one easier—by using a ramp or chock stone.

Route Trails Through Rock Gardens.

Rock gardens are tricky and fun for a variety of users, so route your trail over and through rocky areas. People expect rocks in nature and won't avoid them if they seem natural. The key is that no matter how difficult a rock section might be, it must be easier to travel than the area around it. This gives people no incentive to wander off the trail and prevents trail widening and shortcutting.

Route Steep Trails Over Rock Slabs.

Locate solid rock slabs or faces where a trail can run straight down the fall line without causing erosion. When designing a feature like this into a trail, open the runout to prevent heavy braking, or armor it with rock. Use a grade reversal or dip above the steep section to keep water off the trail.

Utilize Rock Chokes.

A series of boulders staggered on either side of the trail can provide a narrow choke or slot that enhances the ride. This strategy can slow users and add challenge. Make sure the narrowing flows naturally with the trail, or people will find it annoying instead of interesting, and may create a new route around it.

Route Your Trail Over Fallen Trees.

In this last case, we'll deviate from the rock theme for a moment. Trees that have fallen over a trail can be incorporated into the design. Some trail users like logs for the test they present, while others will avoid them by going around—even if it means leaving the trail. In order to accommodate everyone, be sure the log only covers part of the trail, allowing users to scale the obstacle or skirt it. (This won't work on tight singletrack.) Make sure there are good sightlines in both directions and that the direct line is over the log. Try to keep the trail from widening at this point by using rocks or other obstacles to corral the trail.

How to Design a Drop-Off

Start with a grade reversal.

The brief change in the trail grade will help divert water and prevent it from damaging the trail and feature. An added benefit is that the reversal will help curb the speed of approaching riders, so that by the time they reach the drop-off, they're in control and prepared for the challenge.

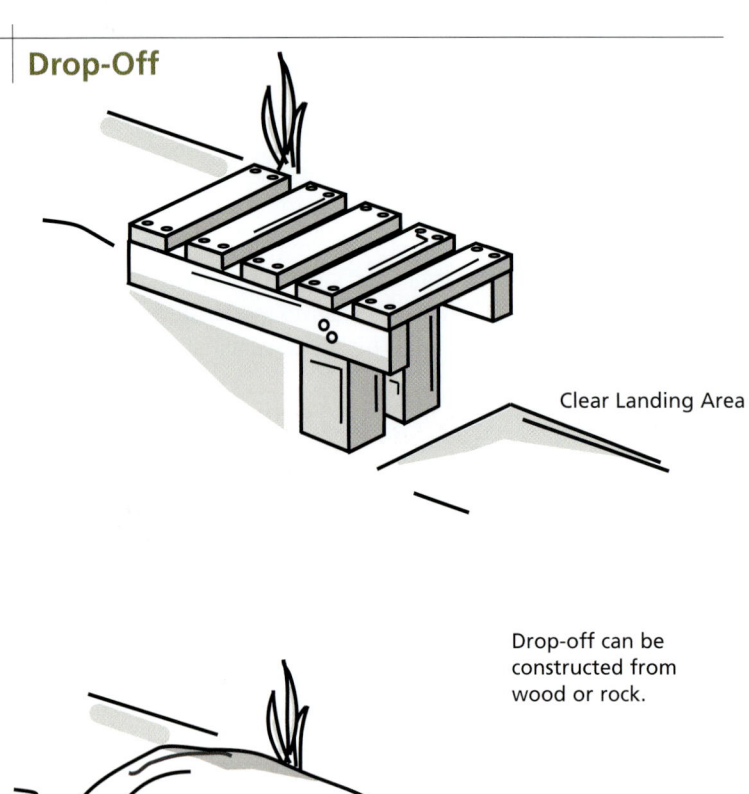

Drop-Off

Clear Landing Area

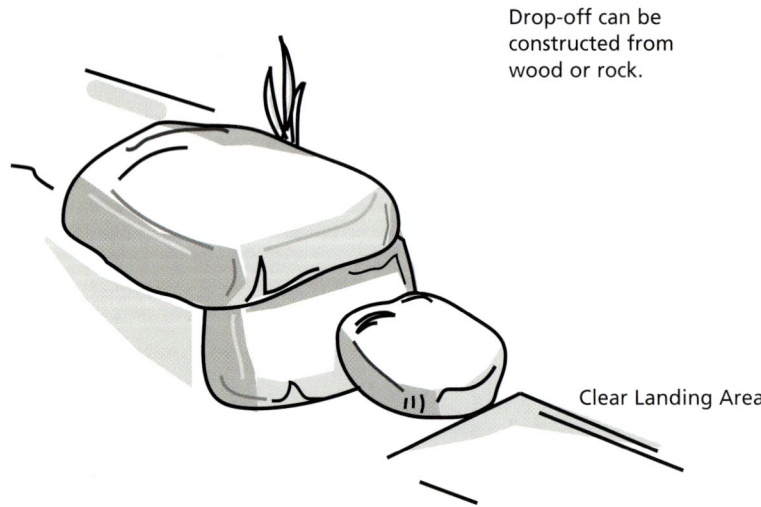

Drop-off can be constructed from wood or rock.

Clear Landing Area

Pay special attention to the landing zone and the fall zone.

This is an area one- to two-bikes long, and almost as wide, that slopes downward from the drop-off anywhere from 5 to 15 percent. Be sure to clear all obstacles from the tread, remove sharp rocks and root wads, and cut back any branches that are in the fall zone. The corridor and ceiling should be cleared to a greater width and height than the rest of the trail in order to provide a clear view of the landing area and allow for various drop distances. By adding a challenging element to the trail, you are increasing the chances of a fall, so it is important to build even more safety into the design here.

To help the landing zone stand up to repeated drops, scrape all organic material (vegetative matter, roots, leaves, etc.) from the surface of the trail tread, and expose the good, hard mineral soil. If you're building a particularly high drop-off, or one that's going to receive a lot of use, you may need to armor the landing with flat-sided rocks.

Trail Solutions

End with a grade reversal.

A grade reversal at the end of the drop will help to shed any water that collects there and will check the speed of riders before they hit the rest of the trail. It is very important that this whole section has good sightlines, for both the dropper's benefit, and for the trail users approaching from the other direction. It's hard to slow down when your wheels are off the ground, so make sure that riders attempting the drop have a clear view of what (and who) is below.

Maintenance on a drop-off amounts to periodically clearing the corridor, keeping sightlines open, removing any dangerous roots or rocks from the tread, and fortifying the drop and landing zone if necessary.

Construction Guidelines for Wooden Technical Trail Features

Before You Start:

- Make sure to get permission from your local land manager.

- All wooden technical trail features (TTF) should be carefully planned. Create a schematic design that shows the trail and all elements of the TTF including scale, location, dimensions, materials, fasteners, filters, fall zones, signs and optional lines. Get your plan approved before beginning construction.

- All wooden features should be designed and constructed with the assistance of an experienced carpenter.

- The TTF should generally follow the same design, management, construction, and maintenance practices used for an exterior deck, a staircase, or a pedestrian bridge.

Select durable wood that is naturally rot-resistant, and remove bark to prevent decay.

Part Eight: Building Challenging Trails

Materials

- Materials should be selected, installed, and maintained for durability, strength, riding predictability, aesthetics, and environmental acceptability.

- Select durable wood that is naturally resistant to moisture, decay, sun, heat, cold, and insects. Some examples include redwood, cedar, white oak, cypress, locust, and manzanita. There are also several environmentally friendly, commercially treated woods that are extremely durable and weather resistant.

- Don't use wooden pallets, scrap lumber, plywood, soft woods such as pine, or other inappropriate materials that will quickly deteriorate or become unstable.

- Don't use dead trees, logs, or stumps unless they are of a sufficient size or type of wood to withstand deterioration. Certain types of weather-resistant dead wood can be used if they are properly prepared.

- Do not use living trees in any way.

- Rough-sawn or hand-prepared wood will blend into primitive locations better than commercial lumber.

Construction Techniques

- Wooden features should be stronger and more stable than the greatest anticipated force and weight. Use cross and diagonal bracing. The strength of the TTF shouldn't rely on the shear strength of the fasteners.

- The surface finish should be such that there are no protrusions or excessively sharp edges that might pose a safety hazard.

- Decking should not extend more than a few inches beyond supports. For example, the decking on a ladder bridge shouldn't extend more than a couple of inches beyond the stringers.

- Decking planks should be spaced slightly to aid drainage. Avoid gaps of greater than a couple of inches on the riding surface.

- Use appropriate fasteners. Select high quality screws, bolts, and nails designed for exterior use. Fasteners must be strong, secure, and corrosion resistant.

- If additional traction is required, add durable, predictable, and aesthetically appropriate texture to the TTF surface. Some of the better methods include using wood with natural texture such as rough-sawn or hand-split timbers, adding texture to wood by scoring it with a saw, covering the riding line with anti-slip paint designed for exterior or marine use, or attaching diamond mesh lath (made from galvanized steel and used for stucco application). Chicken wire and roofing materials typically aren't durable.

- The approach to the TTF should be on dry and stable ground to help prevent water and mud from being carried onto the wood, which can cause deterioration and a slippery surface.

- Special attention should be given to abutments and places where the TTF contacts the ground. Wood should generally not touch the ground directly. Use foundation materials such as rock or pre-cast concrete footings to prevent dirt and moisture from deteriorating the base of the TTF.

- Consider prefabricating the structure before bringing it to the trail. Be sure to make careful measurements in the field first.

In addition to these guidelines, consider the advice in the previous section, Freeriding and Risk Management: 15 Steps to Success, and IMBA's other guidelines for technical trail features and traditional trail design and construction techniques in this book and at imba.com.

Other advice may be found by researching trail-bridge and home-deck building resources, as well as consulting the "Whistler Trail Standards" located on the web at whistlercycling.ca.

Part Eight: Building Challenging Trails

Add Some Ewok to Your Trails

We often hear mountain bikers describe their favorite freeride route as being "like Ewok Village." While certainly not a technical definition, it conjures a clear image of a serpentine trail with flowing obstacles that completely blend with the environment, immersing the trail user in the experience. Such trails are environmentally friendly, aesthetically pleasing and—when built with the utmost care—an artistic expression.

Every trailbuilder should try to design trails and technical trail features that are sustainable and match their environment. A 10-foot high ladder bridge, for example, may fit well in a lush forest, but it's going to be out of place atop a desert plateau. A rock drop, on the other hand, might fit well in that same location and be the preferred approach to increasing the difficulty of the trail.

When building wooden technical trail features, choose wood that blends with the natural surroundings and is common in your local area. Remember that rough-sawn wood looks more natural than factory-prepared lumber. Work to keep sign pollution to a minimum. Never ever attach technical trail features to live trees.

When building wooden technical trail features, try to use wood that blends with the natural surroundings. Location: British Columbia. Photo by Sterling Lorence.

Get in the habit of practicing strict Leave No Trace ethics (visit lnt.org). Avoid trampling sensitive areas and vegetation. Clean all fasteners, wood scraps, trash, and anything else that would let people know you were there. By putting a lot of love into the trail and the surrounding environment, it's possible to create an experience that earns your trail the coveted "Ewok Village" description.

10   Tips For Building a Ladder Bridge

Originally designed to span wet areas, a ladder bridge is a simple elevated boardwalk and one of the easiest wooden trail features to build. Here are 10 tips for making them fun, durable, and safe.

1   Follow IMBA's Freeriding Guidelines.

These tips provide important information on risk management, design, materials, and construction techniques. Before starting, make sure to get permission from the local land manager.

Ladder Bridge

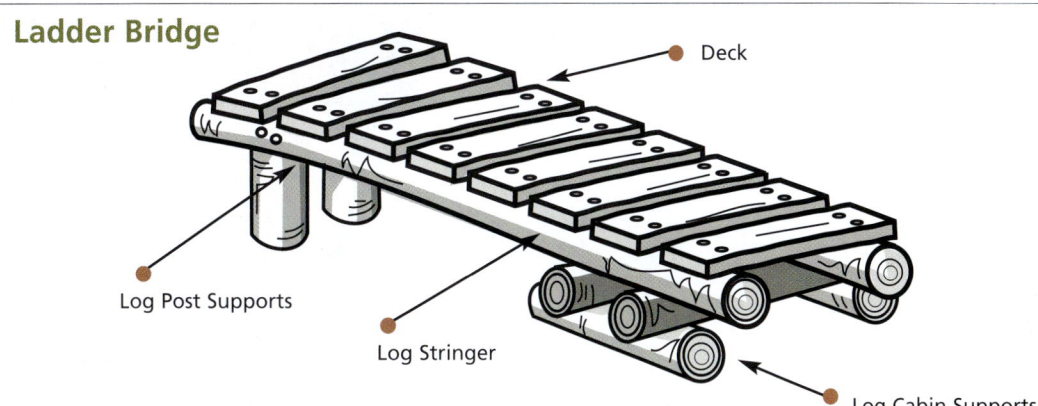

May be constructed from hand-prepared logs or dimensional lumber.

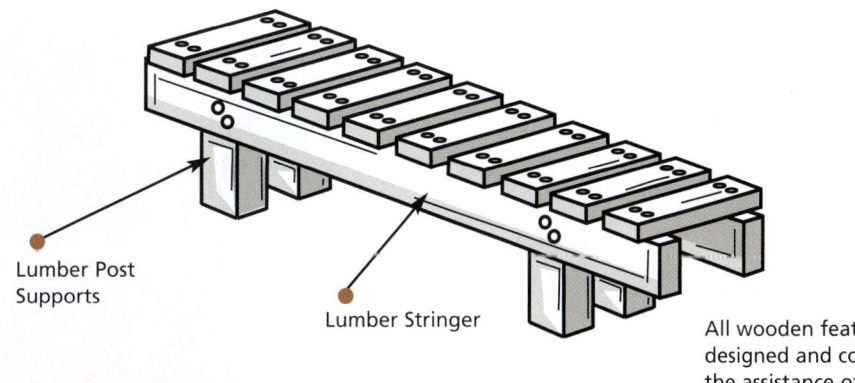

All wooden features should be designed and constructed with the assistance of an experienced carpenter.

2   Locate the ladder bridge properly.

Ladder bridges can be added to trails of varying difficulty. Just be sure that the challenge matches the skill of the expected riders. On beginner trails, ladder bridges should be wide and low to the ground. As skill levels increase, the structures can be higher, narrower, and incorporate turns, camber changes, and drop-offs.

On beginner trails, place the ladder bridge to the side for an optional, more challenging route. On advanced trails, the feature may be located in the main line. However, a clearly visible option around the ladder bridge should always be incorporated into the design.

British Columbia's South Island Mountain Bike Society partnered with local land managers to build this sweet bridge with a super-skinny optional line.

3. Elevate the ladder bridge.

The feature can be raised off the ground in various ways, but be sure to use a durable and sustainable method. Some techniques include large rocks, strong tree stumps that won't rot, well-designed wooden posts, or a log-cabin style crib. Never attach a ladder bridge to live trees, and avoid using rot-prone or flimsy deadfall.

4. Armor the entrance and exit.

The trail surface at the entrance and exit of a ladder bridge will require additional hardening, especially on steeper grades and landing areas. See Part 6 for detailed armoring techniques.

5. Vary length, height, and width to add appeal and challenge.

Part of the appeal of a ladder bridge is simply that it offers a different challenge and aesthetic than is found in the natural environment. A ladder bridge, by design, is not necessarily challenging. The challenge comes from the length and narrowness of the deck and its distance from the ground. Sometimes the mental challenge of balancing on a narrow bridge is greater than the physical risk.

6. Add turns and camber.

A great way to add challenge to a ladder bridge is to incorporate turns. The amount of deck space provided for the turn should be consistent with the style of trail and technical features nearby. On beginner and intermediate trails, the turning radius and deck must be wide, but it can be narrower on advanced trails. Changing the camber of a ladder bridge is another way to add challenge. Banked turns are great ways to add flow and fun.

7. Change the incline and decline.

Ladder bridges with sharp inclines that require pedaling, and declines that demand breaking, can be very challenging. Again, the steepness should match the surrounding trail style.

8. Join ladder bridges together to create alternate lines.

Ladder bridges can be quite elaborate. Consider building alternate bridge lines that offer different levels of challenge. Offshoots can be narrower than the main bridge, provide separate exits or drop-offs, or include more turns.

9. Incorporate drop-offs.

Drop-offs from the end of the bridge to the ground or onto another bridge will add challenge. The height of the drop should match the challenge level of the trail. Make sure to consider the forces of a drop-off in the design of your bridge and landing zone.

10. Combine ladder bridges with other technical trail features.

Ladder bridges can be linked with teeter-totters, A-frames, and other technical trail features to form a flowing series of challenges. Get creative!

Building Downhill Trails

Downhill riding is all about rhythm and flow. As they descend the trail, downhillers go as fast as possible by finding the best lines and riding smoothly. Advanced riders tend to ride faster lines—those that require a higher level of strength, agility, and reaction.

A downhill trail should be technical, with features and lines that challenge riders of all abilities. Here are some ideas to help you create trails that are exhilarating for downhillers.

15 Tips for Building Excellent Downhill Trails

1 Involve Downhillers.

Input from downhill riders is essential to creating a good downhill trail, and the design and construction of the trail should be directed, at least in part, by a downhiller. The ideal rider/consultant has experience building downhill trails and understands the fundamentals of sustainable trail and feature construction. This person should also have peer respect and the ability to ride tough trails confidently and smoothly. He or she must be able to plan and build a trail that will be fun and rideable for the full range of intended users.

2 Determine the Trail Placement.

We define downhill trails as single-use, one-way trails with technical trail features designed for the sport of downhill mountain biking. These trails should not be shared with other users unless those users know and accept that mountain bikers will be riding the trail at high speeds. Downhill trails should be separated from trails designed for other users in order to avoid conflict. Building two downhill trails—one beginner/intermediate and one expert/pro—will reduce conflict between riders of different abilities and speeds and provide each group with a more enjoyable experience.

3 Incorporate Vertical Drop.

An ideal downhill trail will have a vertical drop of least 1,000 feet. An epic trail will have more than 2,000 feet. The more vertical drop the better! However, even locations without big mountains can have great downhill trails if the design is creative and fun.

4 Plan for Shuttling.

Downhill trails are almost always located on mountains that have summit access via automobile or ski lift. Unfortunately, one of the most common problems associated with downhilling is the social impact of automobile shuttling on the outside community. The increased traffic on and parking alongside public roads—not to mention truckloads of bikers doing laps from dawn to dusk—may upset locals. This conflict often results in trail closures; so if you predict shuttling will occur at your trail, take steps to ensure that it won't anger residents and other trail users.

There should be convenient, proper parking and turn-around areas at the top and bottom of your trail. If you are choosing a location for a new trail, be sure the nearby shuttle route does not go through a populated or busy area. Downhillers often drive their own cars to the trailhead and then pile into a truck to shuttle their runs. In some cases, a racing team will use a van with a trailer, making it possible to shuttle up to 15 riders at a time. Your parking area should be able to accommodate these large vehicles and trailers.

Input from experienced downhill riders is essential to creating a good downhill trail. Photo courtesy Giant Bicycles.

If a nearby road will be used for shuttling, aim to create only one entrance and one exit for the entire downhill trail system. This will help minimize conflict with other road users by concentrating mountain bikers and their vehicles at two locations—the top and bottom.

5 Minimize Trail Intersections.

Minimize the number of other trails that crisscross a downhill trail. Given the speed of downhill riders, it is important that downhill trails feature elements that slow riders before they arrive at intersections and meet other visitors. Just be sure the slowing devices blend with the trail style and are not too abrupt or potentially dangerous. A series of two or three insloped turns, also known as berms, work well to slow riders smoothly and in a fun manner. Each turn should point the rider slightly back up hill and lead into a somewhat tighter turn ending at a yield sign. Avoid using excessively restrictive devices to corral or slow riders, as these elements can be dangerous and riders may collide with them. Make sure that sightlines at intersections allow plenty of time for riders and other visitors to anticipate these crossings.

6 Include Open and Flowing Sections.

These wider, faster sections allow riders to choose from a variety of lines, especially through turn entrances and exits. They also test a rider's ability to keep his or her bike stable and balanced at high speeds. Some racecourses are as wide as 50 feet. These sections are often rough and fast (up to 50 miles per hour). While ski resorts have historically supported the use of broad corridors for downhill racing, securing permission to build and maintain them in public parks and forests is difficult.

Part Eight: Building Challenging Trails

7   Include Tight and Technical Sections.

These slower sections challenge a rider's ability to turn quickly, negotiate obstacles, and float through difficult terrain. These sections can include drop-offs and other technical trail features.

8   Design Flow Transitions.

A good downhill trail will alternate between tight and technical and open and flowing trail, as both styles of trail test riders' abilities to choose the best line and then ride that line smoothly. It is important to design smooth transitions between sections of different flow. Using insloped turns when approaching tighter sections will slow riders gradually, reduce skidding, and improve the transition. Putting a steep section directly after a technical section will allow riders to accelerate quickly and easily and to enjoy the entirety of an open and flowing section.

9   Use Grade Reversals.

Keep in mind that the trail shouldn't be downhill the entire way. As with all trails, frequent grade reversals are essential to ensure drainage. Design short uphill sections of about 20 to 100 feet in length every several hundred feet to allow water to exit the trail and to challenge the riders to maintain their momentum. You can use jumps and rollers to create short grade reversals, or you can design a slight, uphill turn in the trail to make a longer reversal. Longer uphills should be preceded by a fast section, allowing the rider to hit the uphill with plenty of momentum.

10   Rock to the Rock.

Design your trail so that it runs through as much rock as possible. Rock adds great technical challenge, is highly durable, and usually requires less maintenance than other natural tread surfaces. Rock is especially useful in building steeps and drop-offs. Rock also enables you to add trail features such as wide, off-camber corners, which normally would erode.

Are racecourses relevant to your recreational trail?

Whether you are building a racecourse or a recreational downhill trail, you need to recognize that professional racecourses affect what many riders want.

Many recreational downhillers also race, and they use recreational downhill trails to train for their races. Even those who don't compete look up to racers and want to ride race-style trails. Consequently, downhillers will build features or entire trails that emulate the technical features of racecourses on the circuit.

It is important that recreational downhill trails provide riders with space to train for the specific features found at races. Otherwise, downhillers may feel the need to go out and build their own trails—which can cause trouble. As racecourses and the sport of downhilling evolve, so must the technical challenge of recreational trails.

Insloped turns, usually called berms by mountain bikers, help riders carry momentum through corners and are a blast to ride. Location: Innerleithen, Scotland.

⑪ Build Insloped Turns (Berms).

Insloped turns, usually called berms by mountain bikers, help riders carry momentum through corners. Berms keep riders on the trail and, perhaps most importantly, they are fun to ride. Berms must be placed in the right spot in the trail corridor and be the correct height, length, and radius. Berms should naturally draw the rider in and should shoot the rider back out of the corner at a greater speed. If a berm doesn't feel right, don't hesitate to change its height, length, or radius so that it does its job. Berms have the potential to trap water, so it is essential to utilize grade reversals to improve drainage before and after the corner.

Berms can be as short as 1 foot and as tall as you want to go. The faster a rider enters the corner, the taller, longer, and wider the berm should be. Berms are often built too far from the turn's apex, which can cause riders to make a tighter turn in order to cut the corner. Move the entire berm toward the apex of the turn if this happens, as the fastest line through a corner should use the berm. See page 154 for more tips on building insloped turns.

Part Eight: Building Challenging Trails

Jumps and drop-offs are key features to include on downhill trails. Location: Les Gets France. Photo by Paul Mckenzie/Clif Bar.

Trail Solutions

12 Include Jumps.

The first priority when building jumps is to create smooth flow through the approach, take-off, air, and landing. Each jump should be clearly visible so riders can choose whether to bypass the jump or hit it, based on a split-second decision. Riders must be able to hit jumps at full speed without being thrown at takeoff or overshooting the landing. If a takeoff ramp is too steep, a rider's rear wheel will be bucked when hitting the jump at full speed.

It is important to make gradual transitions between the approach, the jump face, and the jump lip, and landings should be long, wide, and gradual to allow for a soft touchdown. Jumps can be step-ups, step-downs, or level. Jumps on downhill courses range in length from about 10 to 60 feet, and jump lips can be anywhere from 2 to 10 feet tall. Inexperienced riders often build dangerous jumps. Take the time to find a seasoned rider and trailbuilder to help you construct this type of feature!

13 Include Drop-offs.

Drop-offs are some of the most fun and challenging natural features on a downhill trail. Like jumps, they must be visible and clearly marked to allow riders to smoothly pass around or off the drop—even when approaching at high speed. The approach should be a little slower than the actual take-off so that riders don't have to hit their brakes right at the top. The landing area should be wide and sloped downhill, and it should be carefully located to allow riders to hit the drop at full speed without overshooting the landing zone.

14 Provide Optional Lines.

There should always be an easier, alternate route around a technical feature or jump. On advanced trails, the technical feature can be located on the main line, with an easier option to the side. On intermediate or beginner routes, technical trail features should be outside the main trail flow. Optional lines can potentially be in the same corridor as the main trail; for example, a drop-off could vary in height from one side of the trail to the other. Both lines should be easy to see and should blend with the trail's flow, as riders will be moving fast.

15 Minimize Man-Made Structures.

Ladder bridges, teeter-totters, and other freeriding stunts are not recommended on downhill trails. They are freeride features and do not accommodate high speeds. While a ladder bridge might be used to control erosion on a very steep section of trail, it should not be challenging in its width, and should be positioned so that faster riders can jump over it. There have been occasions when racecourse designers placed logs across a trail in order to increase that trail's difficulty level. This is dangerous and can injure riders.

Don't Forget...

Maintenance. Downhill trails are generally steeper than shared-use, recreational trails. Because of this, and because of greater forces and changes in speeds, downhill trails erode more quickly and require more tread maintenance and drainage structures than other trails.

Afterword

Trail Solutions: Today and Tomorrow

The trailbuilding techniques presented in this book will continue to evolve. Every day, professional and volunteer trail experts create and test new ideas to make paths more durable, more appealing, and easier to manage. Dedicated trailbuilders never stop learning and they share new trail solutions without hesitation.

The challenges of designing, building, and maintaining trails will likely grow. If current population and recreation trends endure, trails everywhere will receive heavier use. New trail systems—particularly in urban locations where there aren't many now—will increasingly be seen as an essential component of high-quality living. That's great. But these paths will also be tougher to squeeze between commercial and residential development and the ever-growing labyrinth of highways.

The good news is that enthusiastic trail professionals and volunteers like you will stay committed to the cause. Trailbuilding offers immediate, tangible rewards that many people simply don't find in their jobs or daily routines. At the end of a project, you see and touch the product of your work. You feel the satisfaction of knowing that your efforts will keep people—you included—healthy and happy for years to come.

We welcome your comments and suggestions on the information included in this book. Write us at IMBA, P.O. Box 7578, Boulder, CO USA 80306 or email us at info@imba.com. We regularly present new and revised trail information on imba.com and we plan to produce future, revised editions of this text.

Appendix A

Natural Resource Impacts of Mountain Biking:

A summary of scientific studies that compare mountain biking to other forms of trail travel

In recent years, hiking and environmental groups have lobbied to ban mountain bikers from trails on the grounds that mountain bikes damage the environment. Some land managers have closed trails to bicycling because of alleged, excessive resource damage.

Do mountain bikers *truly* cause more impact on natural resources than other trail users?

Very little research has been in done in an attempt to answer this question, but the empirical studies that have been conducted do not support the notion that bikes cause more natural-resource impact. What studies *do* demonstrate is that *all* forms of outdoor recreation—including bicycling, hiking, running, horseback riding, fishing, hunting, bird watching, and off-highway-vehicle travel—cause impacts to the environment.

Social scientists have conducted surveys to study the feelings, perceptions, and attitudes of cyclists, hikers, equestrians, and motorized trail users toward one another. This information, along with anecdotal evidence and media reports, shows that trail users don't always get along. User conflict, as a concept, is fairly well understood and demonstrably real.

In a democracy, the allocation of trails based on users' differing interests is a normal, appropriate course of action. Land managers must consider the opinions and concerns of the people who use their trails. But when individuals make unsubstantiated allegations regarding natural resource damage to justify the prioritization of their type of trail use, land managers should be wary.

Objective information, independent of conflicting human desires, must be the basis for sound policy decisions. The results of scientific studies can provide land managers and recreationists with a better understanding of user impacts, and should guide political debate and public policy.

This document examines three main categories: physical impacts to trails or facilities, vegetation damage, and effects on wildlife.

In each case, several studies have examined the topic, but only a handful have compared the effects of bicyclists with other trail users.

---

[1] Science also demonstrates that roads—whether used or not, or regardless of which groups use them—can cause harmful environmental effects. A more limited body of science indicates that trails may cause somewhat similar effects. But this document addresses only the comparison of user groups' impacts, not the effects of roads and trails.

No scientific studies show that mountain bikers cause more wear to trails than other users.

Trails deteriorate over time. To what extent do bicyclists cause this deterioration, and how does the impact of bicyclists compare with that of other trail users? Many people have hypothesized about impact, basing their theories on ideas involving the characteristics of tires versus shoes, skidding, area and pressure of impact, and other factors. But as of 2003, only two empirical studies have scientifically compared the erosion impacts of bicycling with other forms of trail travel.

Wilson and Seney: Hooves and feet erode more than wheels

In 1994, John Wilson and Joseph Seney of Montana State University published "Erosional Impacts of Hikers, Horses, Motorcycles and Off-Road Bicycles on Mountain Trails in Montana" (12). The study tracked 100 passages by each of the four groups over control plots on two trails in national forests. For some of the passages, the researchers prewet the trail with a fixed quantity of water using a rainfall simulator. The researchers measured sediment runoff, which correlates with erosion.

Wilson and Seney found no statistically significant difference between measured bicycling and hiking effects. They did find that horses caused the most erosion of the trails, and that motorcycles traveling up wetted trails caused significant impact. They also concluded, "Horses and hikers (hooves and feet) make more sediment available than wheels (motorcycles and off-road bicycles) on prewet trails, and that horses make more sediment available on dry plots as well" (p.74). Wilson and Seney suggested that precipitation will cause erosion even without human travel, and this factor may significantly outweigh the effects of travel. Trail design, construction, and maintenance may be much more important factors in controlling erosion than excluding specific user groups.

Chiu and Kriwoken: No significant difference between hiking and biking trail wear

In a study whose publication in *Annals of Leisure Research* is pending, two researchers at the University of Tasmania, Australia, conducted an experiment on an abandoned fire road to compare track ("track" is the term for trail in Australia) impacts from hiking and bicycling. For the study "Managing Recreational Mountain Biking in Wellington Park, Tasmania, Australia" (2), the authors had hikers and bicyclists pass test plots 400 times each, and measured the surface profile of the track before, during, and after the passes. They compared flat, steep, wet, and dry conditions. Chiu and Kriwoken found no significant difference in the trail wear caused by the two user groups. They did find significant impact from skidding tires, and they also found that impacts on wet trails were greater than on dry for both types of use.

Goeft and Alder: Erosion trends not clear

Other, non-comparative studies have looked at the erosion effects of bicycling. Goeft and Alder (5) investigated erosion on two trails in western Australia for one year, including various combinations of uphill, downhill, and flat sections as well as curved and straight stretches in their study. They found that trail width varied with time, narrowing a little but not showing a clear trend. Soils on older sections of trail were more compacted than newer. Erosion was influenced by slope, time, and age of trail, but did not show a clear trend.

---

[2] IMBA wishes to obtain and incorporate into future revisions of this document any new or additional empirical science regarding the impacts of mountain biking. IMBA welcomes input. To offer information, please contact info@imba.com.

Bjorkman: Artificially hardened trails erode less

Bjorkman, 1996, (1) cleared vegetation from two very steep slopes (62 %) in a state park in southern Wisconsin and left one bare while protecting the other with artificial hardening surfaces. Trail users traveled over these surfaces and the study measured sedimentation from each slope. The protected path generated 0.11 tons of sediment per acre while the untreated slope produced 10.86 tons per acre.

Crockett: Minimal change from repeated bicycle passage

In 1986 the Santa Clara County Parks and Recreation Department of northern California studied the erosional effects of bicycling on the Edwards Field Trail (3). Forty-five cyclists made a total of 495 passes over 12 transects. Measurements were taken before and after these passes. Trail width increased at some plots and decreased at others, and the cross-sectional area of the transect, which is a measurement of the amount of soil in that spot, also varied. The researcher, Christopher S. Crockett, observed minimal change in the visual trail characteristics in most cases. The data led the county parks department to open trails to mountain biking.

Discussion:

The two comparative studies discerned minimal differences between bicycling and hiking. These studies may not resolve the continuing debate over who does what to trails. This scientific inquiry needs to be repeated in other geographic locations, on other soils, with more passages by each user group.

Because the Goeft and Alder and Bjorkman studies allowed multiple users on the same trails without measuring differences, and the Crockett/Santa Clara study involved only bicyclists, those studies do not provide information to compare erosion processes among users. However, these studies do indicate that the impacts of bicycling on trail condition are minimal.

No scientific studies indicate that bicycling causes more degradation of plants than hiking.

Trail treads are primarily devoid of vegetation, so impacts to vegetation are not usually a concern. However, this issue is relevant with regard to the widening of trails and travel off of established trails.

Thurston and Reader: Hiking and bicycling trample vegetation at equal rates

Again, only one study has compared bicycling with other recreation with regard to the damage to vegetation caused by trampling. In 2001, Eden Thurston and Richard Reader of the University of Guelph, Ontario, published "Impacts of Experimentally Applied Mountain Biking and Hiking on Vegetation and Soil of a Deciduous Forest" (10). The authors set up two identical lanes of travel over natural vegetation in a deciduous forest. They measured plant stem density, species richness, and soil exposure before, during, and after the 500 passages in each lane by hikers and bicyclists. Results: "Three principal findings emerged from this study. First, impacts on vegetation and soil increased with biking and hiking activity. Second, the impacts of biking and hiking measured here were not significantly different. Third, impacts did not extend beyond 30cm of the trail centerline" (Thurston and Reader, 2001, p.405).

Bjorkman: Vegetation on shared-user trails occurs mostly in center of trail
Weesner/NPS: Moderate trail widening controlled by volunteers

Bjorkman, 1996, (1) studied erosion of existing and brand new trails in a state park in southern Wisconsin. Measurements on existing trails indicated a rapid and substantial loss of vegetation along the trail centerline. The disappearance of vegetation 2 meters to the side was much less and slower. Along the centerline, soil compacted steadily, but there was little compaction 2 meters to the side. The width where no vegetation existed increased rapidly at first, then a bit more slowly, was more rapid in shade than in sun, and was more pronounced where the soil had more sand, or less silt. Weesner, 2003, (11) reported the results of National Park Service observations of a trail in southern Arizona over almost a decade. Results: Some trail segments widened moderately and some just a little. Volunteer trail maintenance occurred on some plots and effectively kept the trail narrow.

Discussion:

The Thurston and Reader study provided high-quality information through a solid process. Neither Bjorkman nor Weesner controlled for multiple-uses, and thus those studies do not provide a basis for comparison of vegetative impacts of trail users.

Science has yielded mixed results in comparing the impacts on wildlife of hiking and bicycling.

To date, four studies have rigorously compared bicycling's impact on wildlife with the impacts of other users. The studies involved bison, mule deer, pronghorn antelope, desert bighorn sheep, European alpine chamois, and American bald eagle. A fifth study provided a statistical suggestion regarding grizzly bear.

Taylor and Knight: Hiking and biking cause same impact to large mammals on Utah island

In 1993, Audrey Taylor and Richard Knight published "Wildlife Responses to Recreation and Associated Visitor Perceptions" (9), a study on Antelope Island, situated in the Great Salt Lake of Utah. They measured behavioral responses of bison, mule deer, and pronghorn antelope to the passages of hikers and bicyclists. In each case, an assistant acted as a hiker or cyclist while a researcher collected data as a hidden observer. The recreationists moved at a typical pace, did not stop nor look at the animals, and did not talk. The study measured alert distance, flush response, flight distance, and distance moved. Recreationists stayed on trails for the bison and antelope trials, while the mule deer observations involved recreationists traveling both on and off trails. Taylor and Knight wrote, "…the large degree of overlap between the 95% confidence intervals for hiking and biking is indicative of a lack of biological difference between wildlife responses to these activities" (p.955).

Calculating the amount of trails and the sensitivity distances of wildlife, Taylor and Knight estimated that approximately 7% of the island "was potentially unsuitable for wildlife due to disturbance from recreation." (Only the northern half of the island has trails, and the southern half is off limits to public recreation.)

Taylor and Knight also surveyed recreationists on the island and found that hikers, bicyclists, and equestrians blamed other groups more, and their own groups less, for wildlife impacts. The study also found that all recreationists underestimated the distances at which wildlife were sensitive to human presence.

Papouchis, Singer, and Sloan: Hikers have greatest impact on bighorn sheep

Christopher Papouchis, Francis Singer, and William Sloan, reported in 2001 on "Responses of Desert Bighorn Sheep To Increased Human Recreation" (7). The authors observed 1,029 bighorn sheep/human interactions in two areas, a high-use and a low-use, of Canyonlands National Park, Utah, in 1993 and 1994. They compared behavioral responses, distances moved, and duration of responses to vehicles, mountain bikers, and humans on foot. Hikers caused the most severe responses in desert bighorn sheep (animals fled in 61% of encounters), followed by vehicles (17%) and mountain bikers (6%), apparently because the hikers were more likely to be in unpredictable locations and often directly approached sheep.

Gander and Ingold: Hikers, joggers, and mountain bikers— all the same to chamois

In 1996 Hans Gander and Paul Ingold published, "Reactions of Male Alpine Chamois Rupicapra rupicapra to Hikers, Joggers, and Mountain bikers" (4). The authors measured the effects on male alpine chamois of the passage of hikers, bicyclists, and joggers. Thirty-two passages were carried out by single persons traveling on a trail that runs through a meadow above timberline in a game reserve in the Bernese Oberland of Switzerland. The animals responded similarly to each of the human activities. Subsequent to the passage of people, the chamois tended to avoid the pasture.

Spahr: Hikers have greater impact on eagles than cyclists

In her 1990 graduate thesis, Robin Spahr examined "Factors Affecting The Distribution Of Bald Eagles And Effects Of Human Activity On Bald Eagles Wintering Along The Boise River" (8). Spahr observed people recreating and also "simulated" recreational behaviors on a section of the Boise River in Boise, Idaho, in order to measure the effects on eagles.

Spahr found that walkers caused the highest frequency of eagle flushing, with 46% of walkers causing eagles to flush. Fishermen were second at 34%, with bicyclists at 15%, joggers at 13%, and vehicles at 6%. Bicyclists caused eagles to flush at greatest distances, with a mean of 148 meters, a minimum of 96 meters, and a maximum of 200 meters. Walkers' mean was lower, at 87 meters, but their minimum was closer, at 17 meters, and their maximum was higher than bicyclists', at 300 meters. Mean distance of eagle flushing by vehicles was 107 meters, by fishermen was 64 meters, and by joggers was 50 meters. "The disturbance indexes, which reflect both flushing distance and frequency, indicated that walkers were the most disturbing to eagles. Bicyclists, followed closely by fishermen, were the next most disturbing," Spahr wrote.

Herrero and Herrero: Bikers more likely to suddenly encounter bears

In 2000 Jake Herrero and Stephen Herrero published, "Management Options for the Moraine Lake Highline Trail: Grizzly Bears and Cyclists" (6). The authors' firm was hired by Parks Canada to provide recommendations for managing bicycling on a particular trail in Banff National Park in Alberta Canada. Intended primarily as a management strategy, the report was not an experimental investigation of grizzly bear responses to bicyclists. However, the authors referenced their compiled database of human/grizzly bear interactions and found a statistical suggestion that bicyclists, because they travel quietly and quickly, are more likely to have sudden confrontations with grizzly bears on that trail than are other trail users, such as hikers and equestrians. The authors also found no difference between the effects of bicycling and hiking on bear habitat and stated there was no evidence that bicyclists should be managed differently than other users in that regard.

Discussion:

These studies scratch the surface of a complex topic. The diversity of species and their differing responses to human recreation make generalizations across species difficult. However, this group of studies at least suggests that the impacts of bicycling on wildlife are generally similar to the effects of hiking.

Conclusion

Mountain biking, like other recreation activities, does impact the environment. On this point, there is little argument. But people often debate whether or not mountain bikes cause more damage to trails, vegetation, and wildlife than other forms of recreation such as hiking and horseback riding.

A body of empirical, scientific evidence now indicates that **mountain biking is no more damaging than other forms of recreation, including hiking.** Thus, managers who prohibit bicycle use (while allowing hiking or equestrian use) based on impacts to trails, soils, wildlife, or vegetation are acting without sound, scientific backing.

A land manager's decision to prohibit one user group on the basis of providing a particular type of experience for another group may or may not be justified by evidence provided by social studies, as the wisdom of prohibiting a particular user group in order to satisfy the desires of another is a matter for politics rather than science.

References

(1) Bjorkman, Alan. 1996. *Off Road Bicycle and Hiking Trail User Interactions: A Report to the Wisconsin Natural Resources Board.* Wisconsin Department of Natural Resources: Bureau of Research.

(2) Chiu, Luke and Kriwoken, Lorne. *Managing Recreational Mountain Biking in Wellington Park, Tasmania, Australia.* Annals of Leisure Research, (in press).

(3) Crockett, Christopher S. 1986. *Survey of Ecological Impact Considerations Related to Mountain Bicycle Use on the Edwards Field Trail at Joseph D. Grant County Park.* Santa Clara County (CA) Parks Department.

(4) Gander, Hans and Ingold, Paul. 1996. *Reactions of Male Alpine Chamois Rupicapra r.rupicapra to Hikers, Joggers and Mountainbikers.* Biological Conservation 79:107–109.

(5) Goeft, Ute and Alder, Jackie. 2001. *Sustainable Mountain Biking: A Case Study from the Southwest of Western Australia.* Journal of Sustainable Tourism 9(3):193–211.

(6) Herrero, Jake and Herrero, Stephen. 2000. *Management Options for the Moraine Lake Highline Trail: Grizzly Bears and Cyclists.*

(7) Papouchis, Christopher M. and Singer, Francis J. and Sloan, William. 2001. *Responses of Desert Bighorn Sheep To Increased Human Recreation.* Journal of Wildlife Management 65(3):573–582.

(8) Spahr, Robin. 1990. *Factors Affecting The Distribution Of Bald Eagles And Effects Of Human Activity On Bald Eagles Wintering Along The Boise River.* Boise State University.

(9) Taylor, Audrey R. and Knight, Richard L. 2003. *Wildlife Responses to Recreation and Associated Visitor Perceptions.* Ecological Applications 13(4):951–963.

(10) Thurston, Eden and Reader, Richard J. 2001. *Impacts of Experimentally Applied Mountain Biking and Hiking on Vegetation and Soil of a Deciduous Forest.* Environmental Management 27(3):397–409.

(11) Weesner, Meg. 2003. *Cactus Forest Trail Environmental Assessment, Saguaro National Park, Arizona,* National Park Service.

(12) Wilson, John P. and Seney, Joseph. 1994. *Erosional Impacts of Hikers, Horses, Motorcycles and Off-Road Bicycles on Mountain Trails in Montana.* Mountain Research and Development 47(1):77–88.

Appendix B

Sources for Tools, Bridge Supplies, and Signs

Most tools needed for trailwork can be purchased from local hardware stores and suppliers of forestry gear. Volunteer crews often find the tools they need in the equipment caches of land management agencies. Specialty tools such as Pulaskis and McLeods can be found from one of the following suppliers.

Hand Tool Sources

A.M. Leonard
241 Fox Drive
Piquoa, OH 45356-0816
800-543-8955
www.amleonard.com

A.M. Leonard sells many landscaping tools. The IG7 and AE1 are good hoes for taller trailbuilders.

- Italian Grading Hoe w/41" handle - IG7
- Grubbing Hoe w/54" handle - AE1

Ben Meadows Company
PO Box 5277
Janeville, WI 53547-5277
800-241-6401
www.benmeadows.com

From a trailbuilder's perspective, the selection of flagging tap, pin flags, clinometers, and hand tools is hard to beat. Two favorites of ours are:

- Suunto Self-Damping Clinometers: #102200 Suunto PM5/360PC.
- Adze Hoe: #170602 Wardwood.

BOB Trailers Inc.
3641 Sacramento Dr. #3
San Luis Obispo, CA 93401
800-894-2447
www.bobtrailers.com

Yak bike trailers and tool racks for Yak trailers. The single-wheeled BOB trailer will hold 4–7 hand tools and a chainsaw.

Country Home Products
Meigs Road
PO Box 25
Vergennes, VT 05491
800-687-6575
www.countryhomeproducts.com

Country Home Products is a good source of the DR Field and Brush mowers.

Forestry Suppliers, Inc.
PO Box 8397
Jackson, MS 39284-8397
800-647-5368
www.forestry-suppliers.com

Forestry Suppliers is similar to Ben Meadows in their wide selection of products. Our favorites:

- Suunto PM5/360PC Clinometer: Percent and Degrees, #43830
- Texas SunGlo Flagging Tape

Forrest Tool Company
PO Box 768
Mendocino, CA 95460
707-937-2141
www.maxax.com

Forrest Tools manufactures and sells the MAX Multi Purpose Tool. A combination of shovel, pick, Pulaski, Mcleod, and three other tools, the Max Axe works well and is built to last.

Sherrill, Inc.
200 East Seneca Road
Greensboro, NC 27406
800-525-8873
www.wtsherrill.com

Sherrill is a good source for arborist supplies.

Trail Services
15 Westwood Road
Bangor, ME 04401
207-947-2723
www.trailservices.com

Trail Services provides quality and hard-to-find products for trailbuilding, such as Griphoist winches, slings, blocks, and stone-working tools.

Wildfire Fire Equipment Inc.
www.wildfire-equipment.com

Wildfire Fire Equipment is a great source for trailbuilding tools in Canada.

Bridge Sources

Echo Bridge, Inc.
888-327-4343
www.echobridgeinc.com

Echo Bridge offers custom design, prefabrication, and construction in timber, steel, and/or concrete bridges.

Naturtec
909-793-4501
www.naturtec.com

Naturtec manufactures lightweight modular fiberglass bridges.

Permapost Products Company
800-828-0222
www.permapost.com

Permapost manufactures custom prefabricated treated wooden bridges.

Sign and Trail Marker Sources

Carsonite International
Flexible signs and markers
PO Box 98
Early Branch, SC 29916-0098
800-648-7915
www.carsonite.com

Pannier Graphics
Fiberglass embedded signs
345 Oak Road
Gibsonia, PA 15044-9805
800-544-8428
www.panniergraphics.com

RockArt
Flexible signs and markers
531 North Los Alamos
Mesa, AZ 85213-7832
877-718-7446
www.rockartsigns.com

Scenic Signs
Signs and trail markers
2803 Emery Drive
Wausau, WI 54401-9709
800-388-4811
www.scenicsigns.com

Voss Signs LLC
800-473-0698
www.vosssigns.com

Trail Traffic Counters

Ivan Technologies, Inc.
860-693-0699
ivantechnologies@email.com

Goodson & Associates
913-345-8555
www.trailmaster.com

Appendix C

IMBA-Affiliated Professional Trailbuilders

IMBA Trail Solutions
Boulder, CO
www.imba.com
(303) 545-9011

Trail Design Specialists
Mike and Jan Riter
Conyers, GA
www.traildesign.com
(678) 410-8021

Arrowhead Trails Inc.
Tony and Danna Boone
Salida, CO
www.arrowheadtrails.com
(719) 539-2817

Trail Dynamics, LLC
Woody Keen and Ed Sutton
Cedar Mountain, NC
www.traildynamics.com
(828) 862-5613

Long Cane Trails, LLC
Bill Victor and Michael Burton
Clarks Hill, SC
wmvic32@aol.com
(803) 278-6177

Jim Jacobsen
Forest Knolls, CA
btcjim@aol.com
(415) 488-1665

Alpine Trails, LLC
Troy Duffin
Park City, UT
www.alpine-trails.com
(435) 655-0779

Trail Source, LLC
Tim Wegner and Dale Gundberg
Minneapolis, MN
www.trailsource.net

Concept Construction
Art Tuftee
Seattle, WA
arttuftee@aol.com
(206) 675-8429

Talon Trails
DeWayne Buratti
Austin, TX
duratti@grandecom.net
(512) 797-7433

Trailworks Trailbuilding Services
Lorien Arnold
Victoria, BC
www.trailworks.ca
lothlorien.mtb@shawcable.com

Appendix D

Recommended Reading

Birchard, William, Jr., and Robert D. Proudman. *A.T. Design, Construction, and Maintenance.* Harpers Ferry, WV: Appalachian Trail Conference, 1998.

Birkby, Robert C. *Lightly on the Land: The Student Conservation Assciation Trail-Building and Maintenance Manual.* Seattle: The Mountaineers, 1996.

Demrow, Carl, and David Salisbury. *The Complete Guide to Trail Building and Maintenance.* Boston: Appalachian Mountain Club, 1998.

Hesselbarth, Woody, and Brian Vachowski. *Trail Construction and Maintenance Notebook.* Missoula, MT: USDA Forest Service, Technology and Development Program, 2000.

Flink, Charles A., Kristine Olka, Robert M. Searns. *Trails for the Twenty-First Century: Planning, Design, and Management Manual for Multi-Use Trails.* Washington D.C.: Island Press and Rails-to-Trails Conservancy, 2001.

Hallman, Richard G. *Handtools For Trail Work.* Missoula, MT: USDA Forest Service, Technology and Development Program, 1988.

Schmid, Jim. *Tools for Trail Work.* www.americantrails.org, 2003

Schmid, Jim. *Trails Primer.* A Glossary of Trails, Greenway, and Outdoor Recreation Terms and Acronyms. Columbia, SC: State Trails Program, South Carolina Dept. of Parks, Recreation and Tourism, 2001.

Steinholtz, Robert and Brian Vachowski. *Wetland Trail Design and Construction.* Missoula, MT: USDA Forest Service, Technology and Development Program, 2001.

Glossary of Terms

Abutment: A structure at either extreme end of a bridge that supports the superstructure (sill, stringers, trusses, or decks), composed of stone, concrete, brick, or timber.

Accessible: A term used to describe a site, building, facility, or trail that complies with the Americans with Disabilities Act (ADA) Accessibility Guidelines and can be approached, entered, and used by people with disabilities.

Adopt-A-Trail: A program in which groups or businesses "adopt" trails, providing volunteer work parties at periodic intervals to help maintain those trails. Though no special trail privileges are granted, the trail manager generally acknowledges that a trail has been "adopted" by erecting signs indicating the trail is part of an Adopt-A-Trail program and including the name of the adopter.

All-Terrain Vehicle (ATV): A wheeled or tracked motorized vehicle designed primarily for recreational use or for the transportation of property or equipment exclusively on trails, undeveloped roads, marshland, open country, or other unprepared surfaces.

Americans with Disabilities Act of 1990 (ADA): A U.S. federal law prohibiting discrimination against people with disabilities. Requires public entities to provide accessible accommodations for people with disabilities.

Americans with Disabilities Act Accessibility Guidelines (ADAAG): Design guidelines for making to a range of indoor and outdoor settings accessible to people with disabilities.

Anchor: An object, such as a stone, that defines the sides of the trail, helping to keep users in the center of the tread. Also a large stone that holds other stones in place.

Archaeological Resources (Cultural, Heritage): Any material of past human life, activities, or habitation that are of historic or prehistoric significance. Such materials include, but are not limited to, pottery, basketry, bottles, weapon projectiles, tools, structures, pit houses, rock paintings, rock carvings, graves, skeletal remains, personal items and clothing, household or business refuse, or any piece of the foregoing.

Armoring: Reinforcement of a surface with rock, brick, stone, concrete, or other "paving" material.

Assessment, Trail: Physical assessments undertaken to better understand a trail or corridor. Assessments include an accurate description and documentation of native elements and an inventory of built structures along the trail or corridor.

Average Trail Grade (Overall Trail Grade): The average steepness of a trail over its entire length.

Average Trail Segment Grade: The average slope of a certain trail segment.

Backcut: The vertical part of a bench cut that is blended into the backslope.

Backslope: The cut bank along the uphill side of the trail extending upward from the tread. Usually sloped back by varying degrees, depending on bank composition and slope stability.

Batter: The angle of a retaining wall's tilt into the slope of the hillside.

Bedrock: Solid rock material underlying soils and other earthy surface formations.

Bench Cut: A relatively flat, stable surface (tread) on a hillside made by excavation. When excavated often referred to as full, half or partial bench.

Bench Cut, Full: The total width of the trail tread is excavated out of the slope, and the trail tread contains no compacted fill material. The most durable and recommended style of bench cut trail.

Bench Cut, Half: Half the width of the trail tread is excavated out of the slope, and the outside of the trail tread contains the excavated and compacted material.

Bench Cut, Partial: Part of the width of the trail tread is excavated out of the slope, and the rest of the trail tread is made up of fill material.

Berm: The ridge of material formed on the outer edge of the trail, which projects higher than the center of the trail tread. When improperly designed or unintentionally caused by tread compaction and soil displacement during trail use, a berm can trap water on the trail and lead to erosion.

Blowdown (Windfall): Anything (trees, limbs, brush, etc.) blown down on the trail by the wind.

Boardwalk: A fixed planked structure, usually built on pilings in areas of wet soil or water to provide dry crossings.

Bridge: A structure, including supports, erected over a depression (stream, river, chasm, canyon, or road) and having a deck for carrying trail traffic.

Broadcasting: The process of distributing excavated soil as far downhill and away from the new tread as possible.

Brushing: The process of clearing the trail corridor of plants, trees, and branches that could impede the progress of trail users.

Buffer (Buffer Zone): Any type of natural or constructed barrier (trees, shrubs, or wooden fences) used between the trail and adjacent lands to minimize impacts (physical or visual). Buffers also provide a transition between adjacent land uses.

Capacity (Carrying Capacity): The maximum number of trail users that can pass through a section of trail during a given time period under existing trail conditions. Also refers to the amount of use a given resource can sustain before an irreversible deterioration in the quality of the resource begins to occur.

Capstone: A stone placed in the top or uppermost layer of a structure such as a rock retaining wall.

Center Line: An imaginary line marking the center of the trail. During construction, the center line is usually marked by placing a row of flags or stakes.

Challenge Park (Terrain Park, Skills Area): A special-use area that features a variety of technical trail features.

Check Dam: A log, rock, or wood barrier placed across deeply eroded trails or erosion channels to slow the flow of water enough to allow fine fill material to accumulate behind the structure.

Choke (Gateway): A slight narrowing in the trail used to control user speed.

Circle of Danger: The area surrounding a trailworker that is unsafe due to tool use.

Clearing: The removal of windfall trees, uproots, leaning trees, loose limbs, wood chunks, etc. from both the vertical and horizontal trail corridor.

Climbing Turn: A turn to reverse direction that doesn't have a constructed turning platform or landing. The upper and lower legs of a climbing turn are generally joined by a short section of trail (the apex of the turn) that lies directly in the fall line. As a result, climbing turns located on hillsides with a grade of more than 7 percent are erosion prone and should be replaced with well-built switchbacks.

Clinometer: A hand-held instrument used for measuring trail grade. The user sights through the Clinometer to a reference (usually a second person) and reads the measurement directly from the internal scale.

Compaction: The compression of aggregate, soil, or fill material into a more dense mass by tamping.

Contour Line(s): A line on a topographic map connecting points of the land surface that have the same elevation.

Contour Trail: A trail constructed such that it follows a contour, with its elevation remaining constant.

Control Points: Places that influence where a trail goes. The beginning and end of a trail are basic control points. Other control points include parking areas, trailheads, structures, slopes for turns or switchbacks, road or water crossings, and other trails. Positive control points are places you want trail users to visit. Negative control points are places you want users to avoid.

Corralling: The act of placing anchors on the trail to define the sides and emphasize the turns, keeping users on the tread.

Corridor, Trail: The full dimensions of the trail, including the area on either side of the tread and the space overhead, that need to be cleared of brush and obstacles.

Creep: The slow movement of soil down relatively steep slopes, primarily caused by gravity and water. (Also see Tread Creep.)

Crib Wall: A retaining wall used to stabilize the trail tread and prevent it from collapsing down the fall line. Can be built with rock or rot-resistant wood.

Critical Point: The outside edge of the trail. It's called the critical point because this is where trail maintenance problems (usually related to drainage) begin. Rounding the outside edge helps water drain from the trail.

Crown (Crowning): A method of trail construction where the center portion of the tread is raised to allow water to disperse to either side of the trail.

Crusher Fines: Limestone, granite, or gravel that has been run through a crusher, which, once wetted and compacted, creates a smooth, hard trail surface for high-use areas.

Culvert: A pipe or box-like construction of wood, metal, plastic, or concrete that conveys a stream under a trail without constricting water flow.

Cut and Fill: The process of removing soil from one area and placing it elsewhere to form a base for any given activity.

Deadfall: A tangled mass of fallen trees or branches.

Deadman/Deadmen: A log or logs, heavy timber or timbers, a large block of concrete, a large boulder, or a combination of these materials that is partially or completely buried. Deadmen are used to anchor sections of armored trail.

Deberming: Removing the high ridge of material that has formed along the outer edge of a trail, allowing water to once again flow off—and not down—the trail.

Doubletrack Trail: A trail that allows for two users to travel side by side, or to pass without one user having to yield the trail. Doubletrack trails are often old forest roads.

Downslope: The downhill side of a trail.

Drainage: The way in which water flows downhill and/or off the trail.

Drain, French: A stone-filled ditch that can have porous pipe along the base to collect and disperse water. The top must be kept clear of the surfacing material, allowing water to run freely into the drain.

Duty of Care: The legal "duty of care" that a landowner owes a member of the general public varies from state to state. Generally, liability depends on the status of the injured person. Liability increases from the lowest risk to the highest—from trespasser, licensee, and invitee, to child.

Easement: Grants the right to use a specific portion of land for a specific purpose or purposes. Easements may be limited to a specific period of time or may be granted in perpetuity; or the termination of the easement may be predicated upon the occurrence of a specific event. An easement agreement survives transfer of landownership and is generally binding upon future owners until it expires on its own terms.

Environmental Assessment (EA): A document that complies with NEPA law and regulation prepared early in a planning process (federal), which evaluates the potential environmental consequences of a project or activity. An assessment includes the same topical areas as an EIS, but only assesses the effects of a preferred action, and in less detail than an EIS. An EA results in a decision, based on an assessment of the degree of impact of an action, that an EIS is necessary or that an action will have no significant effect and a finding of no significant impact (FONSI) can be made.

Environmental Impact Statement(s) (EIS): A full disclosure, detailed federal report which, pursuant to NEPA law and regulation, establishes the need for the proposed action, identifies alternatives with the potential to meet the identified need, analyzes the anticipated environmental consequences of identified alternatives, and discusses how adverse effects may be mitigated. An EIS is prepared in two stages: a draft (DEIS) statement which is made available to the public for review and a final (FEIS) statement which is revised on the basis of comments made on the draft statement.

Equestrian: Of horses, horseback riding, riders, and horsemanship.

Erosion: The natural process of wearing down and removing rock and soil by wind and water. Trail erosion can be accelerated by a combination of users, water, and gravity.

Erosion, Gully (Gullying): Concentrations of runoff water cut into the soil forming single or numerous channels, usually on steep terrain.

Erosion Control: Techniques intended to reduce and mitigate soil movement.

Exotic Species: Plants introduced from another country or geographic region outside their natural range.

Exposure: The relative hazards encountered when one takes into consideration obstacles, alignment, grade, clearing, tread width, tread surface, sideslope, isolation, and proximity to steep slopes or cliffs.

Face: The steep, exposed side of a rock or slope.

Fall Line: The direction water flows down a slope (path of least resistance) under most circumstances. Constructing a trail on the fall line encourages water to run down the trail and leads to erosion.

Fall Zone: The area on either side of or below a technical trail feature that provides a clear landing for a rider who has failed to negotiate the obstacle.

Fill (Material): Gravel or soil used to fill voids in trail tread and to pack behind retaining walls and other structures.

Fill Slope: The portion of a trail that is constructed from excavated material. Fill slope can be unstable and thus should not be used to build trail tread. Full bench construction is preferred.

Fire Road: Unimproved dirt road that allows firefighting and ranger vehicles access to the backcountry.

Flagging: Thin ribbon used for marking during the location, design, construction, or maintenance of a trail project.

Flagline: Flagging, tied to trees, indicating the intended course of a trail prior to construction.

Flags, Pin: Wire wands with square plastic flags at one end for field layout and marking of new trail or relocations of trail sections.

Flow: The rhythm or "feel" of a trail. Two basic types include "open and flowing" and "tight and technical."

Footing: The part of a structural foundation that rests on the ground, supporting and spreading the weight of the structure above.

Ford: A natural-water-level-stream crossing that can be improved or armored to provide a level, low-velocity surface for trail traffic.

Full Bench Trail: (see Bench Cut, Full)

Gateway: (see Choke)

Geographic Information System (GIS): A spatial database mapping system (computer and software) that contains location data for trails and other important features.

Geotextile (Geosynthetic, Geofabric, Filter Fabric): A semi-impervious, non-woven, petrochemical fabric that provides a stable base for the application of soil or gravel. Most common use is in the construction of turnpikes.

Global Positioning System (GPS): A system used to map trail locations using satellites and portable receivers. Data gathered can be downloaded directly into GIS database systems.

Grade: The amount of elevation change between two points over a given distance expressed as a percentage (feet change in elevation for every 100 horizontal feet, commonly known as "rise over run"). A trail that rises 8 vertical feet in 100 horizontal feet has an 8-percent grade.

Grade Reversal A reverse in the trail grade—usually a short dip followed by a rise—that forces water off the trail. Grade reversals are known by several different terms, including grade dip, grade brake, drainage dip, and rolling dip. Frequent grade reversals are a critical element of sustainable trail design. Most trails will benefit from grade reversals every 20 to 50 feet, depending on soil type and rainfall.

Groundwater Table (Water Table): The upper limit of the part of the soil or underlying rock material that is wholly saturated with water. In some places an upper, or perched, water table may be separated from a lower one by a dry zone.

Grub (Grubbing): To dig or clear roots and tree stumps near or on the ground surface of the trail tread.

Half Bench Trail: (see Bench Cut, Half)

Half Rule: A trail's grade shouldn't exceed half the grade of the sideslope. If the trail grade is steeper than half the grade of the sideslope, it is considered a fall-line trail and gravity will pull water down the trail instead of across it. This leads to erosion of the trail tread.

Hardening: The manual, mechanical, or chemical compaction of the trail tread resulting in a hard and flat surface that sheets water effectively and resists the indentations that are created by use.

Header, Stone or Rock: A long, uniform stone laid with its narrow end toward the face of a retaining wall or crib used intermittently to structurally tie in the other rocks laid in the wall.

Headwall: A support structure at the entrance to a culvert or drainage structure.

Hybrid: A trail design that blends "open and flowing" and "tight and technical" features.

IMBA: International Mountain Bicycling Association, P.O. Box 7578, Boulder, CO, USA 80306; (303) 545-9011; imba.com. Leading resource for mountain bike–oriented trail design, construction, maintenance, and management information, and mountain biking in general.

IMBA Rules of the Trail: International Mountain Bicycling Association's rules of responsible mountain bicycling are: Ride on Open Trails Only, Control Your Bicycle, Always Yield the Trail, Never Scare Animals, Leave No Trace, Plan Ahead.

Impermeable Material: A soil or material whose properties prevent the movement of water.

In-Kind Contribution(s): Funds donated toward the match for a grant. Can include state, community, or private-sector dollar donations, the value of donated labor or equipment, real property, professional services, materials, etc.

Infrastructure: The facilities, utilities, and transportation systems (road or trail) needed to meet public and administrative needs.

Inside Turns: On a trail traversing a hillside, concave, or naturally banked turns in which the sideslope helps direct trail users around the turn.

Inslope (Insloping): The slope of the trail tread toward the backslope of the trail, causing water to run along the inside of the trail.

Intermodal Surface Transportation Efficiency Act of 1991 (ISTEA): Federal legislation authorizing highway, highway safety, transit, and other surface transportation programs from 1991 through 1997. It provided new funding opportunities for sidewalks, shared-use paths, and recreational trails. ISTEA was superseded by the Transportation Equity Act for the 21st Century (TEA-21) in 1998.

Keystone: A large stone that holds others in place. Also called an anchor.

Kiosk (Sign): A freestanding bulletin board that houses informational or interpretive displays.

Knick: Shaved-down section of trail, about 10 feet in diameter, with an exaggerated outslope. Like a rolling grade dip, a knick is used to shed water off a trail and is a useful remedy for wet spots on relatively flat trails.

Land, Private: Land owned by a farmer, corporation, or individual (private landowner).

Land, Public: Federal, state, or municipal land in trust for the governed populace (public landowner).

Land and Water Conservation Fund (LWCF): A federal matching assistance program that uses money collected from off-shore oil leases to provide grants for 50 percent of the cost for the acquisition and/or development of outdoor recreation sites and facilities.

Land Management Agency: Any governmental agency that manages public lands.

Land Trust: A private, nonprofit conservation organization formed to protect resources such as forestland, natural areas, and recreational areas. Land trusts purchase and accept donations of conservation easements.

Legal Public Access: The right of passage, established by law, over another's property. Can be created by an easement dedicated or reserved for public access. Legal public access exists on public land, public waters, public rights-of-way, and public easements.

Liability (Liable): In law, a broad term including almost every type of duty, obligation, debt, responsibility, or hazard arising by way of contract, tort, or statute. To say a landowner or person is "liable" for an injury or wrongful act is to indicate that he or she is the person responsible for compensating for the injury or wrongful act.

Loam: An easily crumbled soil consisting of a mixture of clay, silt, and sand.

Machine Built: A trail or feature constructed with the use of an excavator, trail dozer, or other piece of equipment.

Management: Includes the overall policy, planning, design, inventory, mapping, construction, and maintenance of a trail or greenway segment or site, as well as the operational aspects of administration.

Master Plan: A comprehensive, long-range plan intended to guide the greenway and trail development of a community or region. Includes analysis, recommendation, and proposals of action.

Maximum Sustainable Grade: The steepest section of a trail that is still sustainable. Although maximum sustainable trail grade is typically about 15 to 20 percent, it is site-specific and fluctuates based on several factors.

Maximum Trail Grade: The steepest section of a trail. (The section must be more than 10 feet in length.)

Measuring Wheel (Cyclometer): A device that records the revolutions of a wheel and hence the distance traveled by the wheel on a trail or land surface.

Memorandum of Understanding/Agreement (MOU/MOA): A signed, written agreement entered into by various governmental agencies and nonprofit groups to facilitate the planning, coordination, development, and maintenance of a trail or trails system.

Microtopography: Small bumps and rises in the landscape.

Mineral Soil: Dirt that's below the top layer of leaves, roots, and other organic material. When making a bench cut, always dig down to mineral soil if possible.

Mitigate (Mitigation): Actions undertaken to avoid, minimize, reduce, eliminate, or rectify the adverse impact from a management practice or the impact from trail users.

Multi-Use Trail: A trail that permits more than one user group—equestrians and hikers and mountain bikers, for example—at a time.

National Environmental Policy Act (NEPA): Federal law (established by Congress in 1969) requiring that every federal agency with public involvement asses the biological and cultural resources in the location of any ground-disturbing activity on federal land and determine if the proposed project will cause any significant environmental impact.

Native Species: An indigenous species (a basic unit of taxonomy) that is normally found as part of a particular ecosystem; a species that was present in a particular area at the time of the Public Land Survey (1847-1907).

Natural Resource(s): In terms of outdoor recreation, these include areas of land, bodies of water, forests, swamps, and other natural features that are in demand for outdoor recreation or are likely to become so.

Natural Surface (Trail): A tread made from clearing and grading the native soil and with no added surfacing materials.

Obstacle(s): Physical objects large enough to significantly impede or slow travel on a trail. Logs, large rocks, and rock ledges are common obstacles.

One-Way Trail (Directional-Use Trail): A trail managed in such a way as to encourage users to travel in one direction. May be reversed periodically.

Open and Flowing: A type of trail design that allows for sweeping turns, higher speeds, and longer sight lines.

Organic Soil: Soil that is made up of leaves, needles, plants, roots, bark, and other organic material in various stages of decay, and that has a large water/mass absorption ratio. Generally the first (or outermost) layer of soil.

Outcrop: A rock formation that protrudes through the level of the surrounding soil.

Outside Turns: Convex or off-camber turns (usually on trails that traverse hillsides) that are more difficult to navigate, as centrifugal force pulls trail users to the outside of the turn.

Outslope: A method of tread grading that leaves the outside edge of a hillside trail lower than the inside to shed water. The outslope should be barely noticeable—usually no more than about 1 inch of outslope for every 18 inches of tread width (or about 5 percent).

Partial Bench Trail: (see Bench Cut, Partial)

Percent of grade: Preferred method of measuring slope, or a hill's steepness. For example, a grade of 10 percent means there is a rise or fall of 10 vertical feet per 100 linear feet.

Ponding: Water accumulation in a low area.

Primary Trails: Through-routes that originate at trailheads. Primarily used for directing visitors through an area while promoting a certain type of experience.

Pruning: The removal of normal vegetative growth that intrudes beyond the defined trail-clearing limits.

Public Land: Any land and interest in land owned and administered by a government.

Puncheon (Bog Bridge): A log or timber structure built on the ground for the purpose of crossing a boggy area. Usually consists of sills, stringers, decking, and often a soil or loose-gravel tread on top of the decking.

Radius: An arc or curve that connects two straight trail segments.

Railing: A horizontal or diagonal structural member that is attached to vertical posts for the purpose of delineating trails, protecting vegetation, providing safety barriers for trail users at overlooks, and assisting users when crossing bridges or using steps.

Rail-Trail (Rail-to-Trail): A multi-purpose, public path (paved or natural) created along an inactive rail corridor.

Rebar: Steel reinforcing rod that comes in a variety of diameters, useful for manufacturing pins or other trail anchors.

Recreational Trails Program (RTP): Federal program providing funds to the States for motorized and nonmotorized trails and trail related projects, based on nonhighway recreational fuel use. (www.fhwa.dot.gov/environment/rectrails)

Recreational Use Statue (RUS): State law (in all 50 U.S. states) designed to limit the liability of public organizations, easement donors, landowners, and others who open their lands for public recreation use without charge.

Reroute: A new section of trail that replaces an existing section. Rerouting is often the best remedy for a poorly designed trail that requires frequent maintenance.

Retaining Wall (Revetment, Crib Wall, Cribbing): A structure used to prevent soil from slumping, sliding, or falling, usually made of log or stone. Often used to provide stability and strength to the edge of a trail.

Riparian: A habitat that is strongly influenced by water and that occurs adjacent to streams, shorelines, and wetlands.

Riparian Zone: The land and vegetation immediately adjacent to a body of water, such as a river, lake, or other natural perpetual watercourse.

Risk Management: An element of safety management that evaluates the effects of potential hazards on safety by considering acceptance, control, or elimination of such hazards with respect to expenditure of resources.

Rolling Contour Trail: A trail characterized by gentle grade, grade reversals, and outsloped tread.

Rolling Crown Switchback: A sustainable turn on a hillside engineered for drainage. The trail is routed onto a crowned deck where it makes a transition to the opposite direction. The upper approach is insloped to drain water out the back of the landing. The lower approach is outsloped.

Rolling Grade Dip (RGD): An undulation in the tread that traps water and diverts if off the trail. Makes trails more interesting and fun to use. Can be added after initial trail construction.

Runoff: Water (not absorbed by the soil) that flows over the land surface and ultimately reaches streams.

Runout: A section of a trail, usually at or near the base of a descent, that provides adequate length and grade reduction in order for the user to safely stop or negotiate turns, intersections, or structures.

Sediment: Soil particles that have been transported away from their natural location by wind or water action.

Sedimentation: Deposition of material carried in water, usually the result of a reduction in water velocity below the point at which it can transport the material.

Shared Use (multi use) Trail: A trail that accommodates more than one user group—equestrians and hikers and mountain bikers, for example—at a time.

Sheet flow: A dispersed flow of water. It minimizes erosion by preventing water from achieving high velocity and carrying away topsoil.

Shim(s): A short, thin wedge of rock used to fill the spaces between larger stones.

Shuttle: Leaving a vehicle at both ends of a point-to-point trip or pre-arranging a shuttle for pickup and drop off at the beginning and end of a trip.

Sideslope: The natural slope of a hillside measured on the fall line.

Sight Line: The visible and unobstructed forward and rear view seen by a trail user from a given point along the trail.

Sign: A board, post, or placard that displays written, symbolic, tactile, or pictorial information about the trail or surrounding area. Signage increases safety and comfort on trails. There are five basic types of signs: Cautionary, Directional, Interpretive, Objective, and Regulatory.

Sill: Stone or timber supports that keep bridge stringers from contacting the ground.

Silt: Non-cohesive soil whose individual mineral particles are not visible to the unaided human eye (0.002 to 0.05 mm). Silt will crumble when rolled into a ball.

Singletrack Trail: A trail so narrow that users must generally travel in single file.

Single Use Trail: One that is open to only one type of trail user group (i.e. hiking only).

Skills Area: (see Challenge Park)

Slope: The natural (or man-made) pitch of the land, as shown on contour maps. Generally refers to the hill, not the trail, as trail "slope" is called "grade."

Slough (pronounced "Sluff"): Material from the backslope that has been deposited on the trail bed and is higher than the center of the trail tread.

Social Trail: Unplanned/unauthorized trails that develop informally from use and are not designated or maintained by an agency. Often found cutting switchbacks or between adjacent trails.

Soil(s): The surface material (mineral materials, organic matter, water, and air) of the continents, produced by disintegration of rocks, plants, and animals and the biological action of bacteria, earthworms, and other decomposers. The four fundamental groups of soils are: gravels, sands, loams, and clays.

Soil Compaction: A decrease in the volume of soil as a result of compression stress.

Soil Stabilizer: Material, either natural or manufactured (such as vegetation, mulch, cement, or synthetic soil stabilizers) used to hold soil in place and prevent erosion due to water, gravity, or trail users.

Soil Texture: Relative proportions of the various size groups of individual soil grains in a mass of soil. Specifically, it refers to the proportions of clay, silt, and sand in soil.

Stakeholder(s): Group or individual who can affect, or is affected by, a trail; examples include trail users, managers, park employees, policy makers, citizens, and community groups.

Stewardship: Taking responsibility for the wellbeing of land and water resources and doing something to restore or protect that wellbeing. Usually involves cooperation among people with different interests and is generally voluntary. It is oriented toward assessment, protection, and rehabilitation of trails and greenways as well as sustainable use of renewable resources.

Stringer(s): A structural component of a bridge. It spans from bank to bank and supports the decking.

Subaru: Sponsor of the Subaru/IMBA Trail Care Crews and maker of great cars! Ask for the heated seats.

Summit: The highest point (top) of a mountain.

Surface (Surfaced, Surfacing): Material on top of the trailbed that provides the desired tread. It can lessen compaction of soil, provide a dry surface for users, and prevent potential erosion and abrasion. In addition to concrete and asphalt, trails can be surfaced with dirt, rock, gravel, sand, mud, snow, grass, and other substances.

Survey, Trail: A physical field assessment of the trail or proposed trail to determine alignment, maintenance tasks, hazards, impact, etc., prior to work or as part of ongoing trail maintenance.

Sustainability: Community use of natural resources in a way that does not jeopardize the ability of future generations to live and prosper.

Sustainable Trail: What every designer and construction crew should strive for: low-maintenance trails that have minimal impact on natural systems.

Switchback: A sustainable turn on a hillside. The trail is routed onto a level deck where it makes a transition to the opposite direction.

Tamping: Using a machine compactor, a tamping bar, or another tool to compact earth.

Technical: A section along a trail that is difficult to navigate; used by mountain bikers to describe challenging sections of trail.

Technical Trail Feature (TTF): An obstacle on the trail requiring negotiation; the feature can be either built or natural, such as an elevated bridge or a rock face.

Ten Percent Average Guideline: Generally, an average trail grade of 10 percent or less is most sustainable. This does not mean that all trail grades must be kept under 10 percent. Many trails will have short sections steeper than 10 percent, and some unique situations will allow average trail grades of more than 10 percent.

Terrain Park: (see Challenge Park)

Tie stone: A header or keystone that spans the breadth of the trail tread.

Tight and Technical: A type of trail design that allows for tight turns and slow speeds while using natural features as technical obstacles.

Topographic (Topo, USGS Topographic, Contour) Map: Maps that indicate built and natural features (buildings, roads, ravines, rivers, etc.) as well as elevation changes and land cover. United States Geological Survey

Maps are available from many government offices, outdoor shops, and map stores, or can be downloaded from the Internet.

Trail Difficulty Rating System: A basic method used to categorize the relative technical difficulty of recreation trails. The IMBA system includes five levels of difficulty.

Trail, Loop(ed): Trail or trail systems designed so that the routes are closed circuits connecting a number of points of interest, giving users the option of returning to the trailhead on a different section of trail than they went out on.

Trail, Out-and-Back: A one-way trail on which users travel to a destination then backtrack to the trailhead.

Trail, Stacked Loop: Trail or trail systems designed with many loops "stacked" on each other, giving users many options for varied routes.

Trail Care Crew (TCC) Program: Subaru/IMBA-sponsored, two-person crews that travel and teach trail users and managers how to design, build, maintain, and manage trails that are environmentally sound and fun to use.

Trailhead: An access point to a trail or trail system that can be accompanied by various public facilities, including hitching posts for horses, an OHV unloading dock, toilets, water, directional and informational signs, and a trail-use register.

Traverse: To cross a slope horizontally by going gradually up and across in lieu of the more direct up-and-over approach.

Tread (Treadway): The actual surface portion of a trail upon which users travel.

Tread Creep: Describes a contour trail sagging or sliding down the hill due to user-caused erosion. Specific causes include bushes or trees protruding into the trail from above, exposure of roots from an uphill tree, an improper bench cut, or poor trail flow.

Turnpike: A trailbuilding technique that uses a combination of gravel, soil, or other filler material to make the tread higher than the surrounding water table. Useful in low-lying areas with poor drainage.

User Fee: Any charge for use of services, facilities, trails, or areas. Examples include trail-use fees, entrance fees, parking fees, shelter fees, or voluntary donations.

Water Quality: The chemical, physical, and biological characteristics of water with respect to its suitability for a particular use.

Water Table: The level below the ground surface where groundwater will fill a test hole.

Waterbar: A drainage structure (for turning water) composed of an outsloped segment of tread leading to a barrier placed at a 45-degree angle to the trail; usually made of logs, stones, or rubber belting material. Water flowing down the trail will be diverted by the outslope or, as a last resort, by the barrier. Grade reversals, rolling grade dips and knicks are preferred on multi-use trails instead of waterbars.

Wetland(s): Lowland areas, such as marshes or swamps, that are saturated with water, creating unique habitat for plants and wildlife.

Wilderness Area: Uninhabited and undeveloped federal land to which the U.S. Congress has granted special status and protection under authority of the Wilderness Act of 1964. Allows foot and horse traffic only—no bicycles, OHVs, hang gliders, or other "machines."

Index

A
adzes, 119
all terrain vehicles, 132
armoring
    Appalachian, 169
    benefits of, 163
    boulder causeways, 165
    flagstone paving, 163
    natural rock outcroppings, 165
    purposes of, 162, 207
    raised tread construction, 164
    rules for, 170–71
    stone pitching, 164
    tips for, 166–67, 172
    water crossings, 179–80
assessment studies, 101
axes, 114

B
bark peeling tools, 119
bench trails, full
    compacting the tread, 143, 147
    cutting the backslope, 142, 146
    design of, 140
    digging the tread, 142, 145
    finishing the tread, 143, 147, 148
    outsloping the tread, 143, 146
bench trails, partial, 140–41
bow saws, 113
bridges, 183–84, 239–41
brush hooks, 113

C
cant hooks, 117
canvas bags, 118
chainsaws, 132
chemical binders, 174
chokes, 80
chopping and sawing tools, 113–14
clay soil, 85
clearing tools, 112–13
climbing turns, 149–50
clinometers, 70–71, 108
come alongs, 118
compact utility loaders, 124

construction plans
    developing, 101
    factors affecting trailbuilding time and cost, 187–88
    securing grants, 189
contour routes, planning, 96
control points, identifying, 94–95
corralling, 80
corridors, trail
    clearing, 138–39
    determining width and height, 137–38
    maintaining, 195–96
    walking and flagging, 100
culverts, 180–82

D
deberming, 201
digging and tamping tools, 116
diverse trail systems, 42–43
downhill trails
    building insloped turns, 245
    designing flow transitions, 244
    determining trail placement, 242
    including jumps and drop-offs, 247
    including open/flowing sections, 243
    including tight/technical sections, 243
    incorporating rock, 244
    incorporating vertical drop, 242
    involving downhillers in planning, 242
    minimizing man-made structures, 247
    minimizing trail intersections, 243
    planning for shuttling, 242–43
    providing optional lines, 247
    using grade reversals, 244
drainage solutions
    deberming and maintaining the outslope, 201
    knicks, 202, 203, 206
    rolling grade dips, 202, 204–5, 206
    waterbars, 206–7
    See also armoring
drawknives, 119
DR Field and Brush Mowers, 132
drop-offs, building, 234–35

E
economic benefits of trails
    answering questions about, 50
    success stories, 51
    tips for maximizing, 52–53
erosion
    building trails to resist, 56–57
    solving user-caused problems, 197–99
    solving water-caused problems, 200
    See also drainage solutions
excavators, 126–27

F
fall-line trails, 60
final alignments, flagging, 102
fire rakes, 115
flagging
    final alignments, 102
    material for, 108
    trail corridors, 100–101
flat terrain, 60, 209
folding saws, 110, 114
fords, 179–80
freeriding
    case study on, 228–29
    definition of, 218
    hype vs. reality of, 219–20
    IMBA position on, 221
    upsides/downsides of, 218
freeriding risk management
    being aware of social issues, 222
    building partnerships and communicating, 222
    deciding between shared or single use, 222

designating a risk management coordinator, 227
developing signage, 225
following construction guidelines, 227
giving answers, 227
placing technical features, 223
providing fall zones, 226
providing for skills progression, 223
providing optional lines, 226
understanding liability and case law, 223
using inspection and maintenance logs, 227
using trail filters, 225
full bench trails, *See* bench trails, full

G
geosynthetics, 175
grade, trail
    avoiding fall-line trails and flat areas, 60
    calculating, 59
    definition of, 59
    half rule, 63–64
    key terms, 61
    maximum sustainable, 66
    outslope, 69
    reversals, 67–68
    10% average guideline, 64–65
    using a clinometer to measure, 70–71
griphoists, 117
grubbing and raking tools, 115

H
half rule, 63–64
hammering and pounding tools, 116
hand pruners, 110
hauling and lifting tools, 117–19
hoes, 115

I
IMBA, 11–12
IMBA's Rules of the Trail, 14
insloped turns
    benefits of, 154–55
    building a turning platform and retaining walls, 157
    building the insloped turning area, 157–58
    choosing a location, 157
    design of, 156
    downhill trails, 245
    fine-tuning the turn, 158

K
knicks, 202, 203, 206

L
ladder bridges, 239–41
land managers
    identifying, 21
    private owners, 18
    public agencies, 18–20
    working with, 18, 22–24
layout, measuring, and survey tools, 120
levels, 109, 120
lifting and hauling tools, 117–19
loamy soil, 85
loops, configuring, 95–96
loppers, 110, 113

M
machetes, 112
maintenance plans
    creating assessment and repair sheets, 192–93
    walking/riding the trail, meeting with land managers, and assigning crews, 194
mattocks, 115
maximum sustainable grades, 66
MAX multi-purpose axes, 120
McLeods, 109
measuring, survey, and layout tools, 120
measuring wheels, 120
mechanized tools, 121
Memorandums of Understanding
    getting examples of, 30
    key elements of, 28
mini dozers, 125–27
motorized carriers, 132

O
one-way trails, 46–47
outslope, 69

P
partial bench trails, 140–41
peaveys, 117
permission, getting and confirming, 88, 102
physical binders, 174
picks, 115
pole saws, 114
post-hole diggers, 116
pounding and hammering tools, 116
power weed cutters, 132
power wheelbarrows, 132
property boundaries, identifying, 88
Pulaskis, 108

R
raking and grubbing tools, 115
razor-tooth saws, 114
Recreational Trails Program, 189
rerouting/reclaiming trails
    tips for, 211–14
    when to consider, 211
retaining walls
    back filling, 161
    breaking the joints, 160
    building a wall, 160
    insloping the wall, 160
    laying a foundation, 160
    placing capstones, 161
    rocks vs. wood, 159
    using appropriate rocks, 159
    using headers, 160
    wooden, 161
reversals, grade, 67–68, 244
ride-on earth movers, 125–27
rigging, 118
rockbars, 109
rolling contour trails, 56
rolling grade dips, 202, 204–5, 206
Rules of the Trail, 14

S
sandy soil, 84, 210
sawing and chopping tools, 113–14
shared-use trails, 44
shovels, 110
signs
    materials for, 79
    types of, 76–78
silty soil, 84–85

single jackhammers, 116
singletrack trails, 48–49
single-use trails, 45
sledgehammers, 110
soil hardeners, man-made, 174–75
soil types, 84–85
speed, controlling, 80
stacked-loop trail systems, 95–96, 99
stream corridors, 176
stump grinders, 132
survey, layout, and measuring tools, 120
sustainable trails
   balancing the values of, 40
   definition of, 13
   essential elements of, 63–69
switchbacks, rolling crown
   building the turning platform and retaining wall, 153
   building the upper leg, 154
   choosing a location, 153
   completing the lower leg, 154
   key features of, 151–52

T

tamping and digging tools, 116
tape measures, 109
technical trail features
   adding man-made structures, 231, 235–37, 239–41
   building a ladder bridge, 239–41
   building wooden features, 235–37
   designing a drop-off, 234–35
   enhancing natural features, 231, 234–35
   incorporating existing natural features, 231, 233
   matching the environment, 238
   rock vs. wood materials, 231
10% average guideline, 64–65
timber carriers, 117
tools, hand
   bark peeling, 119
   clearing, 112–13
   digging and tamping, 116
   essential, 108–10
   grubbing and raking, 115
   lifting and hauling, 117–19
   miscellaneous, 120
   pounding and hammering, 116
   sawing and chopping, 113–14
   survey, layout, and measuring, 120
   tips for safe use of, 106–7
tools, mechanized
   advantages vs. disadvantages of, 121–22, 123
   choosing the right, 127–28
   questions to consider, 122
   tips for using, 129–31
   types of, 124–27, 132–33
Trail Care Crews, Subaru/IMBA, 12
trail design
   building a partnership, 88
   conducting an assessment study, 101
   configuring loops, 95–96
   confirming permission, 102
   controlling speed through, 80–82
   determining trail flow, 97–99
   determining trail users, 88–93
   developing a construction plan, 101
   flagging the final alignment, 102
   getting permission, 88
   identifying control points, 94–95
   identifying property boundaries, 88
   planning a contour route, 96
   questions to ask before starting, 40–41
   spreading visitors out, 83
   walking and flagging the corridor, 100–101
Trail Difficulty Rating System, IMBA
   chart, 75
   criteria to consider, 74
   rating guidelines, 72–73
   symbols used in, 72
trail flow, determining, 97–99
trail proposals, 25–27
trails, types of
   diverse networks, 42–43
   one-way, 46–47
   shared-use, 44
   singletrack, 48–49
   single-use, 45
trail users, determining
   equestrians, 90
   motorized users, 91
   mountain bikers, 91–93
   pedestrians, 89–90
   persons with disabilities, 90
   questions to ask, 88
turns
   climbing, 149–50
   controlling speed with, 81
   downhill trails, 245
   insloped, 154–58
   switchbacks, 151

V

volunteers
   being prepared for, 33
   benefits of using, 31
   keeping, 36
   managing, 34–35
   recruiting, 31–32

W

walk-behind earthmovers, 124
waterbars, 206–7
water crossings
   armored, 179–80
   bridges, 183–84
   culverts, 180–82
   guidelines for, 177–78
   priorities for, 176
   wetlands, 185
weed cutters, 112
wet areas, 209
wetlands, 185
wheelbarrows, 118

Y

YAK trailers, 119